*A*dventure Guide

Grenada, St. Vincent & the Grenadines

Cindy Kilgore & Alan Moore

HUNTER

HUNTER PUBLISHING, INC.
130 Campus Drive, Edison NJ 08818
732-225-1900, 800-255-0343, fax 732-417-0482
comments@hunterpublishing.com

Ulysses Travel Publications
4176 Saint-Denis, Montréal, Québec
Canada H2W 2M5
514-843-9447; fax 515-843-9448; info@ulysses.com

Windsor Books International
5, Castle End Park
Castle End Road, Ruscombe
Berkshire, RG10 9XQ England
01189-346-367; fax 01189-346-368

ISBN: 978-1-58843-624-5

© 2007 Cindy Kilgore & Alan Moore

Maps by Toni Wheeler
© 2007 Hunter Publishing, Inc.

Index by Nancy Wolff
Cartoons by Joe Kohl

Front cover: © 2007 Bob Krist
Back cover: *Tobago Cays*, St. Vincent Tourism Board
All photographs courtesy of Grenada Tourism Board, St. Vincent
Tourism Board, local sites and attractions, or as noted.

For complete information about the hundreds of other travel guides offered
by Hunter Publishing, visit our website at:
www.hunterpublishing.com

4 3 2 1

Contents

Maps

Preface

Posted on the bulletin board at the *Caribbean Compass* news-paper in Bequia is a statement that all travelers should carry with them: *Your attitude is the only difference between an ordeal and an adventure.*

In these islands, everything is an adventure, not just snorkel-ing in crystal-clear water, scuba diving through rich coral gar-dens or hiking old plantation estate roads. Weather creates adventure, so do water taxis, airline schedules and credit cards. Trying to locate the appropriate souvenir or getting to another island when there's no flight or ferry to be had, can be an ordeal or an adventure. How you get through complications will color your travels and build stories you can dine out on for months. It's your attitude that will make the final call.

Whether your visit is to one island or stretches from St. Vin-cent to Grenada, we encourage you to read about all of these is-lands. They are unique little gems one and all. Mayreau may not have the restaurants and shops one finds on Bequia, yet its Saltwhistle Bay is acclaimed as the loveliest beach in the Grenadines. Nightlife on Grenada can provide a different set-ting for every night of your vacation, whereas Mustique has just one place where you can rub shoulders with some of the most visible people on the planet.

Choose to island hop or take root on one isolated beach; the ad-ventures are as varied as the islands and the travelers them-selves.

While each island has its own distinctive personality, they all share common threads. Their histories directly affect what they are today. For an overview, read the introduction to each island and the pieces on island life – flora, fauna, sea life. Also, read the vignettes of personalities scattered throughout this book. We've included a series of tips in the hope that you can be a perfect guest, and remain safe on your Caribbean vacation. Enjoy!

Introduction

Hundreds of islands, islets and cays make up the Caribbean. From the air they look like a string of pearls stretching out over 1,500 miles from Cuba to Trinidad. This necklace of islands is a boundary line separating the Atlantic Ocean from the Caribbean

Sea. All of the islands lie south of the Tropic of Cancer, and offer a consistently warm climate throughout the year. The farther south you go, the less change there is in daily temperature from one season to the next.

The name **Caribbean** derives, of course, from the **Carib** people. It was Columbus who labeled the area *Las Yndias Ocidentales*, the West Indies, when he thought he had discovered the western gateway to

Bequia Harbor (Galen R. Frysinger)

Asia. On his second voyage he named the islands *Antillia*, for the possibility that these could indeed be the lost islands of Atlantis. Mapmakers took the liberty of changing the spelling to Antilles.

History

■ Early Peoples

The earliest known inhabitants of the Caribbean Basin were the **Ciboney Indians**, who arrived around 5000 BC. They lived in caves and ate fish and shellfish. They were followed by the **Arawaks** around the 1st century AD. Both races had migrated north out of South America. At the time of Columbus' voyages into the Caribbean, the Arawak people had been pushed northwards up the chain of islands by a race of people coming from the Amazon Basin, the **Caribs**.

The Caribs conquered the Arawaks island-by-island. Arawak men were killed and the women made slaves or taken as wives. By 1498 there was a large population of Arawaks in Puerto Rico, while the fierce Caribs were just to the east in the Virgin Islands.

We know from Columbus' expeditions that the local people spoke two different languages: men spoke Carib, while women spoke Carib to the men, but Arawak among themselves.

A peaceful people, the Arawaks lived in settlements of thatched huts. They baked bread from cassava, and ate fish and conch, leaving behind large mounds of shells that exist to this day. They smoked tobacco and used it as currency. They made pots, wove baskets and slept in hammocks. Small statues with simple carvings and graffitti on cave walls (petroglyphs) are two forms of their artwork. More elaborate ornamentation has been found in their bangle bracelets and necklaces, hammered from a glittering metal they found in riverbeds – gold.

Columbus, and Spanish explorers who followed his lead, kidnapped and made slaves of the Arawaks for both fields and mines. Forced labor and foreign diseases hastened the end of this gentle people. The Arawaks were wiped out as a nation within 20 years of Columbus' arrival.

The elimination of Arawaks left only the Caribs to subjugate. However, the Spanish didn't intend colonizing the islands, they came to exploit the mineral wealth and bypassed the Carib-infested lands.

The **British** began settlement in St. Kitts in 1624, with the **French** hard on their heels. With these two nationalities and the Caribs trying to share one island, conflict was bound to arise. People eyed other islands, and so started the age of colonial expansion in the Caribbean.

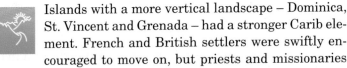 Islands with a more vertical landscape – Dominica, St. Vincent and Grenada – had a stronger Carib element. French and British settlers were swiftly encouraged to move on, but priests and missionaries made the first serious attempts to live among the Caribs. It is from their writings in the 17th century that we learn most about these Indians.

Europeans came to realize they weren't dealing with separate communities of Caribs in isolation, but a whole nation. One heated moment of tension and repercussions reverberated down the chain of islands. The Carib people united in times of conflict, word passing between islands in the night with the stroke of a canoe paddle. When incidents occurred on Guadeloupe and Trinidad, the consequences were felt on Grenada and St. Vincent.

■ Development

Grenada, St. Vincent & the Grenadines form the last hundred miles of the Windwards. They were the final stronghold of the Carib Nation and, thus, the last to be settled by Europeans and assimilated into the plantation system. Today, they are the last stretch of the Caribbean to be absorbed by tourism.

Lesser Antilles

Anguilla

St. Martin/
Sint Maarten

St. Barts

Saba

Antigua

Sint Eustatius

Barbuda

St. Kitts & Nevis

Atlantic Ocean

**LEEWARD
ISLANDS**

Montserrat

Guadeloupe

Dominica

**WINDWARD
ISLANDS**

Caribbean Sea

Martinique

St. Lucia

St. Vincent
and the
Grenadines

N

Grenada

100 KM

60 M

© 2007 HUNTER PUBLISHING, INC

Consequently, these islands tend to be more laid back, with fewer resorts and developed areas for shopping or dining. Instead, you discover small boutiques, cafés and family-run inns and guesthouses, many owned by West Indians. Recently, foreign-owned corporations have begun building upscale resorts comparable in price and luxury with those on islands to the north. Size has been downscaled, allowing them to be more secluded for high-profile or high-stress clients.

After emancipation and until the 1960s, these islands remained a backwater in global events. Whereas the Bahamas, the Virgin Islands and Jamaica were under heavy development, only sailors and a handful of eccentric entrepreneurs ventured to St. Vincent & the Grenadines

Carriacou Workboat (Las Tortugas Villa)

or Grenada. These were men like **Linton Rigg**, a yacht designer; **Colin Tennant**, heir to a Scottish industrial fortune; **Tom Johnston**, advertising executive; industrialist **H.W. Nichols**; **John Houser** of the Hilton group; and **John Caldwell** and **Haze Richardson**, who sought out this unspoiled region, gambling on it becoming an ideal site for yacht charters. These were the visionaries of the islands' future; men who would create something new, while at the same time clinging to tradition. They accomplished this by using native stone and whalebone in construction within the natural contours of the landscape, renovating old plantation buildings, reviving local boat building skills or planting thousands of coconut trees to restore beachfronts. They employed local people in building and management, setting a precedent in these precious islands' development. Unlike the absentee landlords of previous centuries, they stayed in the islands to enrich their own lives by mixing their familiar world with that of the West Indian.

■ Modern Times

A second wave of development is now rolling in on these shores. Corporations have jumped on the all-inclusive-resort bandwagon, enlarging the islands' economies. Regardless, things run at a slower pace on "island time." People are still known by their first names or whimsical nicknames. The changes of the moon, the prevailing wind and the intensity of the sun still dictate events to a certain extent. For travelers escaping the hustle of the corporate world, leaving things up to Mother Nature is the ultimate break from the decision-making process. When you combine that opportunity with a warm translucent sea, blue skies, swaying palm trees and smiling faces – you have a true Caribbean vacation.

The Land

The islands were divided into the **Greater** and **Lesser Antilles** – the Greater being Cuba, Jamaica, Hispaniola and Puerto Rico, while the Lesser Antilles included those islands southeast of Puerto Rico and arching 700 miles down to Trinidad. Together, the Greater and Lesser Antilles make an impressive land mass of 91,000 square miles.

For colonial administrative purposes, the Lesser Antilles were further divided into the **Leeward Islands** and the **Windward Islands**. The most probable derivation of these names dates from the earliest Spanish explorers arriving at Dominica. Heading north, they sailed on the leeward side of the islands; turning south they sailed to the windward side. As early as 1500, they were known as *Islas de Sotavento* (leeward) and *Islas de Barlovento* (windward).

St. Vincent & the Grenadines and Grenada belong to the Windward Islands, along with Dominica, Martinique and St. Lucia. With the exception of the Grenadines, the larger islands are mountainous, with deep valleys lush in tropical vegetation, and have rivers flowing to the sea. All are volcanic in origin, showing either rims of ancient craters or having active volcanoes along their central spine. The Grenadines, on the other hand, lie on a volcanic ridge without tall mountains to trap cloud cover and produce rainfall. The Grenadines are dry, with drought-resistant vegetation.

Exotic plants of bright colors and sensual shapes seem to thrive on the larger islands. Fruits and vegetables are found in abundance – breadfruit, cassava, christophine, paw paw, sorrel, soursop and the dasheen for your callaloo soup, along with a host of others you may never even have heard of, let alone tasted.

Climate

 Every island in the Caribbean has a windward and a leeward side. The lee side faces the quiet waters of the Caribbean and is where most towns have been established around sheltered harbors. The windward is the eastern shore where the Atlantic Ocean beats furiously against the coastline. Here horrendous storms come ashore having traveled from the west coast of Africa or the Canary Islands.

HURRICANES

Most hurricanes occur between June and November, with September being the peak month for storms. Fortunately, the stretch between St. Vincent and Grenada is considered beneath the hurricane belt. That doesn't mean they are invulnerable when Mother Nature chooses to strike. A hurricane's normal pattern is to build up as it crosses the Atlantic from Africa and turn north upon reaching the Gulf Stream. Freak storms do happen, such as

Hurricane Lenny in 1999, which constantly changed directions so that all the Lesser Antilles were hit on their leeward side by wave surges.

The rainy season in West Africa brings low pressure waves and an increasing ocean swell. As the system closes in there is an increase in high-level cirrus clouds or "mare's tails." This is followed by a series of cirrostratus, altostratus, and altocumulus clouds and an increase in winds. As a dark line of clouds approaches, torrential rains begin to fall.

A tropical depression carries winds of 25-33 knots, a tropical storm rages at 24-63 knots, a full-blown hurricane is anything over 64 knots. As a tropical depression appears, it is given a number; if it is upgraded to a tropical storm it is assigned a name. This practice began in 1950. In 1979, it was changed, now alternating girls' and boys' names in French, English, and Spanish.

Hurricanes fall into five categories. Category 1 has winds of 74-95 mph with a wave surge of four to five feet. With Category 3 there will be structural damage, as winds reach 111-130 mph, with a surge of 9-12 feet. Category 4 hurricane winds are 131-155 mph, with surges up to 18 feet and major damage to the islands that are hit. Category 5 is of catastrophic proportions, with winds exceeding 155 mph.

Marine Advisory gives notice in a "Watch" if storm or hurricane conditions are likely within 36 hours. When this changes to a "Warning," then the storm is expected to hit specific areas within 24 hours.

Animals

Wild animals are few and far between in these islands, several species having been hunted out as food, others falling prey to hurricanes and volcanic disasters. The increasing human population and tourist traffic have taken a toll on both wildlife and sealife. While it may sound exotic to sample one of these local species as an entrée, most of them are on the endangered list.

Grey Iguana

Iguanas grow several feet in length and are very shy, with good reason, as they are considered a delicacy on all the islands. The **agouti**, a rodent resembling a mutant guinea pig, is another food source, as is the **manicou**, similar in appearance and behavior to the North American oppossum. The **tatou**, or **nine-banded armadillo**, is nocturnal and endangered, despite its body armor and sharp claws.

Conch shells seem the perfect souvenir, but the eye-catching, vivid pink color quickly fades in direct sunlight. On restaurant menus, conch is also listed as "lambi." This tough, giant snail needs lengthy pounding to make it palatable. Unless harvesting is controlled, conch could soon disappear from menus across the Caribbean. The same applies to lobster. **Lobsters** weren't used as a food source in these islands until the 20th century. In a short time they have been overharvested to the point of becoming a threatened species. A closed season is enforced from May thru October but fines are not nearly as steep as they should be to protect this valuable crustacean.

Sea turtle numbers have suffered due to mankind's appetite and endless desire for decoration. One species, the **hawksbill**, is the world's most endangered reptile. You can experience this creature up close on Bequia at the **Old Hegg Turtle Sanctuary** (see page 143). Trade in turtle shell is illegal, and import is forbidden into the

United States and Canada. While some locals still have a taste for large turtles, more and more people are beginning to respect them.

Then there are the domestic animals: dogs, cats, goats, sheep and chickens. Generally dogs and cats don't have the same appeal to West Indians as they do in North America and Europe. Rarely thought of as members of the family, dogs are kept to sound the alarm against intruders. Cats are, well, cats. Goats and sheep help keep down the dry grass and weeds and are used as a food source. Chickens are also a food source, yet during the night they are a melodious and often irritating glee club. You can't possibly stop the barnyard chorus, so either learn to enjoy it or invest in ear plugs as a precaution.

■ Island Birds

Bananaquit

One morning in Carriacou, we watched a **bananaquit** taking a bath in a sink at the Green Roof Inn. He was making a real fuss. The handsome bird he was flirting with was none other than his own reflection in the mirror.

Darting here, flitting there, combing the area for tasty pecks, the birds will be happy to stand beside your breakfast table – if you don't mind. You could easily cradle the bananaquit in the palm of one hand. You'll probably hear him before you see him, perched upside-down on an exotic flower. These little birds survive on insects and nectar; they nest among the sharp needles of the prickly cactus, keeping predators at bay. He has a black head, wings and tail with a white stripe above each eye. His chest and belly are bright yellow, hence his name. It won't be too long before you see him hoping for a moment's free time with the sugar bowl at a nearby table.

You can be in a restaurant and in comes an attractive black bird with a purple sheen and intense golden eyes; this is the male **Carib grackle**. The female won't be too far away; she is more of a dull brown color, like chocolate that has melted and then reset, but with the same golden

Carib grackle

eyes. This tall and slender bird walks upright, imitating the posture of its human co-habitees. Often they'll be the first birds you hear in the morning, after the chorus of roosters and dogs has finally settled.

DID YOU KNOW?

On Bequia, the grackle is something of a cherished character, as the song he sings sounds like "Bequia sweet, sweet." Only the Bequia grackles do this. On other islands, the grackles sing "Bequia sweet."

We have it on good authority that grackles fly to uninhabited Petit Nevis to sleep. Come breakfast, they're already at the table waiting anxiously, prompting you to leave them a little something.

With tropical flowers abundant, you'll very likely meet the **doctorbird**. This is the most common of the New World's 343 species of hummingbird. Dressed

Doctorbird

in an iridescent cloak of feathers, the male has an emerald or brilliant blue breast. The female sports a pale green sheen on her back, but lacks the dazzling crest.

These birds are high-energy. They weigh less than two dimes, yet they can cruise at 25 mph and dive at an astonishing 85 mph. The doctorbird needs nectar to keep that energy flowing and so pollinates flowers while feeding. Fascinating to observe, all hummingbirds fly like miniature helicopters, their

Introduction

tiny wings flapping 80 times a second when hovering. They are extremely territorial; you may hear them squabbling with each other in high-pitched voices, hovering face-to-face, before one finally gives way to hum elsewhere.

SEABIRDS - AN EYE IN THE SKY

You are sailing. The water shimmers in blues and greens unmatched by even the finest of painters. Flying fish are chased beneath the waves only to take flight above the water. There's a world going on above you as well, and a few of these fine-feathered friends you should know.

Magnificent frigate

The most striking is circling way overhead, the **magnificent frigate bird** or man-o'-war bird. His silhouette is distinctive: long, slender wings spanning eight feet, with a distinctive crook in the wrist. Note the forked or scissor tail. He rides the thermals, gazing down on the water for fish. Frigate birds do not land on the water, nor do they dive. They rely on their speed and agility in snatching fish from the surface with their long, sharp bills. They also resort to piracy, stealing the booty of other seabirds.

Brown booby

Another common bird is the **brown booby**. It is about two feet long, with slender wings, chocolate brown feathers, some-times with a white breast. Boobies fly alongside boats, hover above schools of fish or fly parallel to the water a foot or two above the surf. They dive into the water head first, suddenly, as if shot out of the sky. Having marked the prey, they're in and have eaten dinner before re-surfacing moments later. Popping up, they are quickly airborne again. They are known for catching a ride atop a ship's mast; if you get a chance, check out the booby's face with a pair of binoculars.

Terns and pelicans are equally remarkable. **Terns** are white and, unlike their northern cousins who make the longest migration on the planet, the royal terns stay here yearround be-

Royal tern

cause the fishing is so good. They plunge-dive from insane heights straight into the water; like the frig-ate bird, they often steal directly from the pelican's pouch.

It is riveting to watch **brown pelicans** as they sur-face with a pouch full of sprats and are taunted by gulls squealing for a dropped catch. Looking at the pelican sunning herself on a rock, or watching her dive into the water with an undignified splat, you wonder how she ever manages flight. But she has air chambers connected to her lungs that keep her cool, and also act as shock absorbers for these sudden free-form dives. Efficient fishers and comedians rolled into one, pelicans get the best audience from us humans.

Seabirds are, of course, part of the eco-system, part of the food chain. As fish numbers decrease and pol-lution heightens, their status has become vulnera-ble. Plastic kills seabirds when it gets caught in their bills or tangled in their nests, and suffocation occurs from swallowing. Another killer, not so highly publi-cized, is cigarettes. The filters clog up intestines, re-sulting in the death of fish and birds. Please be aware of your impact on nature and the environ-ment while cruising these pristine waters.

The People

 The people of these two nations are a lovely mixture of Scottish, African, English, French, Portuguese, Indian and Carib. As you continue on in this guide, you will understand this blending of peoples. In the historical sections, the reference to "coloureds" is a colonial term for any mixing of whites with Africans or Caribs. In colonial days, a man born in the Caribbean could be of pure English blood but was described as a mulatto and considered inferior. Today, while the connotations are no longer the same, you'll still hear local people refer to three distinctive types of islanders: black, white and "coloured." There are other qualifications of this, as some coloured people can be "red" and others can be "clear."

■ Languages

The common language is English, although what you'll hear is far from the King's English. With the distinctive West Indian accent, many words in everyday use are drawn from the mixed heritage. Local patois differs from island to island and unless you are a frequent visitor or have an ear for languages, it can be difficult to decipher. Papayas are *pawpaws*, "when did you arrive on the island?" is *when you reach?* To be angry is to be *vex*. In Grenada, *taches* are large cauldrons used to boil up sugar; in St. Vincent they are called *coppers*. *Vay-ki-vay* is something disorderly or careless. Someone from St. Vincent is a *Vincy*. *Liming* is just hanging around. *Mash up* is self-explanatory, as in "Me get so vex wid she, she mash up me car."

What you will undoubtedly notice is the genuine love given to children in the islands. Elderly members of the family and community are also afforded the respect that has now all but disappeared from American culture. The honorable nature of the people is a large factor in the high number of repeat visitors to the islands. Their hospitality is hard to surpass, friendships are held dear and a man's word is still a mark of honor. The most valuable vacation here is one in which you allow yourself to become part of the island community. The companionship you take home in your pocket will far outweigh the photographs snapped, the treasured souvenirs, or the rum consumed in a resort bar. From the lips of a Rastafarian, "One world, one heart."

HOW TO SAY IT

Some names can be tricky to pronounce so here's a guide:

Grenada. . . . . Gren-AY-duh

Lance Aux Epines . . . . Lancy-PEEN

Gouyave . . . . G'WAHve

Sauteurs. . . . . Sew-Terrs

Antoine . . . . An-Twine

Crochu . . . . Crow-Shoe

Anse. . . . . Ants

Carriacou . . . . Carry-A-Coo

Petite Martinique. . . . . Pe-TEET Martin-EEK

Soufriere . . . . Souf-Rare

Wallilabou. . . . . Y-a-boo

Barrouallie. . . . . Barrelly

Colonarie. . . . . Connery

Calliaqua . . . . Cally-Kwa

Vincentian . . . . Vin-Cent-Shun

Bequia. . . . . Beck-Wee

Mustique. . . . . Mus-Teek

Canouan. . . . . Can-Oo-Wahn

Mayreau. . . . . My-Row

Cays. . . . . Keys

Conch . . . . Conk

Caribbean. . . . . Carib-IAN (not Car-RIB-ian)

A WORD TO
THE WISE

The American dollar is accepted throughout these islands, but expect to receive change in the local currency only. For the past decade, the exchange rate between the US dollar and the Eastern Caribbean dollar has been US$1 to EC$2.67.

What's in a Place Name?

On first glance, a map of St.Vincent or Grenada seems studded with towns, especially in the coastal regions. Most of these place names derive from the names given to the original plantations. For instance, **Arnos Vale**, the site of St.Vincent's E.T. Joshua Airport, was an early 19th-century plantation of 449 acres. Parcels of land were sold off, but the whole area still retained the name of the estate. On the northern tip of the island, Sir William Struth had a plantation he called **Fancy**. In that community today the only reminder, other than the name, is a rusty waterwheel. On the southern shore, Struth owned a large estate that he called **Prospect**; ask a taxi driver for Prospect and you'll be taken to an attractive residential quarter to the east of Kingstown.

Not all of the old plantation names have survived as communities; some simply designate areas of cultivated farmland or overgrown rainforest. Other places give more obvious clues to origin, as they are merely names transplanted from Britain; Edinboro, Brighton, Dumbarton, Aberdeen Valley on Mustique, or Carriacou's Dumfries. Early landholders' names also emblazoned the map; Ottley Hall, Mount Wynne, Young Island, Bogles and Campbell's Hill are from the wealthy and powerful British families that were major landowners on the Windward Islands. Today, Ottley Hall is a commercial marina west of Kingstown, Mount Wynne is soon to be transformed from dilapidated ruin into delightful resort. Bogles on Carriacou is a residential area once belonging to Robert Bogles, a leading Glaswegian merchant. Campbell's Hill on Mustique was named for the influential family that held lands from Grenada to St.Vincent. One of the Campbells was bold enough to sue George III over a 4½% tax, keeping the King in court for years.

On Grenada, French names are more prevalent. Though the British tried to change them, the people rejected the new names in favor of what they knew. Gouyave was re-named Charlotte Town 200 years ago, but the name wouldn't stick; it's seen only in the history books. Colorful

La Sagesse Bay

place names are found throughout the island – LaFortune, Rosemont, La Sagesse Bay, Pingouin Beach, Moliniere Point. Each has a distinct reason for existing today.

Visitors to these islands will swiftly discover that a specific street address is not important. Taxi drivers and guides know the hotels, restaurants and points of interest more by their district or parish than by a street address. Telling your taxi driver to go to Prospect, Montrose, Grand Etang, or Crochu should be sufficient information. If he looks at you quizzically after this, then you need to find another taxi!

Water Adventures

■ Scuba Diving

St. Vincent, the Grenadines and Grenada offer wonderful opportunities for scuba diving. There are many dive sites, wrecks and coral reefs with good visibility and easy access. Most islands have at least one dive operator and offer instruction courses. Several resorts have their own dive shops and operators.

It is possible to take resort courses in diving where no certification is required. **Supplied Air Snorkeling for Youths** (SASY) is an option for children aged four and up where the child is tethered to a dive instructor; like riding a horse with a leading rein.

The first element to be stressed with adventures underwater is safety. Whether an experienced diver or a beginner, you will want to check out the dive operator to make sure they are qualified with one of the following:

- ■ **NAUI** – National Association of Underwater Instructors

- ■ **PADI** – Professional Association of Diving Instructors

- ■ **NASDS** – National Association of Scuba Diving Schools

- ■ **SSI** – Scuba Schools International

- ■ **YMCA** – Young Men's Christian Association

Equipment should be well maintained and in good working order. A briefing before every dive is essential to give a description of the site, the duration of the dive, the depth, etc. The dive boat should be equipped with communications, first aid and oxygen, and the captain should stay aboard while you are diving. If you are prone to get cold, neoprene "skins" are a good investment.

A good ratio of clients to staff is desirable; 6:1 is ideal, 10:1 is acceptable. If it is 15:1, then find another operator. One group leader needs to be a Dive Master, if not an instructor, and needs to know the site well enough to guide you.

The dive operator should also want to know about *you*, your experience and proof of certification.

Beginners should look for a course of at least 25 hours, with half that time in the classroom and the other half in the water. If you plan far enough ahead, you may be able to take some instruction in your local area, giving you more dive time in the islands.

■ Snorkeling

First of all, don't leave anything to chance if you are serious about snorkeling in the islands. Before you leave home, visit a local dive shop and purchase a mask, fins and snorkel. Equipment comes in all price ranges. Tell the dive shop employee you are going to the Caribbean so they will make sure everything fits properly. Remember your body will swell with the heat and then shrink in the water. Rings that you can't pull over your knuckles on dry land can easily slip off your fingers in the sea.

Don't rely on buying equipment in the islands. Don't rely on using the gear supplied on boats or by the resort. If they actually have them when you need them, they are often worn thin and who knows where they've been – and you're going to put that snorkel in your mouth?

If you are not a swimmer, you can still snorkel. Simply wear your mask and snorkel and walk around in the clear, shallow waters until you are comfortable enough to don fins. Many reefs are in shallow water close to the beach. This is one of the beauties of a trip to the Tobago Cays. The reefs here can be enjoyed without going more than 20 feet from the shore.

A book on reef fish identification is a worthwhile investment. You can also find laminated cards identifying fish, sea creatures and coral. Keen snorkelers take them in the water for on-site identification.

The underwater world is a spellbinding experience. Within moments of submerging, you'll see fish. It may be a school of transparent ballyhoo coming into focus against the white sands below, or maybe the crunching of parrotfish jaws against the coral that first catches your attention.

Sunscreen is as important a precaution to have with you in the water as it is out. Remember you are only 12 or 13° from the equator. Even whale skin burns in water. You may feel cooler, but you burn quicker. Make sure the sunscreen you are carrying is waterproof. When you see people swimming in T-shirts or even long cotton pants, it is for protection from the sun. The sun can be equally as damaging to eyes so remember to bring sunglasses. The white fiberglass surface of a boat deck is a powerful reflector of the sun's rays, so you should always have means to cover yourself when you feel your body has had enough. Only you can prevent sunburn!

Land Adventures

■ Hiking

 Hiking is the most popular activity. While we have seen people attempt St. Vincent's La Soufrière volcano in sandals, we recommend something a little sturdier. Heavy-duty hiking boots are too hot in this climate and your feet will feel like lead after even the shortest distance. Invest in lightweight hiking shoes with a good grip from your local outdoor specialist. Try to break them in before your journey because brand new shoes can mean brand new blisters! No hiker should be without a windbreaker and rain pants; the interiors of Grenada and St. Vincent are likely to be colder and wetter than the coastal regions. A flashlight, too, could be a lifesaver if you get stranded on the trails in the dark.

 And always remember, strenuous activity will leave you needing water. Drink small amounts often to prevent dehydration.

■ Cycling

 Cyclists bringing their own bikes should be equipped to undertake their own repairs. Spare parts aren't found around every corner in these islands.

■ Golf

 Golfers know the importance of playing with their own clubs. If you are serious about it, then we advise a traveling case with a hard shell to prevent the likelihood of damage in transit. Rental sets are often an assortment of different clubs, but you can still have fun with them. Do bring your own shoes, a glove, tees and some balls if you leave your clubs at home.

■ Tennis

Tennis players have it easier than golfers when it comes to lugging around equipment. You might not want to take your best racket on vacation but remember that half a dozen new balls could come in handy. Giving them to the local children before you head home will leave you extra room in your bag for souvenirs.

Introduction

St. Vincent

Orientation

St. Vincent, the motherland of St. Vincent & the Grenadines, is a large, rugged and densely vegetated island, 18 miles long by 11 miles wide. If you drive or sail along either coast it seems larger. You will find it impossible to drive completely around the island as the road stops abruptly at Richmond on the leeward side and barely rambles past Fancy at the tip of the windward side. Dominating the interior is the majestic and volatile **La Soufrière**. On most days this volcano is hidden by cloud cover, but it has left scars across the landscape and stories that pass from one generation to the next.

Farther south, mountains spill down from the volcano, their steep sides planted in horizontal rows of dasheen, eddoe, tannia, sweet potatoes and yams. The tall coconut, breadfruit, nutmeg and cocoa trees are dwarfed by the mountainsides. The land is rich, the people poor.

St. Vincent & the Grenadines

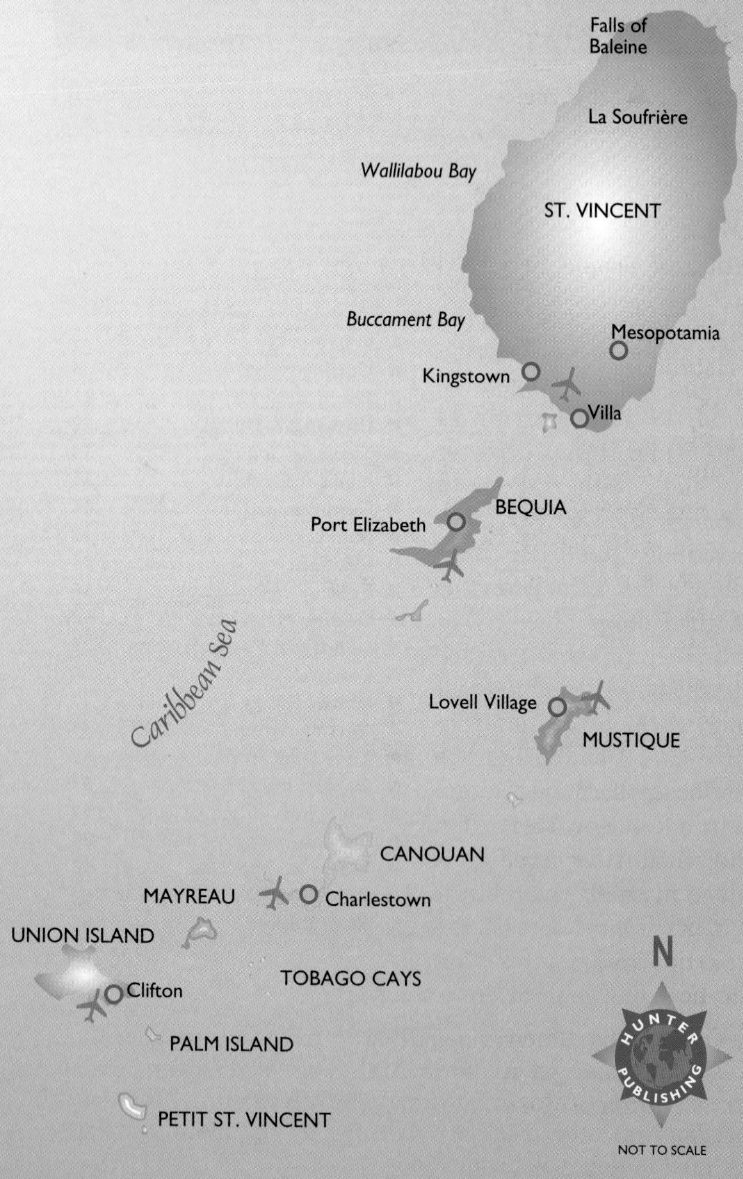

Falls of Baleine

La Soufrière

Wallilabou Bay

ST. VINCENT

Buccament Bay

Mesopotamia

Kingstown

Villa

Caribbean Sea

Port Elizabeth BEQUIA

Lovell Village

MUSTIQUE

CANOUAN

MAYREAU Charlestown

UNION ISLAND

Clifton TOBAGO CAYS

PALM ISLAND

PETIT ST. VINCENT

N

HUNTER PUBLISHING

NOT TO SCALE

As the land slopes closer
to the shore, banana
trees line the roadways,
their familiar fruit cov-
ered by blue plastic bags
for protection against insects. The coastal region
is where most people
make their homes and
businesses. Villages clus-

Waterfront Resort

ter around the fringe of St. Vincent, with the largest concentration of people in the southwestern corner around the
capital, Kingstown. Here, overlooking the harbor, houses dot
the hillsides; they range from modern, concrete homes built to
withstand storms to the last remaining wooden colonials with
tin roofs and wrap-around porches. Looking back to the interior, St. Vincent appears like some prehistoric green lizard, its
volcanic vertebrae stretching from north to south.

Entering Kingstown, you are swallowed up by an energy not
found on the other Grenadines. Human waves move up and
down the streets like the ebbing and flowing of the tide. The
trick to Kingstown is getting into the current and riding the
wave. Stone archways and cobblestones mark the city's noble
old buildings, testaments to the days of sugar, cotton and
slaves. Newer buildings stand in stark contrast, as if the city
were searching for a new identity.

St. Vincent is a mixture of old and new. An ancient mountain
chain adorned with radio towers; container ships keeping
rigid schedules moored next to wooden fishing boats waiting
for the moon to change. In Mangaroo a man rides by on a
sway-backed donkey, his cutlass dangling at his leg, while on
Sion Hill the cars and buses are brought to a standstill in
rush-hour traffic.

St. Vincent is a diamond in the rough. A bit forbidding, definitely unspoiled, yet something in the people, the landscape,
the vegetation or the smell of the air makes you reach for it
time and again as if it were a touchstone you could hold in your

hand. Many men have tried over the centuries, but St. Vincent's wildness doesn't want to be tamed.

When to Go

 It's simpler to advise travelers when *not* to go to St. Vincent since conditions are fairly constant, except in hurricane season. Usually hurricanes pass to the north of these islands, but there have been instances when they have swept right through them. The hurricane season runs from June through November, with September being the most dangerous month. Other than that, the temperature is a pretty constant 84° Farenheit. It becomes more humid as the summer progresses, with more likelihood of rain. The weather in high season – December through April – tends to be fresher, with cooling breezes. More wind means bigger swells in the ocean for those sailing. As a contrast, in early August the seas can be flat and calm.

Some hotels capitalize on the high season and charge extra during busy periods. Times when you need to have a definite advance booking are Christmas and New Year's, Easter and Carnival in June and July. In August some hotels, restaurants and dive operators may close for the off-season.

Getting Here

 Getting to St. Vincent & the Grenadines isn't as hard as it may first appear; it just takes some creative thinking. For many visitors the remoteness is half the attraction. For travelers in the days before the newer airports were built and the motorized ferries arrived, there is disappointment in the ease of travel. Convenience isn't always as attractive as simplicity.

■ By Air

 The first decision is which gateway airport into the Caribbean serves you best. **San Juan, Puerto Rico**, and **Barbados** are the two major hubs for most flights from the US and Canada into the eastern Caribbean. Carriers making connections with inter-island flights in Puerto Rico include Air Canada, Air Jamaica, American Airlines, BWIA, Continental, Delta, Jet Blue, Northwest, United and US Airways. Inter-island operators flying from San Juan to St. Vincent include Caribbean Sun and LIAT. Check the times of departures of the inter-island airlines before booking your flight into the gateway airport allowing enough time, but not a whole day of vacation, between flights. Caribbean Sun offers a non-stop flight to St. Vincent four days a week.

Barbados is only 100 miles due east of St. Vincent. From North America, you can fly to Barbados with Air Canada, Air Jamaica, American Airlines, BWIA, Delta, and US Airways. Inter-island airlines to St. Vincent include Caribbean Star, Grenadine Airways, Mustique Airways, LIAT, and SVG Air. Inter-island planes have either 9 or 18 seats; the flight takes one hour. This is when you'll be glad you packed lightly as the weight restrictions are for your safety. If you need to carry more than your individual allowance, then buying an extra ticket for that flight will secure a place for the extra gear; you wouldn't be the first passenger to be taxiing down the runway only to see your diving gear sitting on the tarmac.

St. Lucia is another option. Air Canada, American Airlines, and BWIA serve the island, landing at Hewanorra International Airport. The trick here is inter-island airlines, American Eagle, Helenair, LIAT, and Caribbean Sun, fly out of Vigie Airport at the northern end of the island.

Grenada is south of St. Vincent and carriers going to the island are listed in the Grenada section of this book (see pages 233-234). While Barbados is an equally good embarkation point, the adventurous traveler will appreciate the scenery and possibility of island hopping when arriving from Grenada. Caribbean Sun, Grenadine Airways, Mustique Airways and SVG Air can connect you between Grenada and St. Vincent.

We highly recommend you purchase tickets for all arrival and departure connections prior to travel as seats fill up fast whatever the season. Leave any excursion tickets for when you have reached your destination.

Remember when using inter-island carriers you are on island time. Flights may be late, changed, or rearranged and nobody will seem concerned about any delay. It's not that they don't care, they're just far more relaxed than people from the north are accustomed to being. Chances are you will arrive in St. Vincent the same day as planned, although it might be at dinner time instead of happy hour.

Gateway Airports

Barbados' Grantley Adams Airport

Grenada's Point Salines Airport

Puerto Rico's Luis Munoz Marin Airport at San Juan

St. Lucia's Hewanorra International Airport with connecting flights departing from George F. Charles Airport in Castries

Airlines Serving the Eastern Caribbean

Air Canada	☎ 888-247-2262, www.aircanada.com
Air Jamaica	☎ 800-523-5585, www.airjamaica.com
American Airlines/ American Eagle	☎ 800-433-7300, www.aa.com
BWIA	☎ 800-538-2942, www.bwee.com
Continental	☎ 800-231-0856 www.continental.com
Delta	☎ 800-221-1212, www.delta.com
Jet Blue	☎ 800-538-2583, www.jetblue.com
Northwest	☎ 800-225-2525, www.nwa.com
United	☎ 800-864-8331 (International) ☎ 800-538-2929 (US & Canada), www.ual.com
US Airways	☎ 800-428-4322, www.usairways.com

Most of these carriers, if not all, fly south and then turn directly around and return to North America. Delays at either end can, and will, cause disruption to connecting flights on your return home. Give yourself plenty of space between flights in the US; it's much nicer to have dinner and catch up on news after vacationing than having to make new arrangements in large airports when you're sunburned and tired.

When you are leaving St. Vincent & the Grenadines, be prepared for the departure tax of EC$40 (US $15) per person. Even if you pay in US or Canadian dollars, your change will be given in Eastern Caribbean currency.

St. Vincent

Airlines Serving St. Vincent	
Caribbean Sun	☎ 784-456-5800, www.flycaribbeanstar.com
Grenadine Airways	☎ 784-456-6793, www.grena-dine-airways.com
LIAT	☎ 784-457-1821, 888-844-5428, www.fly-liat.com
Mustique Airways	☎ 784-458-4380, 800-526-4789 (US), 800-419-1635 (Canada), www.mustique.com
SVG Air	☎ 784-457-5124, 784-456-5610, 800-744-5777, www.svgair.com

Remember to reconfirm your departure flight with a travel agent in the islands several days before you return home.

■ By Sea

Three ferries cross the channel between St. Vincent and Bequia, another links the island with Mustique, and a mailboat (a small freighter) carries both cargo and passengers up and down the chain of Grenadines.

From Bequia you can catch *Admiral I*, *Admiral II* (☎ 784-458-3348) or the *Bequia Express* (☎ 784-458-3472). The journey from Port Elizabeth to Kingstown takes one hour. Ferries leave Monday through Friday at 6:30, 7:30, and 9:30

am, and 2 and 5 pm. On Monday, Wednesday and Friday there is an additional sailing at 4 pm. Saturday departures are 6:30 and 10:15 am, and 5 pm. Sundays and public holidays, the ferries leave Bequia at 7:30 am and 5 pm. One-way fare is EC$15, round-trip is EC$25.

Cruise & ferry terminal, St. Vincent

From Mustique, the *Glenconnor* leaves at 7:30 am on Monday, Tuesday, Thursday and Friday, arriving in Kingstown at 9 am. Departure from Kingstown back to Mustique is at 2 pm. One-way fare is EC$20 per person and must be purchased at The Mustique Company Offices in Kingstown or Mustique.

Barracuda (☎ 784-456-5063, 784-455-9835) is the mailboat calling at Union Island, Mayreau, Canouan and Bequia en route to St. Vincent. On Tuesday and Friday it departs Union Island at 6:30 am, Mayreau at 7:30 am, Canouan at 8:45 am and Bequia at 11 am, arriving in Kingstown at noon. On Saturday, the mailboat departs St. Vincent at 10am, stopping at Canouan and Mayreau before reaching Union Island at 4pm. This is a quick turn around as *Barracuda* unloads and sails non-stop back to St. Vincent. Weather permitting, she arrives at her homeport at 7:30pm, but sometimes later. At that time of night there are no taxis or dollar buses at the jetty. As with any commercial harbor, this is no place to be without a ride. It is unsafe for someone walking around in the dark with luggage. If you do take the service arriving this late, then phone ahead from Union Island for a taxi driver to meet you. Be courteous and let him know if there are any delays, or else, you may find yourself alone on the jetty; taxi drivers don't want to feel vulnerable either. Oneway fare to St. Vincent from Bequia is EC$15, from Canouan EC$20, from Mayreau EC$25, and from Union Island EC$30.

MV *Gem Star* (☎ 784-526-1158, 784-457-4157), a small funky freighter, leaves Union Island at 7:30am on Wednesday and Saturday, making one stop at Canouan before arriving in St. Vincent in early afternoon. The fare from Union Island is EC$30 or US$12.

It is always wise to call the *Barracuda* or *Gem Star* the day before, and again the morning of sailing, and let them know they have passengers. Ferries won't wait on anyone not standing on the jetty. On public holidays, national sports events, or during Carnival, it is advisable to check schedules ahead of time for alterations.

If you are interested in traveling the islands via freighter ships, contact:

Windward Agencies Ltd., windward@sjds.net

Perry's Customs & Shipping, Sharpe Street, Kingstown, ☎ 784-4572920, dhlsvg@caribsurf.com

Freighter World Cruises, 180 South Lake Avenue, Suite 3335, Pasadena, CA 91101, ☎ 626-449-3106, www.freighterworld.com

Traveltips Cruise & Freighter, ☎ 718-030-2400, www.traveltips.com.

Practicalities

■ Customs & Duties

Entering

You may enter St. Vincent & the Grenadines with the following duty-free items: 200 cigarettes or 50 cigars or eight ounces of tobacco; one quart of wines or spirits.

You may not bring in drugs, firearms, ammunition or spear fishing equipment.

All boaters must clear immigrations and customs when entering and leaving the country. In St. Vincent, at Chateaubelair, Wallilabou, and Kingstown; on Bequia at Port Elizabeth; on Canouan at Charlestown; on Mustique at Britannia Bay; and and on Union Island at Clifton.

Leaving

Returning to the **United States**, you may bring back US$600 worth of duty-free goods; one liter of spirits; 200 cigarettes and 200 cigars.

Returning to **Canada** you may bring back duty-free C$300 worth of goods; 200 cigarettes, and 50 cigars, and 200 grams of tobacco; 40 imperial ounces of alcohol.

When leaving the country there is a departure tax of EC$40 per person. This is roughly US$15. Any change will be returned to you in EC currency.

■ Taxes & Tipping

Always check your bill to see whether or not the 10% service charge has been included. Government tax is 7% extra. If it has been included, it might go to your waiter or waitress directly or it may be shared among staff. If you wish to leave a little extra, it will always be appreciated. It is also appropriate to tip guides and taxi drivers if they give good service.

■ Medical Services

Hospitals

Milton Cato Memorial Hospital, ☎ 784-456-1185, has an accident and emergency department, ☎ 784-456-1955. Health centers are located in Georgetown, ☎ 784-458-6652; in Chateaubelair, ☎ 784-458-2228; and at Arnos Vale, ☎ 784-457-4258. Our best advice is not to get sick here! If you do need hospitalization, get to Barbados or Grenada.

Pharmacies

Kingstown has about a dozen pharmacies. Dasco's is on Halifax Street, ☎ 784-457-9431. **Medex**, ☎ 784-456-2989, is on Grenville Street, as is **Royal Pharmacy**, ☎ 784-456-1817, and **People's Pharmacy**, ☎ 784456-1170.

■ Communications

Internet

In Kingstown "**e-msa**," ☎ 784-457-1131, is an Internet and business center open daily from 8 am-11 pm. It's on the third floor of the office building opposite the old Public Library on Granby Street. Bonadie's Plaza on Middle Street, contains **Office Essentials Ltd.**, ☎ 784-457-2235, oel@caribsurf.com, where you can surf the net and check your e-mail.

The **Lagoon Marina Hotel** has a screen for rent, and the **Roy's** has a business center. More hotels plan to provide guests with Internet facilities. On the phone, ☎ 900-266-6328 for Internet access.

Telephone

Cable & Wireless are on Halifax Street, Kingstown, ☎ 784-457-1901. For credit card calls and calling collect to the USA, ☎ 800-225-5872; for other countries, ☎ 800-744-2000.

If you bring your own cell phone, you can use the roaming service, though you can't receive calls if you use credit card roaming service.

You can always rent a mobile phone. For more information contact **Caribbean Cellular**, ☎ 784-457-4600; **AT&T**, ☎ 784-452-5480; or **Digicel SCG, Ltd.**, ☎ 784-453-3000.

To call the USA or Canada, ☎ 01 + area code + number; to call the UK, ☎ 0 + 44 + area code + number; to call other countries, ☎ 0 + country code + area code + number.

For the international operator, ☎ 115; for international inquiries, ☎ 119. For the local number inquiries, ☎ 118.

Phone cards are sold in many shops and stores in EC$10, EC$20 and EC$40 denominations. Peak daytime hour calls to North America and Europe cost an average of EC$4 per minute.

Postal Services

The main post office is in Kingstown on Halifax Street. Opening hours are from 8:30 am-3 pm, Monday to Friday, and 8:30 am-11:30 am on Saturday. Smaller post offices are found in most communities.

■ Banks

On St. Vincent, banking hours are 8 am to noon and 1 to 3 pm, Monday to Thursday. On Friday, banks are open from 8 am to noon and 3 to 5 pm. The **Bank of Nova Scotia** (Scotiabank), **National Commercial Bank of St. Vincent**, and the **First Caribbean International Bank** are on Halifax Street; **RBTT** is on South River Road; and **First St. Vincent Bank** is on Granby Street. All have ATM machines.

■ Electricity

Voltage is 220 volts on all islands, except Palm Island and Petit St. Vincent, where it is 110 volts. Sockets are the British style, three square-pin, although you'll find some that are two round-pin. 110 volt appliances will work with a transformer. Make sure you have an adaptor for any equipment before you leave home; don't count on being able to buy one here.

St. Vincent

■ Pets

Do not bring pets to St. Vincent & The Grenadines. If they arrive via boat, they cannot come ashore.

■ Getting Married

To marry in St. Vincent you must get a license from the courthouse in Kingstown. You must be resident for one full day before any church or civil ceremony can take place. The license is valid for three months.

Holidays & Festivals

■ January

New Year's Day

Mustique Blues Festival – Nearly two weeks of music into early February on Mustique, with interludes on Bequia and St. Vincent. Contact Basil's Bar & Restaurant, ☎ 784-456-3350, VHF Channel 68 or www.basilsmustique.com.

■ March & April

National Heroes' Day – March 14.

Good Friday

Easter Monday

Easter Regatta – On Bequia, the nation's prime annual sailing event. Con-

Bequia Easter Regatta (Bequia Tourism)

tact **Bequia Sailing Club**, ☎ 784-458-3286 or bsc@caribsurf.com.

Easterval – Union Island's three-day festival of music, costumes and games. Contact **Union Island's Tourist Bureau** at ☎ 784-458-8350.

■ May

Labour Day – May first. The **Union Island Maroon Festival** is traditionally celebrated on this date, ☎ 784-457-1502.

Canouan Regatta – Five days of sport on land and water in the middle of May. Contact **Canouan Sailing Club** at ☎ 784-458-8197.

■ June

Whit Monday, Fisherman's Day – Usually the third Monday in June.

Fishing off Palm Island, St. Vincent

■ July

Carnival on St. Vincent, "Vincy Mas" – A 12-day celebration with parades, music, contests, and the biggest street party of the year. Events start in late June (see below). Contact Alliance Française at ☎ 784-456-2095.

■ August

Emancipation Day & Breadfruit Festival – August 1, ☎ 784-457-1502.

■ October

Independence Day – October 27.

Independence Day, Kingstown

■ December

Nine Mornings – Music, contests and general frolic every day from December 16 until Christmas.

Christmas Day – December 25.

Boxing Day – December 26.

Carnival

 Carnival has been celebrated in St. Vincent for over 200 years. Sir William Young, a well-to-do planter appointed by King George III to oversee the Windward Islands' land parcels, has left many glimpses into colonial life through his letters and personal diary. In 1791 he wrote, "December 26. This was a day of Christmas gambols. In the morning we rode out and in the town of Calliaqua saw many negroes attending high mass at the popish chapel. The town was like a very gay fair with booths, furnished with everything good to eat and fine to wear." The harvest was now in and barreled. Sugar was ready for the merchant ships to carry to England.

Carnival, or Vincy Mas

After six months of backbreaking work reaping and processing the cane, slaves finally had respite from 18-hour working days. They would, of course, continue to work 12-hour days, but there was time to rest at night and tend to their own subsistence farming. Feelings were mixed with resentment and relief. Carnival provided an opportunity to let off some steam.

Throughout the West Indies slaves gathered to march upon the estate houses, dressed up in the tattered old clothing of the planters. They danced in the British style, followed by the drumming and dances of their African heritage. The "Mumbo Jumbo," someone on stilts with their identity concealed by a huge mask, towered over and moved among the crowd. Baskets with bells were shaken to create entrancing music. A swordsman would dance out and do battle with an invisible spirit, while the musicians carried on in a comical dance of their own making.

DID YOU KNOW?

Mas is the name used in Grenada for Carnival. In St. Vincent, it is called Vincy Mas. It may have derived from the word Mass, or from the slave word massa (master), as both a religious holiday and the end of planting were being celebrated. According to Richard Allsopp's Dictionary of Caribbean English Usage, however, the word derives from masquerade, the dressing up of bands in costumes.

St. Vincent

Carnival has continued to be a reminder of identity and a connection to one's roots. Fifty years after Young's diary entry, it grew even stronger as a celebration of emancipation and the end of slavery. Gone was the enforced labor of the cane fields under the eye of an overseer, but the stilts, elaborate head masks, and swordsmen remain in the annual revels.

Riots broke out during the 1870 Trinidad Carnival. Colonial administrators anticipated similar incidents in St. Vincent, resulting in Carnival being banned. The Lieutenant Governor defended the decision by referring to the customs of "the Lower Order" dressing in "fantastic attire" carrying sticks and whips "with which they struck at any persons passing by." Today we would consider this the stickiness of a petty official, but in 1872 he was obviously reacting with more than a hint of fear.

Despite the ban, on Saturday, February 8th, Vincentians began their revels in the streets of Kingstown. It was a national celebration the people were simply not willing to give up. In the following days arrest warrants were issued against some of the participants. As a result, violence broke out on Tuesday evening and rioters held off police with sticks, stones and bottles. The Lieutenant Governor called for an emergency assembly the next day and was met by over 300 irate townspeople. Carnival was returned to the people. As a local newspaper recently put it: "This was the spirit in which Carnival was born; out of a struggle from which emerged a people's assertion of their identity."

Calypso plays a major part in Carnival. A singer of these satirical songs covering topical themes is known as a calypsonian. In former times they were required to jig up to the colonial administrator's house and perform. The best was awarded the "administrator's sceptre."

After World War II, Vincentian Raphael Davison brought something new to Vincy Carnival from his adopted home of Trinidad – the steel band. The pans had been used as percussion until a Trinidadian in 1948 devised a method of tuning the pans to carry a melody. Davison refused to take his steel band to the administrator's house to "lick any colonialist boot," and instead took to the streets of Kingstown. And so Vincy Mas, the first street Carnival Jump Up, was born.

St. Vincent

Trinidadian steel bands were kings of Carnival until 1962 when the winning band was the St. Vincent Police Steel Orchestra. By the 1970s the majority of calypso singers were also local.

On Barbados in the 1980s a calypso song had so insulted the Prime Minister that he had it banned island-wide. The following year the Prime Minister of St. Vincent was also under attack from the Calypso King. The Prime Minister responded by saying "Since the tune is good, the song is good. I would never ban a calypso." Good answer.

Vincy Mas takes place in July on an outdoor stage with the bands then taking to the streets in procession. The 10-day celebration begins with Mas Eruption; daily themes and competitions include Calypso, Clash of the Bands, Junior Pan, Ms. Carnival, Soca Monarch and Dimanche Gras, where the King of Calypso is crowned. Carnival ends with Vincentians taking to the streets to party. For some, it isn't too long before they begin planning the next year's costumes, floats and decorations.

Island History

■ The Caribs of St. Vincent

 When the Europeans came to colonize islands of the Caribbean, they weren't exactly welcomed with open arms by the people already living there. The Caribs were a race of strong warriors from the Orinoco basin of the Amazon. They had migrated north through the island chain 800 years before Columbus. Nowhere was their reception of the white man more hostile than on St. Vincent. On attempting to land, soldiers were chased off by ferocious threats from a people 10,000 strong. The island was given a wide berth by European ships. When Caribs were ousted from other islands, it was to St. Vincent that they fled. Here they found safety in sheer numbers and in the hostility of the island to foreigners.

While the Caribs have been represented as savages and cannibals, history has been slow to take the stance that they were protecting their homeland. They were not as intolerant with men of the cloth as they were with soldiers. Père Aubergeon and Père Geuimu, two French priests who could speak the Carib tongue, took up residence in Barrouallie in 1653. They brought with them two attendants and together tried to convert the natives to Christianity. All was not well, however, elsewhere in the islands.

Jesuit missionaries were massacred on Guadeloupe; the governor of Dominica, a respected mulatto, was murdered by his half brother, deputy governor of Antigua. Caribs were kidnapped, soldiers killed in return. The two worlds pushed against each other, and differences in culture and lack of communication brought misunderstandings over the exchange of lands and goods. The Europeans were naive in their optimism that a few beads and trinkets could secure land holdings for any great length of time.

Hostilities peaked in 1654 when a French sailor was killed in Trinidad and a Carib beaten as a result. Word spread through the islands as fast as the tide. At Barrouallie the priests and attendants were attending mass when they were killed by the local Caribs heeding their nation's call to arms – *"Kaori homan!* To every white man death!"* French warships retaliated on St. Vincent's leeward coast by burning villages, ruining crops and taking no prisoners.

 Several years would pass before the Caribs gained an ally from an unexpected quarter. A slave ship heading for Barbados from Africa was blown off course and wrecked on the windward coast. The Africans were given shelter by the Caribs and the two peoples took up residence together. A common enemy ensured their mutual partnership in future struggles. Before long, runaway slaves from St. Lucia and Barbados took their chances on the open sea in the hope of landfall and refuge on St. Vincent. Formerly, the Caribs had returned the runaways to their French or Spanish owners, but by 1700 there was full integration and St. Vincent became the center of the Carib republic. Pure Caribs were known as Yellow Caribs, while those of mixed Carib and African blood came to be called Black Caribs.

 In 1748 the Treaty of Aix-la-Chapelle between France and Britain acknowledged St. Vincent as a neutral territory belonging to the Carib nation. Nevertheless pockets of French settlers sprang up on the leeward side, growing indigo, tobacco, cotton and sugar. Being on the island illegally, they were forced to coexist with the two Carib groups. They provided them with weapons, and according to Sir William Young 50 years later, "sent missionaries among them to dazzle them with ceremonies and entertain them with festivals... to promote a communion of interests and passions, under covert of religion." By the time the British gained possession of St. Vincent, the Caribs had adopted French names.

The Caribs Under British Rule

 In 1763 the Treaty of Paris was signed between Britain and France, with no regard to the Caribs and the previous treaty of Aix-la-Chapelle. Britain would hold St. Vincent, and commissioners were sent out to survey and sell parcels of land. Unlike the 400 illegal French settlers, the British were coming in to work large plots of land for sugar with a multitude of slaves. The British failed to realize that the island was already divided into territories, each with a clan chief. The Caribs used the many rivers as their boundaries. A supreme commander of Carib chiefs was elected only in time of war. When the treaty was signed, this was a man called Chatoyer.

The British, upon confronting the existing French settlers, gave them the option to either repurchase their plantations at the new British price, or abandon them. When the British tried planting in Carib country, the natives burned and plundered. The *St. Vincent Gazette* in 1773 records a treaty between the Caribs and the British. The natives were to pledge allegiance to King George III, lay down their arms, surrender a

King George III

great portion of their lands, and allow roads, forts and batteries to be built. They would have no communication with the French islands, harbor no runaway slaves, and assist His Majesty against any enemies of the Crown. All the clan chiefs signed their French names to the document.

Six years later, the governor, Valentine Morris, was walking a thin line by trying to keep the French at bay, the Carib country intact, and St. Vincent secure with minimal forces. The French on Martinique heard that St. Vincent was virtually defenseless and decided to attack with five ships in a pincer movement. Governor Morris tried to sound the alarm by firing a cannon on Sion Hill. A Lieutenant Colonel Etherington, more concerned with maintaining his own lands in Carib country, removed the cannon's fuse and allowed the French to take St. Vincent without a single shot fired in defense. For the next four years the St. Vincent planters would have to pay for the upkeep of the French fortification. And then another treaty was signed.

With the Treaty of Versailles in 1783 St. Vincent swung back into British hands in the latest stroke of diplomatic ping pong. Game to the British? Not quite, the French Revolution was just around the corner, most notably affecting the islands in 1795. This was when the bloodthirsty Victor Hugues, henchman of **Maximilien de Robespierre**, arrived on Martinique, bringing with him his guillotine, and a plan to unleash simultaneous rebellions on all islands by French and Caribs against the British.

Robespierre, 1791

St. Vincent

In fact, the revolts sparked on different dates, creating a domino effect. Grenada's insurrection had begun a week earlier and the British got wind of the plot on St. Vincent. Chatoyer, leader of the Black Caribs, and his brother, Duvalle, were hurriedly summoned to Kingstown. A plantation in Evesham Vale was burned, and by the next morning Duvalle had devastated the northern windward side of the island. Plantations were burned, British planters and overseers killed, and livestock destroyed. In three days Duvalle pushed down the windward coast until he reached Dorsetshire Hill above Kingstown and ran up the French flag.

On the leeward side, Chatoyer and his warriors took prisoners and preserved the plantations, eventually joining Duvalle on Dorsetshire Hill. All sides came to a clash here and Chatoyer challenged a British officer, Major Leith, to a duel, in which Chatoyer took the fatal blow and fell dead. Many of the French expected an immediate Carib collapse and preempted the situation by retreating. Seeing this, the Caribs in turn disbanded and returned to their villages.

Reinforcements and retribution were on the way from the British. Lieutenant General Sir Ralph Abercrombie first captured St. Lucia on March 17th 1796 and sent all whites and free coloureds to England as prisoners of war. Caribs no longer had their supply of ammunition or their French revolutionary allies.

On June 7th, Abercrombie landed in St. Vincent with 4,000 soldiers. Within days his professional men had rounded up all but handfuls of Black Caribs and transported them to the nearby large islet of Balliceaux. Close to 5,200 waited there nearly two years before being exiled to the island of Roatan off Honduras. Only 2,700 survived Balliceaux to make the trip west.

ASHTON WARNER

Children born into slavery paid little regard to luck. The life ahead of them looked inevitably grim. One infant seemed an exception. Born in Buccament Valley in the early 19th century, Ashton Warner was set free by his aunt. She purchased freedom for the infant and his mother on the death of the owner of Cane Grove Estate.

Shortly after his 10th birthday, Ashton was taken on as a cooper's apprentice at a nearby plantation. Hearing of this indentured child, the manager of Cane Grove arrived to claim him as his own. Despite his mother's appeals and the manumission papers proving Ashton's freedom, he was taken back to Buccament Valley and set to work in the cane field. An appeal was made to the governor of St. Vincent to right the matter; promises were made but never carried out.

Each morning the field hands rose at 4 am in time to walk the four miles to work. At 5 am, the overseer read the roll call. Any late arrivals were stripped and flogged immediately. A half-hour break at 9 was the only rest until noon.

Two hours were allotted for the midday break, but the slaves needed this time to gather grasses for livestock. Any lightweight bundles would result in flogging or possibly a night in the stocks. When it was time to fertilize the fields, Ashton and the others would carry manure on their heads. The damp waste constantly dripped down their faces and soaked their clothing.

Harvest time brought all slaves into the fields day and night irrespective of their age or health. Ashton explained later: "When you are ill and cannot work, your pains are made light of, and your complaints never listened to, nor believed. I have seen people who were so sick that they could hardly stand, dragged out of the sick house, tied up to a tree, and flogged in a shocking manner; then driven with the whip to the work."

In Buccament Valley are the unmarked graves of slaves buried at night. Funerals were allowed only when they weren't working. Across the fields slaves toiled in the heat "with only a rag around their loins in all weathers." At night they wrapped themselves in a single blanket that was changed every five or six years.

Eventually Ashton Warner escaped servitude by jumping a boat bound for Grenada. Keeping careful watch not to be seen by any of Cane Grove's employees, he found work aboard a schooner trading between Grenada and Martinique. An opportunity arose to go to St Kitts and from there he sailed to England, arriving in 1830. The abolition of slavery was the main political topic. Indeed, abolition would come four years later. This wasn't enough for Ashton; he had a name to clear and went in pursuit of the mysterious absentee owner of the Cane Grove Estate. Once and for all he would prove himself a free man with the papers he held in his hands. In London he discovered that the owner had died and the estate was in the hands of the executors of the will.

With nowhere to go, Ashton happened to meet an editor sympathetic to the abolitionist cause. Realizing Warner's story could help speed the road to emancipation, he decided to publish it as a book. With the ink barely dry, Ashton died in London. The editor sold the volume and sent the profits to Ashton's mother, and his wife and child, back on St. Vincent.

Ashton Warner's story has little in the way of good luck; the only fortune is that two centuries later, we have a first-hand account by a Vincentian documenting this era of cruelty. Today, Cane Grove is still a working plantation in Buccament Valley.

■ After Sugar

It is amazing that sugar ever took hold in St. Vincent. The Carib Wars were barely settled when, in 1812, La Soufrière's eruption devastated the land. But fifteen years later, vast quantities of sugar, molasses and rum were being exported from the island. At least four estates were producing around one million pounds of sugar annually. The most productive land was that hit by volcanic ash, which added nutrients to the soil.

By the end of the 19th century, the West Indian Royal Commission advised against relying on the monoculture of sugar. Mother Nature gave the planters the final push towards diversification as hurricanes struck the island in 1831, 1886 and 1898.

In 1902, Sea Island cotton was introduced into St. Vincent. Within two years Kingstown was home to the largest and most refined cotton ginnery in the Carib-

Banana plants

bean. Within 10 years, 1,500 farmers were cultivating 2,000 acres of cotton. But, by 1970, the cotton industry had completely vanished.

Today's major crops are bananas and arrowroot. Traditionally used as a thickening agent in soups and sauces, arrowroot is now used as a finish for computer paper. Bananas are exported weekly to Europe; the fruit is the finest in the Western Hemisphere.

■ Independence

 The old-style regime of government under the British lasted until 1877, when St. Vincent became a Crown Colony. In 1924 this system came under attack from St. Vincent's parliament, who wished to establish electoral government. By the early 1960s the island was incorporated into the West Indies Federation and the

United Nations declared that size was not to be a factor in a country obtaining its independence. By the end of that decade Britain deemed the islands of the Windwards and Leewards as separate states. On October 27th, 1979, St. Vincent & the Grenadines were granted their independence.

The official head of state remains the Queen of England, with the Governor General as her representative on the island. Parliament consists of 15 elected members and six senators. The government is headed by an elected Prime Minister. Milton Cato led the country into independence. The next Prime Minister was Sir James "Son" Mitchell, who held the position through the turn of the millennium. Ralph Gonsalves is the current holder of the office.

■ Coat of Arms

The coat of arms shows an elaborate cartouche depicting two female figures in classical robes on either side of an altar upon a green field.

One figure is kneeling in supplication and making an offering. The standing figure holds an olive branch in one hand. Beneath the cartouche winds a scroll with the motto "Peace and Justice" (*Pax et Justitia* in Latin).

■ The Flag

The flag is a tricolor with vertical bands of blue, gold, and green. In the gold band sit three green diamonds forming the letter V.

The symbolism of color is obvious: blue for the sea, green for the land and the vegetation, and gold for the sun and the warmth of the people. The three green diamonds not only represent the letter V, but also islands in the chain of Grenadines.

Getting Around

■ By Car

 Car rental in St. Vincent is possible, but we're of two minds as to whether it is necessary or advisable. If you are going to hike the volcano or go parrot spotting on the Vermont Nature Trails, don't leave your vehicle parked unattended. We have heard stories of cars being broken into while people were hiking. It's sad to say, but crime directed towards tourists is on the increase. It is better to go with a recognized guide or tour operator on these excursions. If you feel confident about renting a vehicle, then our advice is to travel without valuables; just take food and water and little else. Locking your car again is a matter of debate or instinct; if the door is left open then the chances are you won't return to a smashed window.

You need a temporary driving permit to rent a car. These are issued at Immigration in the airport or at the revenue building in Kingstown on Halifax Street; the cost is EC$50 (about US$19). You must bring a current driving license from your own country and the St. Vincent permit will be valid for six months. Most rentals include insurance, a supplementary charge for Collision Damage Waiver, and will require a credit card for a deposit. Always check the form for small print before signing. Don't forget that driving is British style, on the left.

We chose **Avis Rent A Car** by the airport, ☎ 784-456-6861, and were offered a heavy-duty vehicle, which is fine for a family or group of four. Considering the rough terrain at the north end of the island, we were glad to have opted for the smaller, Japanese-style model. **DAC Rentacar**, ☎ 784-456-9739, dac@caribsurf.com, has air-conditioned cars, 4WD vehicles, motor bikes, and a tour bus! In Kingstown, **Greg's Auto Rentals**, New Montrose, ☎ 784-457-9814, gregg@caribsurf.com, and **David's Auto Clinic**, Upper Sion Hill, ☎ 784-456-4026, are reputable dealers.

St. Vincent

In Arnos Vale, **Ben's Auto Rental**, ☎ 784-456-2907, bensauto@caribsurf.com, and **Kim's Auto Rentals**, ☎ 784-456-1884, stevekim@caribsurf.com, are both well acquainted with the tourist market.

 Driving can test your mettle in and out of town. The coastal and interior roads are full of bends and hairpins. It's best to sound the horn once or twice as you approach these blind curves. Just sightseeing? Then please let the local drivers pass at a suitable place.

The traffic in Kingstown looks worse than it is. The profusion of pedestrians and lack of pavements in places can make you feel as though you're threading a half-ton needle through delicate human fabric. Parking in Kingstown, use the car park next to the new Government Building on the harborfront. It's EC$2 for the first four hours, and EC$10 for all day. Overnight parking is not permitted.

Car rentals cost an average of US$50 per day, and you are expected to return the vehicle with a full tank. The cost of a gallon of gas is around EC$8 (US$3).

■ By Motorbike

 Speedway Bike & Scooter Rental, Arnos Vale, ☎ 784-456-4894, speedway@caribsurf.com, has 125 cc machines for around $35 per day.

■ By Bicycle

 Mountain bikers will appreciate the terrain of St. Vincent & the Grenadines. For cyclists who like to ride sedately on the flat with little strenuous effort, forget it on this trip.

■ By Bus

 The most economical way to get around is by bus. The main terminal is next to the fish market on the harborfront in Kingstown.

It's less than EC$2 to get to Villa and only EC$4 to Georgetown; EC$2 will get you to Buccament Bay, and EC$3 is the fare to Wallilabou.

■ By Taxi

 Taxi drivers can be good guides; some can tell good stories. There are those that know their limitations and will take you to a site where guides are on hand.

A few that we've found to be efficient and friendly include: **Caspar**, ☎ 784-457-1577; **Tom**, ☎ 784-456-4672; and **Harold**, ☎ 784-456-9323. Tours are priced by fixed the hourly rate of EC$50. The fare from the airport to Kingstown is EC$20.

Tour Operators

There are more than a dozen tour operators in St. Vincent taking groups on land and by sea. The hike to La Soufrière, the Vermont Nature Trail, or a visit to Fort Charlotte are best seen with a guide, which all operators supply. We chose **SVG Tours**, ☎ 784-458-4534, run

St. Vincent's windward coast

by Dominique. He is a professional agronomist and guide, who has been living on the island for over seven years. Land, vegetation and wildlife will be given added significance by his explanations. He gives tours to Montreal Gardens, where he has also worked as a gardener, and Hadley Blooms Nursery. His trip to Trinity Falls includes lunch at a farm. **Sailor's Wilderness Tours**, ☎ 784-457-1712, modernp@caribsurf.com, gives hiking and mountain biking tours.

Bathers in Owia Salt Pond

A tour up the windward coast to **Owia Salt Pond** and the village of Fancy gives real insight into the weatherbeaten side of St. Vincent. From the volcano trailhead, north of Georgetown, the ride becomes more and more spectacular. As does the road. **Fantasea Tours**, ☎ 784-457-4477, fantasea@caribsurf.com, has this in its repertoire. Kim and Earl Halbich are happy to create a package for their customers, so they have tours by sea, as well as land adventures.

Falls of Baleine

Hazeco Tours, ☎ 784-457-8634, hazeco@caribsurf.com, another husband-and-wife team, give the same balance of water and land tours. One of their specials is the Adventure Safari, exploring backroads and villages by Jeep. They also arrange boat charters, hotel packages and villa rentals.

The **Falls of Baleine** are most easily reached by water. A typical tour begins from the Villa Bay area and sails or motors up the leeward coast, with a break for snorkeling. The visit to the inland falls is the highlight, followed by lunch. Another snorkel break in a leeward bay rounds off the day. **Dive St. Vincent**, ☎ 784-457-4714, makes this particular tour. **Sea Breeze Nature Tours**, ☎ 784-458-4969, seabreezetours@vincysurf.com, lists the falls, along with whale and dolphin watching. They are the most prominent whale-watch operator in St. Vincent, having a 36-foot sloop and power boat; fishing and snorkeling are also on their itinerary.

Calypso Tours, ☎ 784-456-1746, calypso@vincysurf.com, have a 55-foot power catamaran that can take as many as 75 people to the Grenadines.

WHALE SPOTTING

From a boat you see a large spout of water rise from the waves with a sound like air being pushed through a barrel at high speed. Perhaps a tall, narrow arm stretches out of the sea or a small dorsal fin breaks the surface and then disappears. What was that?

■ Whale Watching

These waters are full of dolphins and whales, but rarely do you see them unless you specifically go looking. Sometimes they happen to pass by and decide to ride your bow or wake; curious about you, they come alongside to take a peek at the humans.

Whale watching here isn't the same as off New England or Baja, where you can expect large numbers. Instead, you'll most likely see dolphins, with a chance sighting of a whale as an added treat. Most watching trips include a commentary on the island, snorkeling, and a trip to the Falls of Baleine.

Humpback whales visit these waters during the winter months, leaving the cold New England and Canadian waters to breed and calve in the warmth of the Caribbean. They range from 45 to 55 feet in length and weigh approximately one ton for each foot. You can recognize their tall, pear-shaped blow lingering for a minute above a calm sea. Their 15-foot pectoral fins stand out of the water while they roll on their back or slap the surface, possibly as a signal to other humpbacks. There's no reason to fear them if they come close to your boat. By cutting the engine, you may be lucky enough to hear their eerie songs through the hull.

Another large whale, resident in these waters throughout the year, is the **sperm whale**. This deep-water whale, immortalized by Herman Melville in his classic novel *Moby Dick*, averages around 55 feet in length and about 60 tons. Its blow comes out at a 45° angle from a single blowhole on the left side of the head. It is from the teeth of the sperm whale that whalemen created scrimshaw, carved pieces of art presented to loved ones after voyages of often several years at sea. Whaleships would sometimes find an impaction in a whale's intestines, now believed to be a collection of squid beaks and other indigestibles. Known as ambergris, it was an important ingredient in perfumes and in the 1800s was worth more than its weight in gold.

Another familiar whale in the locality is the **short-finned pilot whale** or **blackfish**. Only eight feet long and weighing 800 pounds, they are still taken by Barouallie fishermen in small wooden boats. From their bulbous heads you might detect a squeaky vocalization if close by, but their blow is not as noticeable as that of their larger cousins. They travel in family groups or pods, and, like dolphins, are known to ride in the wake of a boat.

■ Day-tours

Bequia, Mustique and Tobago Cays fall within the day-tour category. Nearly every operator has these, separately or in combination, as standard tours.

 Treasure Tours, ☎ 784-456-6432, treasuretours@ vincysurf.com, visits the **Turtle Sanctuary** on Bequia (see page 143), the **Old Fort** on Mount Pleasant and, after some free time, sails back to the mainland. Other interesting options are moonlight tours by sea or on land.

Archipelago Tours, ☎ 784-456-1686, archtours@carib-surf.com, takes passengers to the Tobago Cays, the rainforest, the volcano; you name it, they do it.

Sam's Taxi Tours, ☎ 784-456-4338, sam-taxitours@carib-surf.com, is another smooth operator with a 29-seater bus, as well as smaller vehicles in the fleet.

Similar comprehensive tour service is provided by **Pleasure Island Charters**, ☎ 784-493-2352, pleasureisland@vincy-surf.com.

Sightseeing

■ Kingstown

 Kingstown is very much a working capital and, as some would suggest, does not lend itself to tourism. The hustle and bustle around the harbor and backstreets might prove too frantic for those expecting a leisurely stroll around a typically sculpted and pedestrianized center with street cafés and souvenir shops.

In Kingstown you have to move with the pace of the place, sharing the main streets with cars, dollar buses and porters with large wooden barrows. The sidewalks are lined with

St. Vincent

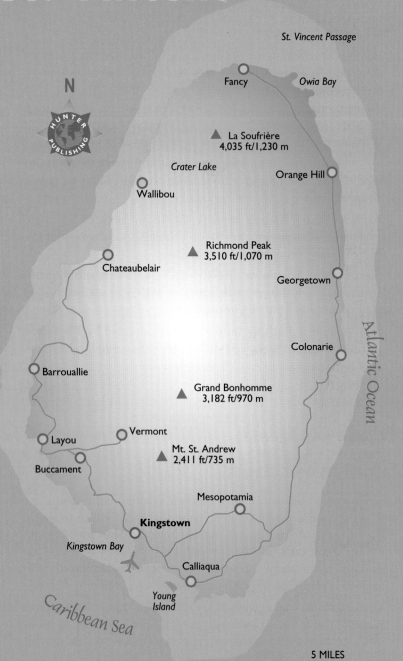

St. Vincent

St. Vincent Passage

Fancy

Owia Bay

▲ La Soufrière
4,035 ft/1,230 m

Crater Lake

Orange Hill

Wallibou

▲ Richmond Peak
3,510 ft/1,070 m

Chateaubelair

Georgetown

Colonarie

Atlantic Ocean

Barrouallie

▲ Grand Bonhomme
3,182 ft/970 m

Layou

Vermont

▲ Mt. St. Andrew
2,411 ft/735 m

Buccament

Mesopotamia

Kingstown

Kingstown Bay

Calliaqua

Young
Island

Caribbean Sea

5 MILES

8 KM

street vendors selling everything from fruit and vegetables to hats, CDs and cassette tapes – not really with the tourist in mind.

Begin on Bay Street, a short walk from the ferry and cruise ship terminal. Under the arched stone walkway is **Basil's Restaurant & Bar** and on the floors directly above is the **Cobblestone Hotel**. These two establishments are housed in a renovated sugar warehouse built in 1814. The bar is a busy meeting spot for local businessmen and gets its fair share of travelers. A rooftop restaurant and bar is ideal for those wishing to avoid the air-conditioning and crowds downstairs.

Two blocks farther north along the harbor is the **central police station**. Although it has a history of fires dating back to 1866, it is thought to be one of the oldest buildings in town. The country's quest for modernization

will probably see its demolition in the near future. This is evident by the new buildings surrounding it – the one harborside is the **government financial complex** completed in the 1990s. Opposite is the new **fruit and vegetable market**, dubbed the "Poor Peoples' Palace," which opened in 2000 – not necessarily a welcome addition as many of the vendors still prefer to be outside in the open air.

Continue past the market and small war memorial along Bay Street. A concrete tower on the left is **Little Tokyo**, a fish market built by the Japanese vendors. The daily catch is impressive in terms of size and variety. They sell tuna, snapper, jack, barracuda, grouper, mahi mahi – everything you can imagine on an island menu. Next to the fish market is the **bus terminal**. The lines designate the area of St. Vincent the bus is heading. Ask any driver and you'll be pointed in the right direction.

On the inland side of the fruit and vegetable market is the **courthouse**, built in 1798. "The Courthouse is built of stone, and contains two rooms on the upper story appropriated for the sittings of the Council and Assembly, with two Committee Rooms; below the Courts of Justice are held. Here also are the Public Offices of the Registrar, and Marshall; this building stands in front of the Market Place, and is enclosed with an iron railing; behind it the Gaol, the Cage, and the Treadmill are placed." Charles Shepherd's description of the courthouse in 1831 still holds true today; only the cage and treadmill fortunately are missing, but the men's prison is still there. Farther north along Grenville Street are two cathedrals – St. George's and St. Mary's – and the Methodist Church.

St. George's Cathedral

St. George's is the usual no-frills Anglican structure. It was built in the early 1800s with the addition of a chancel in the late-Victorian years. An earlier church had stood on the site until the hurricane of 1820. Inside, there are elaborate chandeliers and memorials, such as the one to Rear Admiral Sir Charles Brisbane, governor for 20 years until his death in 1829. Soldiers, planters and other citizens who succumbed to the perils of life in the tropics are buried and remembered here. Perhaps the most understated is William Leyborne Leyborne (not a misprint) who lies beneath a moss-covered obelisk in the graveyard. He was the first governor of the Southern Caribbee Islands in 1770.

The **Methodist Church** is almost directly opposite St George's and was the site of the original Catholic Church. The division between French Catholic and British Protestant was so strong that the church was abandoned shortly after the British took control in 1783. Even when the new St. Mary's was holding its first mass 40 years later, a riot broke out in the street.

St. Mary's Cathedral of the Assumption titillates the eye with its playful Gothic exterior, a creation of the Belgian father, Dom Charles Verbeke, in the 1930s. The interior is 100 years older and more subdued in style, although quiet contemplation is sometimes broken by sounds emanating from the adjoining primary school.

Past St. Mary's, and behind a modern gas station, is the Kingstown General Hospital, now renovated

St. Mary's Cathedral

and renamed the **Milton Cato Memorial Hospital**. This is the one structure we don't mind seeing upgraded into the 21st century. The old building, still standing, is rather gruesome and did little to promote wellness.

Half a mile inland from the hospital are the **Botanical Gardens**. These are the oldest botanical gardens in the Western Hemisphere, dating from 1763. A breadfruit tree grows from a sucker brought to the island by Captain William Bligh. The gardens are open daily from 6 am to 6 pm and are free to the public. Please note that taking a guided tour is not obligatory, but several guides wait for business at the entrance. These gentlemen are expert and knowledgeable guides and we highly recommend you take a tour with them to get the full benefit of your visit. Tours last from an hour to 90 minutes and the fee is set by the government at EC$20 for two people. An additional gratuity will not be out of place. If you have only an hour or two to spend in Kingstown then this is the place you should visit.

Annexed to the gardens is the **Nichols Wildlife Complex**, which sounds fancier than it actually is. The few resident animals and birds are housed in kennel-like facilities. At least you can get a good look at the St. Vincent parrot. If you're planning to visit the Vermont Nature Trails (see page 65), this gives you a preview of the endangered bird you might see in its natural habitat.

Until recently, the gardens housed an archaeological museum in the old curator's house. Arawak and Carib artifacts were collected from all over the island and kept here under the auspices of Dr. Earle Kirby. The old **Carnegie Library** building on Granby Street is the proposed home for the collection in the near future.

View from Fort Charlotte

The road behind the Hospital and Kingstown cemetery leads up to **Fort Charlotte** at the northwest point overlooking Kingstown Harbour. Near the top, the road narrows to one lane. On the garden wall of a house is a historical marker commemorating King Ja Ja of Opobo, an African king who was in exile in St. Vincent in the late 1800s.

At 636 feet above sea level, Fort Charlotte offers a terrific view down the chain of Grenadines. On a clear day Grenada is visible. The fort was begun after the British takeover in 1763, but not completed until 1806, and named after the wife of George III. You'll notice that none of the cannons are pointing out to sea. The fort was built to protect the city from inland attacks by the French and the Caribs. A drawbridge provided extra protection. Once there were 34 pieces of artillery here; today only a handful remain.

Cannon, Fort Charlotte

The only bloodshed in the fort was in 1824 when a Royal Scots Fusilier was killed by a guard at the drawbridge. The private was duly executed at the scene of the crime. Inside the former officers' quarters is a series of paintings depicting St. Vincent's history painted by William Linzee Prescott in 1972. Beneath the fort facing the harbor are some ruins. Once barracks for troops, they were also used as a mental hospital, poor house, and leper colony.

BLIGH & THE BREADFRUIT

Everyone knows of Captain Bligh and the mutiny onboard the *Bounty*. You may be surprised by his connection to St. Vincent.

Bligh's wife, Betsy Betham, had a wealthy uncle involved in the sugar trade and in possession of several merchant ships. On occasion he would hire Bligh to captain his car-

goes to the West Indies. When Joseph Banks, director of Kew Gardens in England, wanted breadfruit brought from the Pacific, he called upon Betsy's uncle, Duncan Campbell. Campbell could provide the ship, a 230-ton, three-masted merchantman *Bethia* (later renamed *Bounty*), and he had a captain in mind, William Bligh.

HMS Bounty *(Gregory Robinson)*

Following the famous mutiny, the path was cleared for him to sail again. The planters wanted the breadfruit in the West Indies as a cheap source of nutrition for their slaves. The second expedition had Bligh in charge of the *Providence*, and accompanied by an armed brig for support.

As the crew of the *Bounty* had experienced, traveling with a cargo of live plants was no easy ride. The *Providence* was 91 feet long and no more than 24 feet wide. The crew had to carry the plants below at night and bring them on deck in the morning. Any salt water had to be washed off the plants immediately. Cabins became greenhouses, and the officers and men were forced to share conditions more cramped than usual.

In January 1793 the two ships, under the watchful eye of William Bligh, sailed into Kingstown harbor with 2,126 potted breadfruit plants that would be divided between St. Vincent, Jamaica and Kew Gardens in England. The young trees were instantly planted out and Bligh continued on to Jamaica. A year later the trees began to bear fruit and the mission had succeeded up to a point. What the planters had not expected was that Africans weren't interested in eating this foreign food.

By this time, the Botanical Gardens were well established and St. Vincent was teetering on the brink of war with the French and Caribs. The curator of the gardens also happened to be the only military surgeon on the island. This is why the hospital is directly below the entrance to the gardens.

Unfortunately, St. Vincent has a drug problem. Marijuana is only the half of it; the past few years have seen growth in the use of crack cocaine. Penalties for possession and trafficking of narcotics are stiff. Don't get involved.

■ The Leeward Highway

The road that passes the hospital in Kingstown and then the Botanical Gardens is the Leeward Highway. It twists and turns, climbing and falling through the communities north of the city: Lowmans, Camden Park, Questelles and Chauncey. At Pembroke the road divides; to the right, it heads inland towards the Vermont Nature Trails, while to the left it continues toward Buccament Bay.

The **Vermont Nature Trails** have a parking lot with a kiosk where you can get a map. Guides are usually waiting to take travelers through the trails for a small charge. Chaperoned or not, you need to bring rainwear as the air is much more cool and damp than in town.

The canopy of massive old-growth trees gives shade for exotic plants to grow and is rich with bird life. The trails are part of a wildlife reserve established in 1987 to protect the endangered **St. Vincent parrot**. Its numbers in the wild are down to an estimated 400 due to loss of habitat and interest from collectors. Parrot poachers face fines of up to EC$2,000 and a possible jail sentence. Just after dawn and just before dusk are the times you're most likely to catch sight of the parrots. The wings are green with yellow and purple flashes, and the tail is green and blue with a yellow band at the tip.

Petroglyph (Karl Eklund)

Back on the Leeward Highway, a sign points to the beach and the restaurant, Buccama On The Bay. Take this turn to see the **petroglyphs**. About one mile down the road is a telegraph pole with steep cliffs behind it. The petroglyphs are carved into the base of the cliff and highlighted with white paint. They are believed to date back to the Arawaks, though nobody knows for sure. Some figures are geometrical and make you wonder what was being recorded by their creators.

The main road goes past the Emerald Valley Casino (open evenings only), which lies in what was once a golf course and previously a canefield. At the end of the road are the ruins of a sugar works. The road winds on to **Layou**, a few minutes away. Another petroglyph is in Ferret along the Rutland river. It is on the property of Mr. Victor Hendrickson, who charges US$2 per person to see it.

Here you are weaving in and out of lush valleys and dramatic landscape. On the black sand beach at Mt. Wynne is another petroglyph known as the **Calendar Stone**. A tall brick chimney marks the site of **Peter's Hope Estate**. Its buildings are in fair-to-good condition and there are rumors of a prospective resort in this valley with them as a centerpiece.

The newly paved road rounds a corner and sitting below you like a town on an Alpine lake, is **Barrouallie**. Yet another petroglyph is here to see. This time it's in the playground of the Anglican secondary school. Known as the **Ogham Stone**, the rock is large, the carving fills the face and it is quite beautiful. If the schoolchildren are around, they'll point it out for you and may even highlight it with chalk. You can return the favor by buying them a soda.

Barawally

Twelve miles north of Kingstown, about half the length of the western coastline, is the town of Barrouallie, or "Barawally." This is the earliest recorded European settlement on St. Vincent. Jesuit missionaries arrived here from Martinique in 1653, but were murdered in retaliation for the beating of a Carib in Trinidad.

By 1730, tension had eased enough to allow French settlers to farm alongside the local Carib populace in the town they called "Barawally." It was then laid out in the fashion of French town planning, with two parallel main streets divided by a park.

Facing the park, but with its back to the black sands of Prince's Bay, the police station resembles the one in Colonarie on the opposite side of the island. Both date from the late 1700s and were used as military outposts. Note the barrel-shaped roof, which was devised for protecting ammunition from fire and other disasters.

With British occupation in 1763, the town was renamed Prince's Town. When the French regained control in 1779, albeit for only four years, the earlier name was used again, but with a new French spelling. Many French settlers remained on the leeward coast despite the British takeover, but they lost their church to a hurricane in 1780. An Anglican Church was built in 1800, and no Catholic place of worship was ever restored to Barrouallie.

The houses surrounding the park are from the 1930s but look more typical of the colonial period. The upper stories are of wood, with elaborate fretwork, or gingerbread, sitting on a ground floor of stone. These stone foundations doubled as storage and warehousing and the floors above were the living space.

Regina Maris *(Center for Whale Research)*

Out in Prince's Bay is a cay called **Bottle and Glass**, used as the local whaling cay for butchering and rendering the catch. Whale hunting in St. Vincent & the Grenadines began in the mid-19th century by visiting Yankee whaleships following the migrating humpbacks and in pursuit of the deep-water sperm whales. Many Vincentians signed on as crew members of New England whalers. The rapid decline of the sugar trade made their new skills economic lifesavers.

Early in the 20th century, William White purchased a traditional New England whaleboat and the industry took root. Though humpbacks and sperm whales are still found in these waters, Barrouallie fishermen go out looking for another migratory whale, the short-finned pilot whale, also known as the blackfish. The height of the Barrouallie fishery was the 1970s. At that time 50 or more whaleboats could be seen resting on the black sands. Twenty years later, only two traditional whaleboats were left.

Today Barrouallie fishermen push off from the shore to chase the pilot whale in speedboats. Unlike the humpback, the pilot whale is not an endangered species nor is its hunting governed by any international regulations. Still, there are some groups that would have it otherwise. It is a rare, but highly controversial event whenever a whale is brought ashore at Bottle and

Glass Cay. The meat is distributed locally, but this little town lost in another century incurs the wrath of modern-day conservationists worldwide.

ARCHIE FRANCIS

The first time we met Archie Francis he was sitting by the sea in Barrouallie mending his fishing nets. He was as black as the night is dark. For some reason I knew he would be sitting on that same beach whenever we returned to the leeward coast. That was almost two years ago. Sure enough, there was Archie, this time in the shade of an almond tree not far from the fishing boats and the drying nets.

In the time since we had last visited Archie, he had relinquished his nets to the care of two of his 11 children. His son has a small speedboat and his daughter, of whom he is extremely proud, fished from a seven-foot wooden boat propelled solely by wooden oars. She was following closely in the footsteps of her father and he liked that. But Archie's heyday wasn't ballyhoo, but blackfish.

Long-finned pilot whales

Blackfish are really mammals; whales to be exact. The term "blackfish" has been used for hundreds of years to describe several species of small, toothed whales. It means the same in this remote water as it does in Newfoundland and Iceland. What these three areas have in common is whaling. And with

St. Vincent

that shared past, they share certain language, boat designs and fishing techniques. In St. Vincent, there was a time when it seemed nothing changed – until the speedboat appeared.

What Archie knew almost by instinct was harpooning the blackfish or pilot whale, pygmy killer whale and orca. Occasionally too, the moody and unpredictable sperm whale. Once sperm oil could be reproduced synthetically, there was no longer a market. Unlike the blackfish oils that the Vincentians drink as a curative for lung disorders, the sperm oil passes right through a person. Archie was determined to have us understand that, when drunk, it literally goes in one end and directly out the other.

We were enthralled by Archie's tales of whaling. You can whale-watch from New England or off Canada's shores and hear articulate naturalists' commentaries or listen to marine biologists explain certain behavior pattern. Yet, there is nothing like hearing a West Indian whalerman tell you the same thing, but from the eye of the hunter. The blackfish swim into the bay at Barrouallie in family groups of four or five members. Archie describes the mother and calf as "husband and wife," because of the way they stick beside each other. An interesting view, as time has always shown that the mothers stick beside their young long after the male has taken flight.

He said they came into the bay "swee, swee, swee, like talking on a telephone," describing a system known by biologists as echolocation. The blackfish use it to navigate and find food by interpreting returning echoes. The sperm whale, he said, went "clock, clock, clock." At his side his granddaughter studied his face as he imitated the sounds of the whales. Thus education and a bit of instinct are passed along.

His face lit up as he came to the hunt. He said they would all fight for one another. "Fighting for each member of de family," a sense of compassion for the whales came into his voice. Then the hunter spoke as the harpoon slipped through his hand and each whale, the entire family, was struck. The boat would carry them to Kingstown where the meat would be sold.

The blackfish aren't a protected species; neither are dolphins. Both can be hunted here without international interference. Today whales have more allies than whalermen do; often what is overlooked is that the sea is their farm. When you see a town like Barrouallie, the deteriorating homes, the weather-beaten fishing boats lying in the sand, and hear the laughter of an elderly man telling tales, while a young child sits mesmerized watching his face, that is when you have to view the world in a different light.

Beyond Barrouallie, you soon reach **Wallilabou Bay**. A hidden driveway veers off to the left down to the beach and a small hotel, restaurant, bar and dive shop. This was chosen as a location for Disney's *Pirates of the Caribbean*,

Pirate village

filmed in early 2003, and again in 2005. A few hundred yards up the road is an art and craft studio with gift shop and place serving cold drinks attached. Another minute up the road, are the small **Wallilabou Falls**. Stop and relax for a while as the road to come has steep curves and hairpins.

Cresting over to the next valley you may, on a clear day, get a view of the volcano, **La Soufrière**, though it is generally shrouded in clouds.

The region of **Gordon's Yard**, **Spring Village**, and **Cumberland** is very secluded; the scenery is dynamic, with hardly a building showing in the landscape. Then you reach **Chateaubelair**. On the black sand beach small wooden fishing boats

St. Vincent

wait for the weekend to pass. We have heard stories of yachts moored in the bay being boarded in the dead of night and of boats off-loading drugs on this part of the coast. The sight of two men, each carrying a large cutlass and not looking very happy, prompted us to keep going.

View from Chateaubelair

North of Chateaubelair, the road travels beneath a portion of an antiquated aqueduct and past a multitude of banana trees with their trademark blue plastic bags around the clusters of fruit. Once you reach **Richmond Beach**, you've gone as far as you can go by car. There's a rum shop, of course, where you can get a cold drink and meet hikers who have just crossed over from the windward side via the volcano.

Three waterfalls are within this northern region and are best visited with a local guide. **Petit Wallilabou Falls** is a two-tier waterfall with a pool at the bottom. **Trinity Falls** is in the rainforest one hour's hike from Richmond Beach. It's comprised of three falls – hence the name Trinity – warmed by hot springs, but with a reputation for strong currents and loose boulders. The most spectacular is the **Falls of Baleine**. They are 7½ miles up the leeward coast beyond Richmond. The best way to reach them is by boat and then a climb up to the 60-foot falls with pools below. Most tour operators have this in their itineraries, with the boat trip starting in Kingstown. The Falls of Baleine can also be reached by hiking a rugged two miles from the village of **Fancy** at the tip of the Windward Highway.

Trinity Falls

■ The South

The south has the majority of hotels, restaurants, dive shops and marinas. Most of these are either on the beach or only a short ride from it. In Villa or Indian Bay, you can hop onto a dollar bus and be in Kingstown in a matter of minutes. The beaches are of golden sand, the water is

Young Island Resort

warm and inviting; why would you want to leave?

Young Island is a 35-acre private resort. Sir William Young was the chief commissioner when the British were surveying and selling plots of land on St. Vincent. He had the first choice and owned what is Villa today. The gumdrop of an island that bears his name was traded by Chatoyer, the Carib chief, in exchange for Young's prize white stallion. The resort was developed in the 1960s by American, John Houser. It has been locally owned and managed since 1980.

A huge white concrete cross stands on a tiny islet in Indian Bay. It is the mausoleum of a local builder, Sylvester DeFreitas. His last request was to be buried standing upright facing the setting sun. Whether this legend is entirely accurate nobody can say. A windowlike opening in the cross certainly feeds the imagination.

From the Arnos Vale roundabout, take the road inland to **Mesopotamia**. Heading into the interior, the valleys roll in and out of ragged hillsides. It is far greener here than along the coastal fringe. "Mespo" and the Marriaqua Valley are the breadbasket of the nation. St. Vincent's 30,000 acres of farmland are worked mostly by independent farmers; many are here in this fertile area. Only a 30-minute drive from Kingstown, it feels a million miles away. The pace is slower, the air is cooler, the only things rushing are trucks with boxes of freshly picked bananas. They have to get them quickly to

St. Vincent

Kingstown and aboard the refrigerated Geest ship in the harbor (Geest is the European company that buys St. Vincent's banana crop).

Across the cut from Young Island is **Fort Duvernette**. This small hill jutting out of the water to 250 feet was fortified after the Carib uprising of the 1790s. Over 100 steps are cut out of the rock leading to two vantage points. The lower level has four 24-pound cannon and an eight-inch mortar; at the top more cannon lie dormant.

Young Island (Lynn McKamey)

The village of Mesopotamia has a Shell gas station, a police station and a church. Follow the sign for Richland Park and thereafter the signs for Montreal Gardens.

Montreal Gardens

AUTHOR
PICK

From the village of Mesopotamia, it's a 15-minute drive up to the gardens. The latter part of the route is single-lane dirt road. Montreal Gardens are set in an elevated bowl that spills out from a backdrop of mountains. These beautifully sculpted gardens are a must if your visit to St. Vincent is to be complete.

They have been lovingly and artfully created by English gardener, Timothy Vaughan. He fell in love with the island at first sight in 1991. A taxi driver brought him to an abandoned garden of flower beds and he saw potential in the place. After inquiries had been made, an opportunity arose to resuscitate and manage the gardens.

They sit at 1,500 feet above sea level in a climate that is cooler than the coast and wet. The average annual rainfall is 13 to 14 feet and the temperature averages 75°F. These are perfect conditions for bloomers such as anthuriums and heliconia; they are here in abundance.

Pink anthurium

Timothy Vaughan is no mean gardener; with a degree from Kew Gardens, he later worked in a zoological garden in France. It has taken 7½ years to finish the 7½-acre site. The time scale is no coincidence. "In Victorian times the big European houses used to have one gardener for every acre," he told us. "Nowadays it's more like one gardener for every 30 acres."

The garden is a blend of three aspects: sunny, formal, and rainforest. Foliage is given prominence, rather than flowers, but there is no lack of color. Pathways and walls of volcanic stone lead you downhill from formal patterns to bridges, tunnels, and grottos in the rainforest. A river winds through the arrangements with elfin speed. There's an elegance even to the carpentry of handrails, posts, and shelters. Two local craftsmen have done some notable work alongside Vaughan. Elfred Wyllie is the stonemason, and Alick Toney the master carpenter. It is quickly pointed out that a team of others work on the project.

No one visiting Montreal Gardens will be disappointed. They are peaceful, yet provocative.

Justicia secunda

St. Vincent

Heliconia

You cannot help but feel calm as you flit from bush to bloom. You start thinking what you can do with your own little bit of backyard. If you want to purchase any cut flowers, that's also possible. The restrooms at the entrance to the gardens are in as pristine condition as the gardens themselves.

No signs are found on the plants and shrubs, such as can be seen at the Botanical Gardens in Kingstown. Vaughan wanted "not so much a botanical garden as an artist's garden." His canvas is complete now, but always growing and adapting. He was trimming a large ornamental hedge while we talked. He worked his pair of shears as if coaxing a butterfly into flight. All the time he was working he was smiling. We complimented him on his creation. He gently reminded us that he is just a gardener. The gardens are open 9 am-4 pm, Monday to Saturday, December through August. There is a small entrance fee. ☎ 784-458-1198.

■ The Windward Highway

Once you have passed Villa, it's striking how many homes have been built along the Windward road. On the tightest bends and steepest slopes, there is a drive leading up to one or a group of houses. Peruvian Vale, like so many of the communities you'll pass through, was a large sugar estate at one time. It is more common now to find bananas, coconuts, and arrowroot, although some sugar cane is still grown here.

Farther north as the road bends is **Argyle**, site of a proposed jetport. If the government is successful in compulsory purchase of land and removal of residents, a major change will come to this beautiful area. This is a prime example of the dilemma faced by these small islands in regard to tourism: To what extent should natural beauty be sacrificed to ensure easier access for a greater number of visitors?

Sixteen miles from Kingstown is Union. **Hadley Blooms** is a working plantation and nursery and open to visitors. Victor Hadley is the sixth generation of his family to work the estate since his ancestor, Ephraim Hadley, came from Bristol, England, with a land grant from Queen Victoria. In that time, the crop has changed from sugar to sea cotton to arrowroot to bananas, and finally at an agricultural climax, tropical flowers.

Windward Coast

Hadley Blooms is clearly marked from the main road and the drive leading downhill to the nursery is lined with banana trees. With a good amount of rainfall, the drive can get muddy and it may be advisable to park your vehicle and walk to the office. From here anthuriums, wild ginger and heliconia are exported worldwide.

The plants are tricked into believing they are at a higher elevation. A canopy of tight, black netting gives this effect. A few acres of orchids are also grown here. You can purchase cut flowers at the source. What may cost you US$10 here would cost you easily US$50 at home. It isn't necessary to make an appointment to visit, but we advise it nonetheless, ☎ 784-458-6326.

Farther up the Windward Highway, you reach **Black Point Tunnel**; 350 feet long, it was cut out of the rock by slaves of Colonel Thomas Browne in 1815. He owned the Grand Sable Estate in Georgetown and the tunnel sped up the transportation of his crop to Byera Bay. It was then shipped to Kingstown, and exported to England. Driving through the tunnel, roll down your windows and go slowly. Every few feet there are recesses carved into the rock where the slaves placed candles while they were digging.

St. Vincent

Georgetown is the second largest town after Kingstown. It has the appearance of a ghost town; the arched walkways echo the buildings of Kingstown, but no crowds fight for walking space on the streets. The **Anglican Church** is surrounded by an indifferently kept churchyard. Inside, it is pleasingly elegant, with memorials to the Rev. Brown and his father, Thomas. **Ferdie's Footstops** is the place for lunch. They serve good local food and have a few rooms to rent, which are popular with those hiking up the volcano, La Soufrière.

Volcanoes

The Windward Islands are volcanic. Lying between the Grenadian Shelf to the west and the Trinidad shelf to the east, the volcanoes on Martinique and St. Vincent are believed to be in their final stages of activity.

St. Vincent's volcano is called **La Soufrière** (meaning sulphur) and eruptions have occurred in 1718, 1812, 1902, 1971 and 1979.

1718 – A crater was formed known as "old crater." Ash spread up to four inches deep as far away as 300 miles to the north.

1812 – A new crater was formed northeast of the old one; explosions were heard 100 miles away in Barbados.

1902 – An eruption occurred on May 7th. The previous day Mt. Pelée on Martinique, only 90 miles to the north, had erupted with such force that the leeward coastal town of St. Pierre was engulfed in a fireball. So fierce was the inferno that there was little left standing and only one survivor (a jail inmate in an underground cell). La Soufrière's eruption was similarly destructive. Earthquakes had been felt for almost a year before the event. A volcanic cloud rose to a height of 30,000 feet. Most of northern St. Vincent was devastated, with trees and buildings torched and all vegetation destroyed. A 50-foot-deep river of lava flowed to the windward coast and over 1,500 people were killed. Ash was recorded falling the next day on a sea-going vessel 900 miles away off West Africa. This type of explosion and the one from Mt. Pelée, are known as "nuées ardentes" or "glowing clouds." Both events were witnessed by an international team of scientists, and their findings are considered to have advanced significantly the bounds of modern volcanology.

 1971 – This was known as a "quiet" eruption. Steam and gas were emitted from the crater between November and March 1972. A dome of lava grew in the lake. This type of eruption, scientists believe, marks the start of the end phase of a volcano's active life.

1979 – This was the most recent bout of activity. For weeks the volcano steamed and gassed. As a precaution, 20,000 citizens from the windward and leeward sides of St. Vincent were evacuated from their homes and housed temporarily in the south of the islands. Schools on St. Vincent and Bequia were closed for the duration. Local banana crops were devastated, as were arrowroot and carrot crops. Livestock was lost, even stolen. Some farmers slaughtered their own animals rather than lose them to lava or larceny.

■ The North

North of Georgetown is the **Rabacca Dry River**. It was created by lava flowing down the riverbed in 1812 and it remains a dry and barren passage which the road crosses for over 100 feet. The river now flows underground from about a mile upstream. Heavy rains can bring the river alive and make it impassable, blocking off the northern end of the island for days at a time.

St. Vincent

The 1902 eruption of Soufrière claimed 2,000 lives in this small neighborhood. Now a ruin on the estate, a stone building with a cellar was shelter for 40 workers during the eruption. They were the only survivors.

Beyond Rabacca is the turning to the trailhead for **La Soufrière**. It is two miles to the trailhead along a narrow dirt road through a banana plantation. This is the banana trucks' freeway, so take care. Continuing north on the coast road, the next great house is the **Orange Hill Estate**. It has weathered volcanic eruptions and hurricanes, making it one of the few surviving colonial plantation houses on the island. The estate boasts the largest coconut plantation on St. Vincent, with 120,000 trees and an annual yield of 80 nuts apiece. The 3,000 acres include 5,000 kola-nut trees and close to 200 acres of citrus trees. Kingstown's grocery stores are filled with jams, jellies, marmalades, lime juices and cordials produced at Orange Hill.

The stone arches of an old aqueduct spans the road, marking **Carib Country** from here on. The land promised to the Caribs over 200 years ago encompassed the entire northern half of the island. Piece by piece, it was chiseled away through the years by planters greedy for this lush and fertile mountainous region. Today the remaining Carib people own very little of the land originally deemed theirs during colonial rule. They live perched above the channel that divides St. Vincent from St. Lucia like seabirds nesting on steep and rocky cliffs.

At **Owia**, there's an **arrowroot factory** open to visitors. Arrowroot is used as a thickening agent in sauces, baby foods, puddings, soups and more recently as a coating for computer paper. Ironically, in this poor community, the world's largest supply of arrowroot is processed. Owia has a salt pond where natural tidal pools are formed by sea action and lava formations.

The road is similar to a roller coaster track with potholes as obstacles.

Arrowroot

Forty-five minutes north of Rabacca Dry River is **Fancy**. The village has been touted as St. Vincent's poorest community, as if this were something worthy of acknowledgement. We found a community of friendly faces with beaming smiles. The rum shop was in full swing, as was a playground of children, where an old water wheel served as their jungle gym.

Waterfalls lace the steep cliffs beside the road and locals bathe in the cool, fresh water. The road curls around the contours of the cliff walls, occasionally pocked by fallen boulders. The road is framed on the other side by a long, straight drop to the sea. The Pitons of St. Lucia are clearly defined 22 miles away. Telegraph poles striding across the landscape are the only reminders of civilization.

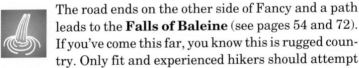

The road ends on the other side of Fancy and a path leads to the **Falls of Baleine** (see pages 54 and 72). If you've come this far, you know this is rugged country. Only fit and experienced hikers should attempt this two-mile trail. If you are going to rent a car to come all this way, check out the tires first. The nearest option for a bed and a hot meal is **Ferdie's Footsteps** in Georgetown.

St. Vincent

Shopping

The advent of the cruise ship terminal has concentrated stores for the tourist in one place. **R&M Adams Book Centre**, ☎ 784-457-5174, has titles by Caribbean authors and, of local interest, even books by Mr. Edgar Adams himself.

EDGAR ADAMS

Visiting the new cruise ship terminal in Kingstown Harbour, St. Vincent, we were delighted to find a new bookstore with titles we had been interested in for nearly 10 years – St. Vincent's history in print. Behind the counter stood Edgar Adams, historian and author of some of those books.

As a boy, Edgar would accompany his father to the boatyard and watch as he built and repaired the boats that traded between the islands. He realized it was natural to connect boatbuilding with agriculture, the source of much of the ships' cargo. The boats and the produce were dependent on one another. *Linking the Golden Anchor with the Silver Chain*, the title of Adams' most recognized work, aptly describes this relationship and is a great introduction to the history of these islands.

With seven books to his credit, the eighth underway and number nine taking form in his head, Edgar Adams admits to a certain frustration with the lack of a local reading public. In some respects, he is handling this by publishing local folktales in small volumes. He is continuing the age-old tradition of teaching by storytelling and at the same time instilling local culture in today's Vincentian children.

Nothing deters St. Vincent's chief popular historian. In the sparkle of his eyes you can tell there is a story waiting to be told, if only you can ask the leading question. Dare to mention to Mr. Adams the paintings in Fort Charlotte or the sunken ships in the harbor. Hear how the story flows through his lips like a river to the sea.

Quay Treasures, ☎ 784-456-1371, has antiques and curios. Other shops sell art, jewelry and clothing. At the time of writing, there are still some units vacant. In Kingstown, **Voyager**, on Halifax Street, sells duty-free items.

The cluster of hotels around the Villa and Indian Bay area have shopping more specifically for the tourist. The **Lagoon Marina Hotel** has a small boutique with swimwear and beach things, the mini-mart by the jetty has provisions for yachties. **Young Island Dock Shop** on Villa beach has shirts, dresses, swimsuits, straw baskets, sun cream and aloe, jewelry, maps, books, Cuban cigars, chocolate and film.

At Basil's is next door to the Lime 'N' Pub on Villa Beach. Evidently this world shopper has more goods to offer than space on Mustique! Visiting his shops is a journey into Indonesia without leaving the Caribbean. If you can't fit that carved headboard into your suitcase, Basil will ship.

Kingstown has any number of small shops with clothes and shoes geared to the local populace. Opposite the new fruit and vegetable market is **Jax Enterprises**, and on the harborfront is **Y. De Lima**. Both are department stores. The new market building itself is a hive of activity on two floors, with produce on the ground floor, while upstairs there are clothing boutiques. The **Bounty Restaurant** on Egmont Street has an art gallery with many works by Vincentian artists such as Josette Norris, Gary Peters, and Peter Providence.

C.K. Greaves, one of the larger supermarkets in town, is on the road leading to the cruise terminal. This crowded street also has the delectable **Sweetie Pie Bakery**, with cookies and pastries. Opposite the airport is the well-stocked **Sunrise Supermarket and Bakery**.

Wallilabou Anchorage

At Wallilabou on the leeward coast are a few shops of interest. **Moma's Art & Craft** and **Wallilabou Craft Centre** (☎ 784-456-0078) sell local wickerwork hats and baskets, painted calabash shells, dolls, carvings and T-shirts, along with cold drinks and the occasional liqueur. Any financial support, whether it's a wicker hat or a cold soda and a visit with the local shopkeeper, will be genuinely felt. While in the neighborhood, stop in at **Wallilabou Anchorage's** gift shop for a selection of swimwear and wraps. Here you can wander on the set of Disney's *Pirates of the Caribbean*, hear some firsthand stories and visit their pirates' museum.

Shops on St. Vincent are generally open 8am to noon, then re-open between 1 and 4pm, Monday through Friday. On Saturday they're open only until noon. The airport has a couple of boutiques for last minute shopping and the **Gonsalves Liquors** duty-free outlet for tobaccos and liquor.

Adventures on Water

■ Scuba Diving

St. Vincent has over 20 dive sites, all on either the leeward side or the south coast. Steep cliffs form much of the coastline and, thus, it is almost impossible for yachts to drop anchor and then go diving. We highly recommend that you go with one of the island's dive operators. Bill Tewes of **Dive St. Vincent** is the Daddy of diving here. He discovered and named many of the sites and installed a lot of the marker buoys above them. If you are on a yacht, please, please do not tie up at these buoys; they are meant for dinghies only and the chances are you'll break the mooring.

Horse-eye jacks (Dive Grenada)

Rock Fort, off Young Island, going to a depth of 90 feet, has black coral and lots of fish. In the bay near the airport, **The Forest** goes from 20 feet to 90 feet and looks like a forest busy with wildlife.

Bottle Reef and **The Steps** are below Fort Charlotte, at the west end of Kingstown. They descend to between 80 feet and 100 feet and both have wall and garden features and many fish. The Steps is often used as a night dive.

Spotted trunkfish (Dive Grenada)

St. Vincent

Farther up the leeward coast, **New Guinea Reef** is famed for its abundance of black coral and **Orca Point** contains fine, colorful sponges. At Layou, **The Wall** spreads from 20 feet to 135 feet down, with a coral garden near the surface and lobsters lurking at the wall.

These prices are for diving with rented equipment. Bringing your own dive equipment makes the costs about 10% cheaper.

Average Prices for Diving	
One-tank dive	US$50
Two-tank dive	US$90
Night dive	US$60
Five-day package	US$220
10-day package	US$425

■ Snorkeling

Dive shops offer snorkeling trips at an average of US$10, or US$20 if you need to rent snorkeling gear.

Dive Operators

DIVE ST. VINCENT

Young Island
☎ 784-457-4714, fax 784-457-4948
bill2s@divestvincent.com, www.divestvincent.com

DIVE FANTASEA

Villa Beach
☎ 784-457-5560, fax 784-457-5577
divefantasea@vincysurf.com, www.divefantasea.com

SUNSAIL

Villa Beach
☎/fax 784-458-4308
sunsailsvg@caribsurf.com, www.lagoonmarina.com

DIVE WALLIALABOU
Wallilabou
☎ 784-456-0355
walldivexp@caribsurf.com, www.diveexperience.com

PETIT BYAHAUT
Petit Byahaut Bay
☎ 784-457-7008
info@petitbyahaut.com

■ Sailing

 These islands are a dream location for sailors. Whether you are a total novice and want to try it on for size, or you are an old hand with boom and rudder, you can go sailing round bays and cays, and up and down the chain. You can charter a yacht, monohull, catamaran or trimaran. The average length is 40 feet. Opt for a captain and crew, or go it alone. You can take lessons, go on day-trips, or take a week or more under sail. You can even buy into a "time share" with a Moorings catamaran!

BOAT BUILDING

Arawaks and Caribs were the first skilled seamen in these islands. In their dugout canoes they moved easily from island to island. Swift communication between tribes meant they were able to hold off European invaders from the Windwards successfully until the late 1700s.

France started a small settlement in what is now Kingstown, St. Vincent. They laid out a village with three parallel roads along the seaside – today's Bay Street, Middle Street, and Halifax Street. They also set up a ship carpenters' yard in the harbor for repairing vessels after the long journey across the Atlantic. This shipyard was in use until 1962 when it was consumed by the Kingstown Deep Water Har-

St. Vincent

bour Project. The last boat, the schooner *Lady Dawn*, had been built six years earlier.

Building was not confined to Kingstown. Beaches throughout the Grenadines became building sites for schooners and sloops.

Early copies of *Shipping News* record the movements of local vessels: "*Two Friends* and *The Lark*, with cargoes of coffee, cocoa, cotton, tobacco and corn bound for Grenada and Barbados." Occasionally the cargoes included slaves.

An 1839 edition of the *St. Vincent Chronicle & Public Gazette* describes the construction of the *Katherine* on Union Island and praises the local shipwright, Robert Thomson, for work that "could not have been excelled by any master shipwright in England."

No complete records of boats built in the islands exist before 1923. From then until 1990, 153 vessels were built by 95 different builders. With large, sandy beaches, shallow water and a supply of white cedar wood, Bequia was the birthplace of nearly half these craft. A boom in building came as a direct result of the end of slavery. Sugar and cotton were in decline so people turned to the sea for trade and survival.

The 18-ton *Sir William Snagge* was the first ship built on Canouan, by Benjamin Compton of Hampshire, England. Compton's daughter, Mary Frances, married his apprentice, William Mitchell, and their sons took to the trade. Harry Mitchell was famed for his schooners out of Bequia. His own son, Reginald, built the largest schooner ever from that island; *Gloria Colita* was 165 feet long and weighed 178 tons. At her launching in 1939, her weight broke the supporting rollers and for two weeks she lay in the sand. Shortly after being commissioned, she was found drifting in the Gulf of Mexico with no one aboard and the only lifeboat gone. Her cargo of lumber was intact and further inspection of the hull revealed no sign of damage. The mystery has yet to be solved.

The era of sail has come to a close. One of the last to be built on Bequia was the *Water Pearl* for Bob Dylan. The best example of these sturdy ships still at work in the islands is the *Friendship Rose,* built in 1966 on Bequia by Eric Adams. For 30 years she served as the main passenger, cargo, livestock and mailboat between Bequia and St. Vincent. Nowadays she is a graceful day-tripper sailing tourists to Tobago Cays, Mustique or the Falls of Baleine.

 Most extended sailing trips are pre-booked in North America or Europe with the larger companies. It is possible to charter boats in the islands, but in high season you could find your choice limited.

Small operators in the islands are more geared to walk-in business as they offer specific day-trips and short-term cruising. Some of them are listed under the *Tour Operators* section, page 53.

Prices for bareboat yacht charters differ according to size of craft, number of berths, and other variables. At the cheaper end of the scale, based on four people sharing, expect to pay US$80 per person, per day, for a week's charter on a 40-foot monohull. If you want a skipper, add US$100 per day, plus food, to the total cost. For a live-aboard instruction cruise, add US$100 per day to each passenger's cost.

 Caribbean Compass *is a free monthly newspaper distributed in the islands. It contains useful information for sailors and articles on recent and upcoming events.*

BAREFOOT YACHT CHARTERS

Blue Lagoon

☎ 784-456-9526, fax 784-456-9238

www.barefootyachts.com, barebum@caribsurf.com

SUNSAIL

Ratho Mill

☎/fax 784-458-4308

sunsailsvg@caribsurf.com

TMM

Blue Lagoon

☎ 784-456-9608, fax 784-456-9917

sailtmm@vincysurf.com

GRENADINE ESCAPE

☎ 784-457-4028

www.grenadine-escape.com

Lara and Guy Hadley have a crewed yacht and speedboat for sailing, island-hopping and snorkeling. US$50 per person, per day. Lunch is US$10 per person.

Yacht Services & Ports of Entry

St. Vincent has three ports of entry: Chateaubelair, Wallilabou Bay and Kingstown Harbour. Sailing into Indian or Calliaqua Bays, you must complete formalities in Kingstown, both at the airport and again at Immigration in the harbor. This is frequently noted by sailors as a real pain as you must taxi or take the dollar bus from one place to the other – and undoubtedly stand in line for some time. The preferred method is to sail into Bequia first, as Customs & Immigration are housed together directly in front of the harbor jetty. Mustique is another possibility, where formalities can be cleared at the airport or Basil's Bar. If you are sailing from Grenada,

St. Vincent's Byahaut Bay

Union Island is the closest port of entry. Should the Customs & Immigration at the jetty be closed, you can try at the airport.

YACHT SERVICES

BAREFOOT YACHT CHARTERS

Blue Lagoon
☎ 784-456-9526, fax 784-456-9238
barebum@caribsurf.com
Full-service facilities, repairs, mail and fax available.

HOWARD'S MARINE
Villa
☎ 784-457-4328, fax 784-457-4268, VHF Channel 68

KP MARINE LTD.
Calliaqua
☎ 784-457-1806, fax 784-456-1364
kpmarine@caribsurf.com

LAGOON MARINA
☎ 784-458-4308, VHF Channel 68

WALLILABOU ANCHORAGE
☎ 784-458-7270, fax 784-457-9917
wallanch@caribsurf.com, VHF Channel 16/68
Port of entry, moorings and provisions.

St. Vincent

OTTLEY HALL

☎ 784-457-2178, fax 784-456-1302

ottleyhall@caribsurf.com

A 22-berth marina just west of Kingstown harbor with covered drydock and all modern service facilities.

CHARLIE TANGO

Yacht and assistance service.

☎ 784-458-4720, fax 784-457-4847

■ Deep Sea Fishing

Fishing is not so much a sport in St. Vincent as a way of life. For the towns on the leeward side, it is still a big slice of their income and their food. Kingstown has a large fish market in the harbor near the dollar bus terminal. Walking through, you get a good idea of what's waiting for you out in the ocean. Marlin, barracuda, snapper, sailfish, yellowfin tuna, wahoo and mahi mahi are just some of the varieties.

For the sportsfisherman, tag and release is now the correct way to proceed. St. Vincent has a three-day international gamefishing tournament in late May. The first-place boat wins US$900, the most tag-and-release points wins US$300, and the champion angler takes home US$375. For more information, contact: **Saint Vincent & the Grenadines Gamefishing Association**, ☎ 784-457-9111, svggfa@caribsurf.com.

Fishing Charter Specialists

BLUE WATER CHARTERS

☎ 784-456-1232, fax 784-456-2382

55-foot Sport Fisherman fishing and cruising excursions half-day, full day and overnight.

CRYSTAL BLUE CHARTERS

☎ 784-457-4532, fax 784-456-2232

www.wefishin.com

Bait, tackle and refreshments included on fishing trips over a half- or full day. Tours to Tobago Cays, Falls of Baleine, Bequia and Mustique on this 34-foot Pirouge.

SEA BREEZE NATURE TOURS

☎ 784-458-4969

seabreezetours@vincysurf.com

36-foot sloop and powerboat available for charter fishing.

FUN TOURS

☎ 784-457-5802

Fishing charters.

Where to Eat

Prices are per person having an appetizer and main course at an evening meal, including 7% government tax and 10% service charge. Lunch tends to be priced lower than dinner, even with the same dishes. Neither drinks nor dessert are included in this scale.

Restaurant Directory

KINGSTOWN
BASIL'S BAR, Bay Street, ☎ 784-457-2713
BOUNTY RESTAURANT, Egmont Street, ☎ 784-456-1776
COBBLESTONE INN ROOFTOP, Bay Street, ☎ 784-456-1937
MANGO TREE, McKies Hill, ☎ 784-456-1897
OCEAN RISE, Ferry Terminal, ☎ 784-456-1120
ROY'S INN, Kingstown Park, ☎ 784-456-2100

St. Vincent

SOUTH COAST

AIRPORT RESTAURANT, Arnos Vale

ALLEGRO BAR & RESTAURANT, Villa Beach,
☎ 784-458-4972

BAREFOOT RESTAURANT AND BAR, Calliaqua,
☎ 784-457-5362

BEACHCOMBERS, Villa Beach, ☎ 784-458-4283

FRENCH VERANDAH, Villa Beach, ☎ 784-457-4000

LAGOON MARINA, Ratho Mill, ☎ 784-458-4308

LIME 'N' PUB, Villa Beach, ☎ 784-458-4227

PARADISE INN, Villa Beach, ☎ 784-457-4795

SUNSET SHORES, Villa Beach, ☎ 784-458-4411

WILKIES RESTAURANT, Villa Point, ☎ 784-458-4811

VILLA LODGE HOTEL RESTAURANT, Indian Bay,
☎ 784-458-4641

YOUNG ISLAND RESORT, Young Island, ☎ 784-458-4826

LEEWARD COAST

BUCCAMA ON THE BAY, Buccament Bay, ☎ 784-456-7855

WALLILABOU ANCHORAGE DINER, Wallilabou,
☎ 784-458-7270

WINDWARD COAST

EASTSIDE RESTAURANT & BAR, Rabacca River

FERDIE'S FOOTSTEPS, Georgetown, ☎ 784-458-6433

PEBBLES RESTAURANT, Mount Pleasant, ☎ 784-458-0190

■ Kingstown

BASIL'S BAR

Basil's Bar (Lynn McKamey)

Bay Street

☎ 784-457-2713

US$15-$25 MC, Visa, Amex

Daily breakfast, lunch and dinner

The relief of air-conditioning from the sweltering heat of the city greets you at Basil's Bar. The food isn't spectacular, but worth the price in quality and quantity. Some items such as sandwiches, burgers, chicken dishes, steaks, and spaghetti are on both lunch and dinner menus, with the predictable but baffling price differences. The bar is a thriving meeting place for regulars, local businessmen and -women. A great place to meet friends coming off or heading to the ferries.

Cobblestone Inn & Basil's Bar, Kingstown (Lynn McKamey)

St. Vincent

BOUNTY RESTAURANT

Egmont Street

☎ 784-456-1776

Under US$15

Monday to Saturday, breakfast and lunch

Curried chicken, macaroni, stewed breadfruit, rice and peas, served buffet style. Sandwiches and snacks available. Tasty local cuisine at a very good price, with local artwork as décor.

COBBLESTONE INN ROOFTOP

Bay Street

☎ 784-456-1937

Under US$15 MC, Visa

Daily breakfast and lunch

Full breakfast, pancakes, French toast, and omelettes are served until 11 am, and then lunch begins with soups, salads, sandwiches, burgers and chicken or fish with fries. It's cheaper than the air-conditioned competition downstairs, and also quieter. We prefer this light and open space, particularly at the beginning of the day.

MANGO TREE RESTAURANT

 New Haddon Hotel, McKies Hill

☎ 784-456-1897

US$15-$25 MC, Visa

Daily breakfast, lunch and dinner

Elegant tables with white linen and silver give the Mango Tree an upscale atmosphere. Slight deviations from the usual offerings are vegetable spring rolls, vegetable samosas, sweet and sour prawns, and vegetable callaloo lasagne. The dinner menu has poached salmon, beer-battered shrimp, grilled pork chops with applesauce, and prawns thermidor.

OCEAN RISE
Ferry Terminal
☎ 784-456-1120
US$15-$25 MC, Visa
Daily breakfast, lunch and dinner

This restaurant at the cruise-ship and ferry terminal gives emphasis to East Indian cuisine. Tandoori chicken or fish, or hotter vindaloo dishes, papadam, naan bread and onion bhajis are served. This is not as out-of-context as it may appear. Many East Indians were brought to the Caribbean as indentured workers after slavery was abolished.

ROY'S INN
Kingstown Park
☎ 784-456-2100
US$15-$25 MC, Visa
Daily breakfast, lunch and dinner

Roy's Inn (Karl Eklund)

If you don't get the chance to stay here, you can at least have a taste of the first-class dining by making a reservation. A five-course dinner is offered at a very reasonable price. After soup, it was difficult to chose between the conch samosa and Vincy fish cakes as a starter. For main courses, we selected sautéed kingfish and grilled beef tenderloin, both served with vegetables. We rounded off the evening with chocolate mousse and an Irish coffee. On Fridays from noon until 2pm an "all-you-can-eat" Jamaican lunch is prepared. Piano music accompanies evening dinner guests, except on Sundays.

■ South Coast

AIRPORT RESTAURANT

E.T. Joshua Airport, Arnos Vale

Under US$15

Daily breakfast, lunch and dinner

From eggs and bacon to bakes and saltfish, rotis, burgers and hot and cold drinks. The balcony is usually crowded with people watching planes carrying friends and relatives. We once came here out of choice as it was before our hotel's breakfast time and we needed an early start. For departing passengers, it is a better alternative to waiting downstairs in the busy lobby or at the boring gate.

ALLEGRO BAR & RESTAURANT

Villa Beach
☎ 784-458-4972
US$15-$25 MC, Visa

Daily breakfast, lunch and dinner

The proprietor is from Canada via Grand Cayman and the Lime 'N' Pub. Fresh fish features heavily on the dinner menu, with mahi mahi, tuna, or coconut prawns breaded in a honey lemon sauce.

Sunday brunch is served from 10 am to 3 pm. Daily specials of appetizers, main courses and desserts appear, but some people opt for the large pitcher of sangria and forget about eating altogether. Tending to be busier in the evenings, Allegro completes the nice mix of restaurants along the beachfront.

BAREFOOT RESTAURANT AND BAR

Calliaqua
☎ 784-457-5362
US$15-$25 MC, Visa

Tuesday to Sunday, 11 am-10 pm

Barefoot Yacht Charter has its own jetty west of Indian Bay and the main offices and restaurant sit above it. We tried the saltfish fritters as a lunchtime snack; they proved so tasty we were lured back that evening for pizza. A large selection of toppings enables you to build your own. Specials include barbecue pork ribs, stewfish and coucou, and curried goat. Takeout is also available.

BEACHCOMBERS

Beachcombers Hotel, Villa Beach

☎ 784-458-4283

US $100-$300 MC, Visa

Daily breakfast, lunch and dinner

Octopus, mussels, crab backs, grilled mahi mahi and jumbo shrimp should please all seafood fans. Pork chops, chicken creole, rotis and sandwiches for landlubbers.

FRENCH VERANDAH

(Lynn McKamey)

Mariners Hotel, Villa Beach

☎ 784-457-4000

US$26-$35 MC, Visa

Daily lunch and dinner

Priced a little high in our estimation, but with beautiful furnishings and atmosphere. This is a venue for grownups who want a quiet and romantic dinner. Don't expect to get up and boogie.

LAGOON MARINA

☎ 784-458-4308

US$26-$35 MC, Visa

Daily breakfast, lunch and dinner

The lunch menu has some tasty bites such as warm goat cheese salad, hot wings, and garlic prawns. We ordered

St. Vincent

Caesar salad, which arrived as merely cut greens and chicken, but the chicken roti was huge and satisfying. Dinner starts with fish nuggets, batterdip shrimp, or callaloo soup; main courses include curried goat, shrimp and fish kebabs on rice with curry dipping sauce, or creole mushrooms and vegetable and potato bake. And just try resisting the baked banana with Guinness-flavored ice cream.

LIME 'N' PUB

Villa Beach
☎ 784-458-4227
US$26-$35 MC, Visa
Daily breakfast, lunch and dinner

AUTHOR PICK

It is rare to find a restaurant menu with a wide choice of dishes, all of which are high quality and always available. The Lime's menu covers six pages from hors d'oeuvres, soups, fish and seafood to meats, pasta, pizzas, desserts, exotic coffees and cigars. Drinks and cocktails are listed separately. The English owner/chef runs the bar like a pub and the restaurant like a star-rated château of gastronomy. A few selections: Pâté Maison, creamy rich pâté with garlic and cognac on hot buttered toast. Blackened tuna steak, in paprika, coriander and black cumin with local herbs, tasted so delicate and almost meaty, it could fool you into thinking you were eating steak au poivre. Grilled pork medallions come in a port and ginger sauce with mushrooms. Specialties include pigeon, rabbit, duckling, and mountain goat.

Daiquiris, coladas and punches pepper the cocktail list; the piña colada is made with coconut ice cream. The signature drink is the Lime Sensation, a blend of lime squash, rum, Malibu, cranberry juice, pineapple and grenadine.

Other places will come and go, change owners, menus and paint jobs, but the Lime 'N' Pub gives the impression that it has been here always and forever. Reservations for dinner are recommended in high season. We have no hesitation in grading this as "Best Food" on St. Vincent.

PARADISE INN

Villa Beach

☎ 784-457-4795

Under US$15 MC, Visa

Daily breakfast, lunch and dinner

Entrées are priced to include appetizer and wisely limited to a few choices. Chicken, scallops, and jerk pork were offered with potatoes and red beans when we called in.

SUNSET SHORES

Sunset Shores Beach Hotel, Villa Beach

☎ 784-458-4411

US$26-$35 MC, Visa

Daily breakfast, lunch and dinner

International menu with seafood highlights. On the expensive side for dinner, but the kitchen is open throughout the day and we found lunch to be a better value.

VILLA LODGE HOTEL RESTAURANT

Villa Lodge Hotel, Indian Bay

☎ 784-458-4641

US$15-$25 MC,Visa

Daily breakfast, lunch and dinner

Dishes that caught our eye were Vincy Ducana, an appetizer of potato and coconut in a codfish sauce; pasta with conch and brandy sauce; and linguine with zesty sausage.

WILKIES

Grand View Beach Hotel, Indian Bay

☎ 784-458-4811

US$26-$35 MC, Visa

Daily breakfast, lunch and dinner

Old World-style dining in elegant plantation house surroundings. We tried the chicken breast in creamy hollandaise sauce

St. Vincent

with rice, fresh organic green beans, and fried puffballs (our description), and it was very good indeed. An appetizer of shrimp in garlic and ginger sauce was piquant enough to set up the palate, yet leave room for the main course. For dessert, the fruit cake with chocolate sauce was out of this world. We really enjoyed this dinner – and breakfast the following morning.

YOUNG ISLAND RESORT
Young Island
☎ 784-458-4826
US$26-$35 MC, Visa
Daily breakfast, lunch and dinner

Breakfast, lunch and dinner are served in either a thatched-roof gazebo or a dining room surrounded by a lush garden. Lunch is à la carte daily, except on Tuesday and Sunday when it is a barbecue or curry buffet. Dinners are five-course meals and guests are asked to dress appropriately. Start with local ballyhoo on a bed of fried plantains and follow with a grilled lobster with couscous and pine nuts edged with a salsa of grapefruit and avocado. End the feast with either the chocolate espresso torte with caramel sauce or the stacked key lime pie with strawberry coulis. If you are not staying at the resort, call to make reservations.

Beach Bar at Young Island Resort

■ Leeward Coast

BUCCAMA ON THE BAY

Buccament Bay, Leeward Coast

☎ 784-456-7855

US$26-$35 MC, Visa

Daily lunch and dinner

One of the classiest beach restaurants to be found. A jetty caters to yachties pulling into this large but secluded bay. Heavy leather veneer armchairs in the bar give it a club feel. Game hen and seafood platter are among the restaurant specials.

WALLILABOU ANCHORAGE DINER

Wallilabou, Leeward Coast

☎ 784-458-7270

US$15-$25 MC, Visa

Daily breakfast, lunch, and dinner

Set in a quaint, open-air building with small cannon as decoration in a beautiful bay setting. This is where scenes from Disney's *Pirates of the Caribbean* were filmed in early 2003 and again in 2005. The set remains in place today (sans Captain Jack Sparrow and the mysterious fog). As you would expect, seafood dominates the menu, but curried chicken wings and a veggie platter can be had as well. No doubt, talk at the bar is a combo of pirates and Hollywood.

■ Windward Coast

PEBBLES RESTAURANT & BAR

Mount Pleasant, Windward Coast

☎ 784-458-0190

Under US$15

Daily lunch and dinner

A set lunch is provided for passengers on pre-booked taxi tours. If you are making your own way here, then be sure to phone ahead to avoid disappointment. The setting is a peaceful scenario caught between the Atlantic Ocean and the ruins of an old sugar cane estate. Our lunch consisted of fresh crab cakes followed by whole grilled snapper with vegetables and salad. The attentive host made the journey all the more intriguing.

FERDIE'S FOOTSTEPS
Georgetown, Windward Coast
☎ 784-458-6433
Under US$15
Daily breakfast, lunch, and early dinner
Ferdie caters mainly to touring parties and volcano hikers, as this is the only restaurant north of Mount Pleasant. If you are coming from or going over the volcano, you want to make a stop here as you are going to be famished. And Ferdie likes to leave his customers satisfied; so huge portions are the norm. We managed to convince him to make us a simple fried fish sandwich and we still left quite full and happy. If you're heading up the Windward Highway, this is a destination point in itself.

EASTSIDE RESTAURANT & BAR
Rabacca River, Windward Highway
Under US$15
This is a lean-to kitchen on the side of the road to catch people getting off the bus and hikers traveling to or from the volcano. It's the last chance at food before heading into Carib Country. No phone, no credit cards, no set schedule; when it's open, it's a welcome sight to weary hikers.

Where to Stay

Prices are per room, per night, based on double occupancy in regular high season, early December through mid-April. Some hotels will add a surcharge for Christmas and New Year. From May through December, some establishments drop their prices by 10-15%. Discounts are sometimes given for extended stays or repeat customers.

Accommodations Directory

KINGSTOWN
THE COBBLESTONE INN, Bay Street, ☎ 784-456-1937, fax 784-456-1938
CRYSTAL HEIGHTS GUEST HOUSE, Bay Hill, Cane Garden, ☎ 784-456-4386, fax 784-456-6389
HERON AT SOUTHBRIDGE, South River, ☎ 784-457-1631, fax 784-457-1189
HIGHFIELDS GUEST HOUSE, Leeward Road, ☎/ fax 784-457-7563
NEW HADDON HOTEL, McKies Hill, ☎ 784-456-1897, fax 784-456-2027, www.newhaddonhotel.com
NEW MONTROSE HOTEL, Montrose, ☎ 784-457-0172, fax 784-457-0213
PHOENIX APARTMENTS, Grant Street, ☎/fax 784-458-9859
ROY'S INN, Kingstown Park, ☎ 784-457-2100, fax 784-457-2233

SOUTH COAST
BEACHCOMBERS HOTEL, Villa Beach, ☎ 784-458-4283, fax 784-458-4385
BREEZEVILLE APARTMENTS, Indian Bay, ☎ 784-458-4641, fax 784-457-4468
COCONUT BEACH INN, Indian Bay, ☎/fax 784-457-4900
GRAND VIEW BEACH HOTEL, Villa Point, ☎ 784-458-4811, fax 784-457-4174
HARMONY RETREAT, Prospect, ☎ 784-456-9113, fax 784-456-9301
KINGS INN, Villa, ☎ 784-457-4086, fax 973-966-0317

St. Vincent

LAGOON MARINA & HOTEL, Ratho Mill, ☎ 784-458-4308, fax 784-458-8928

MARINERS HOTEL, Villa Beach,☎ 784-457-4000, fax 784-457-4333

PARADISE INN, Villa Beach, ☎ 784-457-4795, fax 784-457-4221

RIVERSIDE APARTMENTS, Indian Bay, ☎ 784-457-4308

ROSEWOOD APARTMENT HOTEL, Villa, ☎ 784-457-5051, fax 784-457-5141

SEA BREEZE GUEST HOUSE, Arnos Vale, ☎ 784-458-4969

SKY BLUE BEACH APARTMENTS, Indian Bay, ☎ 784-457-4394, fax 784-457-5232

SUNSET SHORES, Villa Beach, ☎ 784-458-4411, fax 784-457-4800

TRANQUILLITY BEACH APARTMENT, Indian Bay, ☎ 784-458-4021, fax 784-457-4792

TROPIC BREEZE HOTEL, Queen's Drive, ☎ 784-458-4618, fax 784-457-4592

VILLA LODGE HOTEL, Indian Bay, ☎ 784-458-4641, fax 784-457-4468

YOUNG ISLAND RESORT, Young Island, ☎ 784-458-4826, fax 784-457-4567

WINDWARD COAST

FERDIE'S FOOTSTEP, Georgetown, ☎ 784-458-6433

PEBBLES, Mount Pleasant, ☎ 784-458-0190, fax 784-456-4456

LEEWARD COAST

PETIT BYAHAUT, Petit Byahaut Bay, ☎/fax 784-457-7008

WALLILABOU ANCHORAGE, Wallilabou, ☎ 784-458-7270, fax 784-457-9917

■ Kingstown

THE COBBLESTONE INN

Bay Street

☎ 784-456-1937, fax 784-456-1938

www.thecobblestoneinn.com,
info@thecobblestoneinn.com

Under US$100 MC, Visa

The Cobblestone was once a warehouse for sugar and then arrowroot before it was transformed into an inn. The colorful facelift given to the old inn remains faithful to the architecture of the original 1814 building and the signature arches of colonial Kingstown. Nineteen air-conditioned rooms with bath, shower, TV and telephone. Two restaurants and bars complete this tight complex on the waterfront. The busy downstairs restaurant and bar has a long enduring history of being a meeting spot for politicians and sailors alike.

CRYSTAL HEIGHTS GUEST HOUSE

Bay Hill, Cane Garden

☎ 784-456-4386, fax 784-456-6389

crystalheights@caribsurf.com

Under US$100 No credit cards

Nine rooms with shower and ceiling fan.

HERON AT SOUTHBRIDGE

South River Road

☎ 784-457-1631, fax 784-457-1189

innsvg@caribsurf.com

Under US$100 MC ,Visa

Right in the heart of the harbor, this is all that's left of the old Heron Hotel, which was a delight in its day – and should have been preserved for historical value. Five basic air-conditioned rooms with shower, TV, and ceiling fan. The present Heron is ideal for backpackers and those who are waiting for the ferry south to the Grenadines. The inn faces stiff competition from the recently renovated Cobblestone, a stone's throw away. The restaurant and bar do a roaring trade with locals at lunchtime. Taxis congregate across the road, so transportation is at hand, unless it's early morning. As a safety precaution, remember this is on the edge of St. Vincent's busy commercial port.

HIGHFIELDS GUEST HOUSE

Leeward Road
☎/fax 784-457-7563
Under US$100 No credit cards
A family-run guest house with 14 small but tidy rooms and facilities, all with private bathrooms. The location is a bit out of the way for walking into town, but it is on the main bus route for adventures heading up the leeward coast.

NEW HADDON HOTEL

New Haddon Hotel

McKies Hill
☎ 784-456-1897, fax 784-456-2027
www.newhaddonhotel.com
US$100-$200 MC, Visa

The two properties have recently been upgraded. **Haddon Lodge** has rooms with all the facilities expected by a business traveler. King-size beds, large bathrooms, lounge, TV, telephone, and comfortable chairs; a blend of dark wood furnishings and cool tile is predominant throughout this complex. The self-contained **Haddon Suites** across the road are designed for executives on extended stay, with space enough to bring the whole family. These suites are larger than an average, big-city apartment. The **Mango Tree Restaurant** complements the accommodations. Although aimed at the business traveler, the Lodge rooms should be within the bud-

Kingstown

New
Montrose

McIntosh St

Wilson St

Leeward Highway

Giles St

Cemetery
Hill

N

Points of Interest

1. Botanic Gardens
2. Catholic Church
3. St. George's Cathedral
4. Methodist Church
5. Bus Station
6. Fish Market
7. Finance Office
8. Port & Marine Authority
9. Deep Water Wharf
10. Ferry Boat Jetty
    Grenadines Wharf

Queens St

Tyrrel St

① 2 ✝

① 3 ✝

Long Lane Lower

Lower Bay St

Higginson St

① 4 ✝

Melville St

Bedford St

Hillsboro St

Halifax St

Long Lane Upper

Egmont St

Upper Bay St

South River Rd

① 5

① 6

Kingstown Bay

① 7

James St

Granby St

① 8

① 9

① 10

Sharpe St

get of vacationing couples. The only drawbacks are the lack of a beach and the road running between the two buildings; a couple of speed bumps would make a world of difference.

NEW MONTROSE HOTEL

Montrose

☎ 784-457-0172, fax 784-457-0213

www.newmontrosehotel.com, info@newmontrosehotel.com

Under US$100 MC, Visa

Only a few minutes walk from the Botanical Gardens. Twenty-five rooms with shower, TV, and telephone. The manager, Leroy Lewis, is committed to guest comfort and satisfaction. As a member of an organization of hotels practicing eco-tourism, in-room notices politely remind guests of water conservation practices. **Mont Rose Restaurant** serves both hotel guests and the public, and each month the hotel hosts large Saturday-night parties; yet on Sunday morning no trace of the night's activities can be seen as staff is busily preparing brunch. Room service, laundry, internet access, are available. Island tours and scuba adventures can easily be arranged with front desk staff. If any one word sums up New Montrose Hotel, it's "dependable."

PHOENIX APARTMENTS

Grant Street

☎/fax 784-458-9481

phoenixapt@vincysurf.com

Under US$100 MC, Visa

One- and two-bedroom self-contained apartments with TV and telephone. Spacious and comfortable, these apartments are only a five-minute walk from the Botanical Gardens.

ROY'S INN

Kingstown Park

☎ 784-456-2100, fax 784-456-2233

Under US$100 MC, Visa

Once the residence of the first French governor of St. Vincent, this hotel has always been a favorite among Vincentians for weddings and special events. With two dining rooms, large dinner parties can be held at the same time as a small intimate dinner date. Not surprisingly, government vehicles fill the parking lot as the view from the hotel terrace is a selling point for any international conference. Each of the twenty rooms and two honeymoon suites has been thoughtfully and taste-fully decorated. All bedrooms are air-conditioned, have ceiling fans, TV, telephone, and large bath. A fully-equipped fitness center, including sauna and massage therapy, occupies an an-nex by the pool; a game room and tennis court are on-site.

■ South Coast

BEACHCOMBERS HOTEL
Villa Beach
☎ 784-458-4283, fax 784-458-4385
www.beachcombershotel.com beachcombers@cariaccess.com
Under US$100-$200 Breakfast included. MC, Visa

Located at the western end of Villa Beach in beautifully kept gardens. Twenty-three airconditioned rooms with shower, TV and telephone. The dining pavilion divides the rooms from the beachside pool area. A US$10 per night fee is charged for air-conditioning; this is becoming more common as a supple-mentary charge in some smaller hotels. Look for discounts for extended stays. The dining pavilion divides the rooms from the beachside pool area. Sauna and massage are available on-site.

BREEZEVILLE APARTMENTS
Indian Bay
☎ 784-458-4641, fax 784-457-4468
www.villalodge.com
US$100-$200 MC, Visa

Connected to the popular Villa Lodge Hotel complex (see page 119), these eight self-catering apartments have the use of the hotel pool and restaurant. Breezeville is on the landward side of Villa Point, with a view down to Indian Bay on one side and

Arnos Vale on the other. Conveniently situated on the dollar-bus route to Kingstown and only a short stroll down to the beach.

COCONUT BEACH INN

Indian Bay

☎/fax 784-457-4900

www.coconutbeachinn.com, coconutbeach@vincysurf.com

Under US$100 MC, Visa

This funky 1960's West Indian establishment has 10 small rooms with double bed, shower, ceiling fan, and no other clutter. For the location on the beach at Indian Bay, this is very competitively priced, a great deal if you rent the whole place for the week – with 15 or more persons, its $22 a night each guest. The restaurant serves basic West Indian fare, and the **Jolly Roger Pub** can draw a good evening crowd.

GRAND VIEW BEACH HOTEL

Villa Point

☎ 784-458-4811, fax 784-457-4174

www.grandviewhotel.com, grandview@caribsurf.com

US$100-$300 MC, Visa

Nineteen air-conditioned rooms with bath, shower, TV, telephone and ceiling fan in an excellent location on Villa Point. The rooms are named after tropical flowers, as is the custom with many hotels, but Grand View continues the theme with a painted frieze around each room. The building dates to the late 1700s when it was a battery supporting Fort Duvernette on Young Island. Converted for the cotton industry in the 1870s, it finally became a hotel in 1962. The owner, Tony Sardine, was born here – it was his father who opened Grand View as a hotel. We found this property quiet and graceful. The dining was first class. The pool, refreshing and private, with a bird's-eye view below to Indian Bay, Villa and Young Island. The restaurant and bar terrace looks westwards towards Arnos Vale and the setting sun. A tennis court, squash court, and fitness center complete the picture.

HARMONY RETREAT

Prospect

☎ 784-456-9113, fax 784-456-9301

harmonyhotel@vincysurf.com

Under US$100-$300 MC, Visa

The owners formerly rented to long-term medical students, but are now keen to accommodate regular guests, particularly large groups. Forty-two air-conditioned rooms with self-catering facilities, shower, and TV, are available in one-, two-, and three-bedroom apartments. Prospect is a mile plus from the Villa Beach area and set high on the hillside so transportation is necessary. Arrangements may be made for meals. The pool is cool and inviting, with bougainvillea trailing overhead. Trails lead to the ruins of the old Harmony Hall Estate sugar mill. From this high vantage point, there is a magnificent view of Bequia, Mustique, Battowia and Balliceaux. Quiet and pleasing, Harmony is definitely a retreat.

KINGS INN

Villa

☎ 784-457-4086, fax 973-966-0317

kingba@aol.com

Under US$100 MC, Visa

Considered a B&B – West Indian style, five air-conditioned rooms with private bathrooms built around a large, shared living area with kitchen and TV room – Kings Inn is in a residential area that provides peace and quiet at a very affordable price. In an elevated position with a scenic view over Calliaqua, what you save on the room you'll probably spend on transportation, unless you fancy a long trek down to the beach and back again.

St. Vincent

MARINERS HOTEL

Villa Beach

☎ 784-457-4000, fax 784-457-4333

www.marinershotel.com, marinershotel@caribsurf.com

US$100-$200 MC, Visa

There are 20 air-conditioned rooms with bath, shower, TV, telephone, Internet

Mariners Hotel (Lynn McKamey)

access, ceiling fan, and private balcony. This prime location on Villa Beach has its own jetty and pool, giving it an exclusive atmosphere without the slightest hint of snobbery. The rooms are bright, attractive and airy, the restaurant cool and shady. Mariners is as luxurious and discreet as other places in higher cost brackets, and it's only a short stroll along the beach to restaurants, dive shops, and boutiques. Dive packages are available with pickup/dropoff at the jetty.

View of Mariners Hotel (Lynn McKamey)

PARADISE INN

Villa Beach
☎ 784-457-4795, fax 784-457-4221
www.paradiseinnsvg.com
Under US$100 MC, Visa

Shirley Layne-Jones, the owner/manager, is proud of her staff and their reputation for good service. She offers 12 air conditioned rooms on the beachfront with bath, shower, TV, telephone and ceiling fan. For first-time visitors to St. Vincent, we heartily recommend this inn, as you are ensured individual attention from all quarters. The front office specializes in making arrangements for day-trips by land or sea. Special hotel rates are given for groups, senior citizens, and returning guests.

ROSEWOOD APARTMENT HOTEL

Villa

☎ 784-457-5051, fax 784-457-5141

www.rosewoodsvg.com

rosewoodsvg@caribsurf.com

Under US$100 Breakfast included. MC, Visa

Ten self-contained air conditioned rooms with bath, shower, TV, telephone and kitchenette. Sitting above Villa, the inn is only a few minutes' walk down to the beach and restaurants.

A bus stop at the bottom of the drive gives it easy and inexpensive access into Kingstown or along the coast. Janet Woods, the owner/manager, is a former Director of Tourism, so she knows the business inside and out. Rosewood charms its guests so much that many return time after time.

SEA BREEZE GUEST HOUSE

Arnos Vale

☎ 784-458-4969

seabreezetours@vincysurf.com

Under US$100 MC, Visa

Sea Breeze has five rooms with bath, shower, ceiling fan and shared kitchen facilities. This is on a busy corner in Arnos Vale where traffic never seems to cease, so be prepared for noise. The beach is a 10-minute walk. The owners, competent naturalists, operate the most reliable whale and dolphin watching, snorkeling and nature tours.

SUNSET SHORES

Villa Beach

☎ 784-458-4411, fax 784-457-4800

www.sunsetshores.com, sunshore@caribsurf.com

US$100-$200 MC, Visa

The 32 air-conditioned rooms, with bath, shower, TV and telephone, are in immaculate condition, and fresh flowers are in place upon your arrival. The three wings of the hotel are arranged around a pool and garden, with direct access to Villa beach. We were impressed with all aspects of this hotel. The rooms, food and service warrant the prices charged. The manager, although busy with arrangements in the conference center, found time to give us a personal tour.

St. Vincent

SKY BLUE BEACH APARTMENTS

Indian Bay

☎ 784-457-4394, fax 784-457-5232

skyblue@caribsurf.com

Under US$100 MC, Visa

Eight clean air-conditioned apartments with shower, TV, and telephone. Sky Blue is just behind the Coconut Beach Inn so has easy access to the beach. The blue and yellow color scheme is bright and attractive. Medical students tend to rent here over long term, but you might find at least one of the apartments available at a favorable price. With a restaurant and bar, the food was given a "thumbs up" by our taxi driver.

LAGOON MARINA & HOTEL
Ratho Mill
☎ 784-458-4308, fax 784-458-8928
www.lagoonmarina.com, sunsailsvg@caribsurf.com
US$100-$200 MC, Visa

The 19 air-conditioned rooms are large, with two queen-size beds, bath, shower, TV, telephone and ceiling fan. Spacious balconies look out over either the garden or the 50-berth marina; this is part of the Sunsail yacht charter organization. Most customers have already booked their boat before leaving home, but Sunsail also caters to walk-in clients. Sunsail works on having you aboard and under sail within three hours of arrival. Sailing, diving, snorkeling, kayaks and windsurfing, can all be arranged. The boutique and mini-mart should have all the items on your shopping list. The restaurant serves breakfast, lunch and dinner.

TRANQUILLITY BEACH APARTMENT HOTEL
Indian Bay
☎ 784-458-4021, fax 784-457-4792
Under US$100 MC, Visa

This hotel has 12 apartments of one-, two-, or three-bedrooms; all are equipped with shower, TV, telephone, cooking facility and refrigerator. The beachside location on Indian Bay is the major advantage of this group of buildings.

TROPIC BREEZE HOTEL
Queen's Drive
☎ 784-458-4618, fax 784-457-4592
www.tropicbreezesvg.com, tropbrez@caribsurf.com
US$100-$200 MC, Visa

There are 17 rooms in this hotel, which we had a little trouble finding due to its out-of-the-way location. Rooms are comfortable and spacious; some have kitchenettes. In a garden setting, the restaurant serves breakfast, lunch and dinner. From the large swimming pool, you overlook Villa and down the chain of Grenadines. Weekly apartment rental is a spectacular deal.

VILLA LODGE HOTEL

Indian Bay

☎ 784-458-4641, fax 784-457-4468

www.villalodge.com

US$100-$200 MC, Visa

Villa Lodge, 11 rooms with bath, shower, TV, telephone, and ceiling fan, and its companion, Breezeville Apartments (see page 111), occupy the same spit of land as the Grand View Hotel. The poolside restaurant area looks over Arnos Vale, the sports field, and the airport. The white stucco hotel is decorated in pastel colors typical of the Caribbean. Lush gardens are planted throughout the property, and the staff is friendly and helpful. Special package deals are offered for a variety of events happening on the island throughout the year to entice travelers. Easy access to bus stop at end of drive should further entice travelers; for a few EC dollars the bus passes right by on its way up the windward coast, or ride the bus into Kingstown and change buses to visit the leeward coast.

YOUNG ISLAND RESORT

Young Island

☎ 784-458-4826, fax 784-457-4567

www.youngisland.com

US$300-$500+ All-inclusive MC, Visa

Young Island is considered a national wildlife reserve. Locally owned and managed, the resort encompasses all 35 acres of this private island, just 200 yards off St. Vincent's southern coast. The 30 traditional West Indian cottages built of local stone are all ocean-view, and are set either on the beach or overlooking it from a hillside vantage point. King-size beds, sitting rooms, garden showers, wicker furnishings and rattan rugs are marks of classic Caribbean lifestyle. Some of the cottages have private plunge pools and the communal freshwater swimming pool has the appearance of a natural pool in a jungle scene. Tennis, windsurfing, snorkeling, sailboats, and massage are all a part of your daily choice, or just enjoy the hammock on your own private patio. The screams you hear at night are the resident peacocks.

■ **Windward Coast**

FERDIE'S FOOTSTEP

Georgetown, Windward

☎ 784-458-6433

Under US$100 no credit cards

Ferdie's has six rooms at a very cheap price, used mainly by those wanting to set off early to hike the volcano. All are as sparse as you would expect for a backpacker's base camp; it's the only lodging available north of Pebbles (see below). Ferdie's restaurant is a favorite with tour groups at lunch time, so give yourself plenty of time to take in some of the local flavor.

PEBBLES

Mount Pleasant

☎ 784-458-0190, fax 784-456-4456

Under US$100 No credit cards

Noel Fraser has spent 40 years in the hotel industry. He decided to go it alone by running Pebbles Guest House and res-taurant. Two rooms with basic furnishings and shower are available. It is a short hike down to the seaside. An old sugar mill provides a good landmark to ensure you don't get lost in this isolated location.

■ Leeward Coast

PETIT BYAHAUT

Petit Byahaut Bay
☎/fax 784-457-7008
www.petitbyahaut.com
US$301-$500 All-inclusive MC, Visa

Petit Byahaut is St. Vincent's eco-resort. Five rooms, each unique in design and simplicity, with shower and ceiling fan. You won't find any of that fancy stuff here – like phones, TV, roads or keys. Accessible only by

sea, this 50-acre valley is surrounded by jungle-covered peaks. Four miles up the leeward coast from Kingstown, you are in what feels like a small tribal community. Activities include diving, snorkeling, kayaking, Sunfish sailing, and hiking. Transfers from the airport by water taxi are included in Petit Byahaut's rates; three-night minimum stay.

WALLILABOU ANCHORAGE

Wallilabou
☎ 784-458-7270, fax 784-457-9917
www.wallilabou.com, wallanch@caribsurf.com
Under US$100 MC, Visa

Twelve rooms with shower and floor fans. Perfect for the adventurous soul – no TV or telephone to distract you from your getaway. With the dive shop on hand and trailheads close by, divers and hikers alike will appreciate this location. Adventures start straight outside your door. The atmosphere is so laid back you can easily unwind. This exotic bay was chosen by

St. Vincent

Disney to film scenes from *Pirates of the Caribbean*. Since the production finished, Wallilabou Anchorage has kept the set and are building a pirate museum. Restaurant on premises serves Caribbean dishes at 1960's prices.

Keep quiet about the date you are leaving. Thefts often occur the night before departure, when you have no time to deal with the authorities. This is a worldwide rule of thumb.

After Dark

In Kingstown, **New Montrose Hotel** hosts a monthly party with live band. The capital's young professional crowd rocks all night long. **Club Marcomay**, ☎ 784-475-5044, is a local dancehall, lounge and sports bar with live jazz on Saturday evenings.

The Villa area is the evening social central for travelers. The **Lime 'N' Pub** leads the way, and it's the one we return to year after year. As in any pub, dining is not compulsory. **Wilkie's Restaurant & Bar** at the Grand View Beach Hotel has live acoustic music on a regular basis. **Young Island Resort** has music nights in high season. On Friday evenings you can join them with the sounds provided by their own **Bamboo Melodian Band**. Call for reservations, ☎ 784-458-4826.

Basil's Bar on Bay Street is always a hot spot, with people gathering from breakfast until closing. Taxis are available at the corner, but have the bar order you one so you don't have to brave the streets after dark. Seriously.

Gamblers can try their chances with Lady Luck at the **Emerald Valley Casino**, three miles north of Kingstown in Penniston Valley. Eight tables for blackjack, roulette, craps and Caribbean stud poker, 50 slot machines and video poker games are available if you are so inclined. Shuttle bus service

St. Vincent's Emerald Valley
(Lynn McKamey)

collect at points from Villa to Kingstown in route to the casino. The inbound trips begin at 9 and 11 pm; the return trips are at 1 and 3:30am. The casino is open from 8pm to 4am every day except Tuesday. The physical location of the casino is in a beautiful lush valley. Check with your hotel for more information or call ☎ 784-456-7834, 456-1523.

A WORD TO
THE WISE

As a courtesy to locals and fellow travelers, we suggest gentlemen dress in long pants for evening functions.

Volcanic Islands

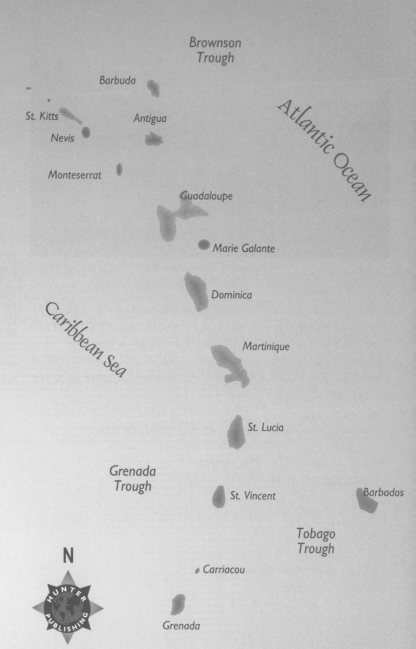

Brownson Trough

Barbuda

St. Kitts

Antigua

Nevis

Monteserrat

Atlantic Ocean

Guadaloupe

Marie Galante

Dominica

Caribbean Sea

Martinique

St. Lucia

Grenada Trough

St. Vincent

Barbados

Tobago Trough

N

Carriacou

Grenada

HUNTER PUBLISHING

NOT TO SCALE

© 2007 HUNTER PUBLISHING, INC

St. Vincent's Grenadines

Between St. Vincent and Grenada lie rocks, cays, islets and islands, like a string of pearls stretching over 60 miles. Of these, nine are inhabited: Bequia, Mustique, Canouan, Mayreau, Palm Island, Union Island, Petit St. Vincent, Petite Martinique and Carriacou.

Each island has its distinct personality. They share excellent sheltered anchorages, hillsides sloping to beaches of white sand, and translucent, sapphire seas rich in coral reefs and other sealife. Their climate has two seasons – under normal conditions.

They can be assured a dry season following hurricane season, which runs from June to November. The summer months should bring enough rainfall to fill cisterns and water tanks.

There is such a variety of drought resistant exotic plants that the thirsty earth often goes unnoticed by visitors.

Bougainvillea is a vine with papery flowers of purple, white, orange or pink. Like the hibiscus, it can wind around arbors and fences, giving a false feeling of a balanced lush environment. **Periwinkles** bloom with pink or white flowers, adding to this misconception. When the fragrant **frangipani** tree is in bloom, or the **flam-**

Frangipani

boyant spreads its red canopy over the hillside, it is difficult to remember that the region is so arid; in fact it is dry enough for hoteliers and restaurateurs to be constantly balancing water usage with the number of guests. To the short-term visitor, water does not seem to be such a big issue, especially as the islands are surrounded by so much. So much... salt water.

The people are lovely. Walk along the road and nearly everyone will greet you with a hearty "Good Morning" or "Hello." You've never met, but you are made to feel welcome. The people remember, maybe not names, but certainly faces. You can visit for two years in a row and then not return for years. When you do, the taxi driver wants to know where you've been. You won't be recognized for being on the cover of a magazine, or in an advertisement for toothpaste, or for the clothes you've designed or the size of your bank account. You are acknowledged for being here, for finding their island home. That makes you special. And that's what makes the Grenadines special.

Bequia

■ Orientation

Bequia's attractive buildings and bus shelters have a seafaring motif on their gingerbread trim. Houses are painted in pastel colors characteristic of the Caribbean. The blending of these soothing shades with exotic flowering trees and shrubs counteracts the dryness and hardness of the land. Infrequent rainfall is the only source of fresh water. The parched earth yields some fruit trees and enough vegetation for sheep and goats to graze.

It was natural, with the ending of slavery and the fall in the sugar trade, that Bequia men would look to the sea to farm. **William Thomas Wallace**, the son of a Scottish naval officer, was raised on Friendship Bay. As a youth he must have been intrigued by the New England whalers as they sailed after humpback and sperm whales.

 From these large sailing ships they lowered small, double-ended boats in which they could follow quietly behind a whale. Hand-held harpoons with ropes attached were thrown and would fasten the boat to the beast. After the kill, these light boats were hoisted back aboard ship, until the next sighting.

In 1857 Wallace took a berth on one of the whaling ships. He traveled as a shantyman, playing tunes on his fiddle, but keen to learn the whaling trade at its heart – in Provincetown and New Bedford, Massachusetts. A decade later, he returned to Bequia with a wife and two seasoned double-ended whaling boats.

By 1870, Wallace was training the men of Friendship Bay. Folklorist Horace Beck describes his task: "He had to teach the locals how to build the boats, how to rig them out for whaling, how to look out for whales, how to approach a whale, how

Friendship Bay

to harpoon it, fight it, kill it, bring it ashore, butcher it, and process it." He drew images of whales in the sand and the men practiced throwing poles representing harpoons. Once this was mastered, a man was allowed in Wallace's crew.

Shortly after his return, another family, the Ollivierres from Paget Farm, took to whaling. The collapse of the New England whaling industry didn't affect its Grenadine counterpart. At

Bequia

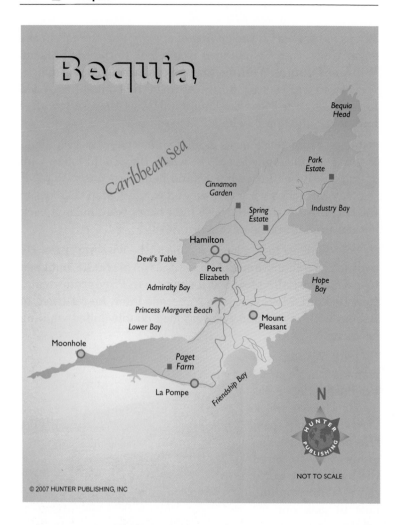

Bequia

Caribbean Sea

Bequia Head

Park Estate

Cinnamon Garden

Spring Estate

Industry Bay

Hamilton

Devil's Table

Port Elizabeth

Admiralty Bay

Hope Bay

Princess Margaret Beach

Mount Pleasant

Lower Bay

Moonhole

Paget Farm

Friendship Bay

La Pompe

N

NOT TO SCALE

© 2007 HUNTER PUBLISHING, INC

one time there were five whaling fisheries on Bequia. These whalers saw it as a source of food for a hungry island, whereas the Americans were hunting only for whale oil.

Bequia turned a new leaf in the middle of the 20th century when its first hotel, the Sunny Caribee (now the Plantation House), was constructed where sugar cane once grew. In the 1960s, a hotel was built in Friendship Bay, and then the Mitchell's homeplace, **The Frangipani**, converted to taking in guests. Electricity and telephones followed in hot pursuit. Yet whale boats were still built in the same style as Wallace's *Iron Duke* and *Nancy Dawson*. Whaling begat boat building on Bequia. Schooners and sloops were constructed along the waterfront.

Wallace had brought the language and responsibilities of crew members from New England. An etiquette on the water was established, based on rules in effect even today and recorded in Kingstown's courthouse. Three boats now leave from Friendship Bay and Paget Farm with the tools and techniques that Wallace introduced. Although they are highly criticized for this cultural tradition, the taking of whales occurs infrequently and is monitored by the International Whaling Commission and several wildlife conservation organizations.

Boat building has ceased for the most part on the shoreline. A number of men build their own speedboats and fishing boats, but generally on the hillsides close to their homes. The beach sites have been taken over by tourism. Today, men of Bequia

Admiralty Bay

are involved in a variety of maritime professions, from piloting ferries to captaining international merchant ships, cruise ships and sailboat charters. They run water taxis in **Admiralty Bay**, and set out from Paget Farm in plywood speedboats to supply hotels and restaurants with the catch of the day.

Though much of Bequia's way of life stems from Wallace and his voyage to New England, it is like an invisible undertone. What you notice as a visitor to the island are the buildings smothered in bougainvillea and shaded in almond trees. What warms you is the sight of sailboats bobbing at their moorings in the harbor and the friendly smiles of people you meet on the street. The threads of the past are there for you to unravel – as in Friendship Bay, where men of all ages revive the childhood art of building "gumboats." Carved to perfection from local wood, they are raced on weekends in competition along the bay. As with their ancestors' endeavors at sea, to a Bequia man this is serious business.

■ Getting Here

By Air

 These days Bequia is one of the easier Grenadines to get to by air. Flights to the **James F. Mitchell Airport** can be arranged from Barbados, Carriacou, Union Island, Mustique or St. Vincent.

Airlines Serving Bequia	
Grenadine Airways	☎ 784-456-6793, www.grena-dine-airways.com
Mustique Airways	☎ 784-458-4380, 212-202-4087, www.mustique.com
SVG Air	☎ 784-457-5124, 800-744-5777 (within Caribbean), 800-624-1843 (US & Canada), www.svgair.com

If there aren't any scheduled flights when you need to depart, do not despair; given notice, several of these airlines will land in Bequia to pick up passengers in transit to St. Vincent, Barbados, Grenada, or between the Grenadines. Or you can ferry over to St. Vincent and catch a flight from ET Joshua Airport.

When you are departing the country of St. Vincent & the Grenadines, you must pay a departure tax at the airport. The tax is EC$40 (US$15) per person. Change will be given in Eastern Caribbean dollars.

By Sea

Three ferries serve Bequia from St. Vincent daily and the mailboat service calls four times every week.

 Admiral I, ***Admiral II***, and the ***Bequia Express*** are the regular ferries between Bequia and St. Vincent. Sailing time is one hour and the one-way fare is EC$20 per person or EC$35 round-trip if passage is on the same day. Tickets are purchased aboard the ferry and no reservations are taken, although you may want to inquire about space if you are boarding with cargo other than personal luggage. ☎ 784-458-3348, fax 784-457-3577, admiraltrans@ caribsurf.com.

Departures from St. Vincent are Monday to Friday at 8 am, 9, 11, 1 pm, 4:30 and 7. On Monday, Wednesday and Friday there is an additional departure at 6 pm. Saturday departures are at 9 am, 11:30, 12:30 pm and 7. On Sundays and public holidays the only two scheduled departures are at 9 am and 7 pm.

The mailboat ***Barracuda*** carries cargo and passengers throughout the Grenadines. The journey time from St. Vincent is one hour; departures from St. Vincent are on Monday and Thursday at 10:30 am.

On Tuesday and Friday, the *Barracuda* leaves Union Island at 6:30 am, Mayreau at 7:30 am and Canouan at 8:45 am, and arrives in Bequia at 10:45.

Barracuda stops only long enough to unload cargo and let passengers depart. Do not assume the vessel will back in and let the ramp down.

If it appears to be pulling up alongside the jetty, be ready to exit from a side door on the cargo level. Tickets are purchased aboard the boat. Passage from St. Vincent to Bequia, or Canouan to Bequia, costs EC$15 per person; Mayreau to Bequia is EC$20 per person and Union Island to Bequia is EC$25 per person.

Schedules are always subject to change, and there may be no service at all on holidays or during major sports events.

Bequia

■ Police, Immigration & Medical Services

Bequia Police Station, ☎ 784-458-3350, is in Port Elizabeth behind the hospital.

Customs & Immigration is in the large, yellow building opposite the jetty in Port Elizabeth. It is easier to clear in and out of St. Vincent & the Grenadines here than on St. Vincent. Office hours are 8:30 am-4 pm, Monday to Friday; 8:30 am-12 pm on Saturday; and 9 am-12 pm, 3-6 pm on Sunday.

Bequia Hospital, ☎ 784-458-3294, is behind the harborfront in Port Elizabeth.

Chiropractor **Gregory Thomas** is on all at ☎ 784-458-3973; in emergencies, 784-457-3785.

■ Internet & Telephone

Anglican Church

There are more Internet cafés on Bequia than on St. Vincent at the moment. In the harbor opposite the fruit and vegetable market, the **RMS Internet Café**, ☎ 784-458-3556, rms@ caribsurf.com, provides fax, phone and photocopying, in addition to service on six screens. They are open daily from 8 am to 8 pm. At the rear of the Anglican Church, **ACS Computer Services**, ☎ 784-458-3967, has e-mail, phone, fax; they also do photocopying, scanning and laminating of documents.

At the Gingerbread, **Surf'N'Send**, ☎ 784-458-3577, surfnsend@vincysurf.com, has four screens and is open from 8:30 am-5 pm, Monday to Friday, and 8:30 am-2:30 pm on Saturday.

 Screen time at these Internet shops costs between EC$15 and EC$20 per hour.

The **Frangipani Yacht Service** has phone, fax and a snail mail pick-up. **Keegan's Guest House** on Lower Bay also has an Internet café.

Solana's Boutique, ☎ 784-458-3554, is the local agent for Federal Express.

Phone cards are on sale from most shops and stores in EC$10, EC$20, and EC$40 denominations. To dial the USA, paying by credit card, or making a collect call, ☎ 800-225-5872; for other nations, ☎ 800-744-2000.

■ Postal Services

The post office is in the yellow **Customs & Immigration** building opposite the jetty in Port Elizabeth. It is open from 8:30 am-3 pm, Monday to Friday, and 8:30-11:30 am on Saturday. Postcard stamps cost EC$1.

Bequia

■ Banks

RBTT is in Bayshore Mall on the harborfront, and is open from 8 am-2 pm, Monday to Thursday, and 8 am-5 pm on Friday.

NCB is near the Hospital in Port Elizabeth, and opens from 8 am-1 pm, Monday to Friday, and 3-5 pm on Friday afternoons.

■ Tour & Taxi Operators

The Bequia taxi drivers are the best guides you will find on the island. They are all local, friendly and helpful. Their tours can carry you to the **Old Hegg Turtle Sanctuary**, to **Mount Pleasant** for a panoramic view, to **Moonhole** to marvel at homes carved out of rock in the 1960s, or drop you off at secluded beaches (and pick you up at a designated time). Drivers wait for fares under the almond trees in the heart of Port Elizabeth, but don't be shy about flagging down an empty taxi. Tours cost EC$50 (US$19) per hour.

Every one of the Bequia taxi drivers we've met and traveled with deserves a mention here, but the list is exhaustive. Eager to serve your needs are: **Elson Taxi**, ☎ 784-457-3181; **Bill Taxi**, ☎ 784-458-3760; **Pikie Taxi**, ☎ 784-457-3833; **Rudy Taxi**, ☎ 784-458-3125; **Locklyn Taxi**, ☎ 784-457-3895.

■ Dollar Bus

Half a dozen dollar buses run the circular route from Port Elizabeth to Paget Farm on the south side. They don't usually go all the way to the airport but, if asked nicely and for a dollar or two more, the driver may well oblige. Busy times are early morning and when school lets out. Heading for Lower Bay, you are dropped at the top of Lower Bay Road; it's a shorter but no less steep walk down to Friendship Bay. There are dead times during the day when you seem to wait forever for a bus to come by, but they'll come. Only a few drivers venture out on a Sunday. Fares range from EC$1-EC$4.

THE DOLLAR BUS

It's cheap. It's what the islanders use to get around. The 15-seater Volkswagen-type minibus has additional flip-down seats to accommodate 18, or sometimes as many as 27 passengers!

It has been described by one fainthearted tourist as, "a roller coaster ride in a tin can with a human shield." The dollar bus can get you where you want to go quickly, assuming you arrive safely. There are regular stops, or you can try flagging them down anywhere on the road. A bus boy works the door, packing the people and their bags into the vehicle, taking the money and so on. This leaves the driver to get on with driving, which he does rapidly. Buses are thrown around hairpins, over-revved up hills, with brakes squealing on bends.

Inside the van, schoolchildren carry on with their games and laughter, oblivious to the panic you are feeling in your seat. Your knees are drawn up to your chin from lack of legroom, you clutch the side of the van with taut fingertips. Claustrophobia can creep up on you as you stare at the small quarter-light window close by, wondering how on earth you're going to climb through.

Had enough? Want to get out? Just tap quickly on the side of the van, loud enough for the driver or his helper to hear. Pay when you get out. The reason why "Excuse me, but I think I'd like to get out here" won't do, is that the dollar bus usually has a voluminous sound system operating. The thudding bass

Bequia

lines can be so overpowering that you can almost forget about the speed the bus is traveling.

Some buses look plain and functional, but some have padded interiors, even in the ceiling space. Upholstery is covered with thick plastic for that deluxe look. Dashboards are shrine-like with figurines, bric-a-brac and the latest nodding novelty. Red, green and gold colors abound. Every dollar bus has its "home" name displayed on a windshield stripe: *Top Gun, One Love, Righteous, Jamming*. These frequently reflect the character of the driver.

■ Car Rental

 If you can't resist the urge to have a car handy, be aware that on such a tiny island, there are no such things as parking places. A local driving permit is a must, and is valid for six months. You can purchase one for a fee of EC$50 at the police station in Port Elizabeth; you must present an existing license. Driving is on the left.

Phil's Rentals, ☎ 784-458-3304, julies@caribsurf.com, has a fleet of Suzukis with air-conditioning; he operates out of Julie's Guest House in Port Elizabeth. **B&G Jeep Rental**, ☎ 784-458-3760, gideontaxi@vincysurf.com, and **Handy Andy Rental**, ☎ 784-458-3722, mitchell1@vincysurf.com, are the main competition. **Lubin Ollivierre**, has car rentals in Friendship Bay, ☎ 784-458-3349, friendshipgapt@vincysurf.com. A pleasant change from all these air-conditioned vehicles is the Mini Moke, as seen in the 1960's TV cult classic, *The Prisoner*. To rent one, ☎ 784-458-3279.

■ Exploring

Bequia is the largest of St. Vincent's Grenadines (Carriacou is a larger island, but it is part of Grenada). The island covers about seven square miles. For exploring, you hardly need a car unless you are pressed for time, in which case you should take a taxi tour. It makes more sense to use the dollar buses, which can take you from the harbor to the south side. In the middle of Port Elizabeth, the Tourist Office is housed in a circular building. This is where the buses begin the route to the south side. Otherwise, take to the roads on foot, but remember the noonday sun is wicked. Carry bottled water and sunscreen in your pack.

Walking barefoot around the streets is a perfect way to pick up parasites and infections.

The road to south side winds up and out of Port Elizabeth. A little out of town, a road to the left climbs up in hairpin turns to **Mount Pleasant**. This is where Irish and Scottish settlers, known as "Redlegs," came in the 1800s. They were poor whites from Barbados who had finished their indentured servitude. Their descendants still live in this area. It's not hard to understand what has kept them here for generations. The air is cool at this altitude, the scenery spectacular.

Port Elizabeth

Bequia

The south side road climbs higher, with superb views of **Admiralty Bay**. As it crests the gap to Friendship Bay, a road heads downhill to the right. This is the Lower Bay Road. **Lower Bay** is usually the first beach that lands travelers. It has its nightlife fans as well as its sunbathers. Water taxis easily transport people to Lower Bay from the harbor. If there isn't one patroling the beach looking for customers, ask at the nearest beach bar and they'll call one for you over the radio.

Lower Bay, toward Port Elizabeth

To get to Lower Bay on foot is a good hike in itself. Take the **Belmont Walkway** all the way to **Plantation House**. There the trail goes up through scrub, with a few man-made steps. Then it becomes a goat path down to **Princess Margaret Beach**. The late Princess Margaret had visited the beach in the 1950s and its name was changed, much to some locals' displeasure; they still insist on calling it by its original name, Tony Gibbons Beach. Princess Margaret Beach has no development as yet, though you will find **Whistling Willy's** boutique, workshop and sometime restaurant. Willy and his colleagues make small items of jewelry and sell them from a makeshift stall. If you get to know him and bring food, you might get invited for dinner.

At the other end of Princess Margaret Beach, another goat path leads you up and over to a paved road and Lower Bay. The point dividing the two beaches has good snorkeling. At the far end of Lower Bay, almost hidden in the bush, is **Claude Victorine's studio**. Ring the bell and soon a French voice will sing out from the bougainvillea and hibiscus, inviting you into an attractive chattel house. There you'll discover beautiful and colorful pieces of fairytale artwork on canvas and silk.

Back at the top of Lower Bay Road and at the gap leading to the south side you have a choice. The road to the left meanders down to **Friendship Bay** and its beach hotels. This beach is generally quieter than Lower Bay; perhaps the seagrass deters fussy customers.

The main road to the right goes through **La Pompe** to **Paget Farm**. On the right-hand side of the road you come to **The Boathouse** – home, studio and gallery of L.D. Lucy and Kingsley King. These artists are an amazing couple who will dazzle you with their work and their sincere hospitality.

Wind on along the road a half-mile or so and a light blue, wooden gate is framed by a large archway made from the jawbones of a humpback whale. This was the home of the late harpooner, **Athneal Ollivierre**, who was respected by whalermen and conservationists alike throughout the world. This was one of the traditional whaling homes for generations and still today you are likely to meet an elderly whalerman sitting on the wall looking out to sea. Don't be shy, they are always ready to relive the days of yore and carry you back to a time reminiscent of Herman Melville's tale of *Moby Dick*.

 From the road, which leads to **Paget Farm**, you can see the whaling cay, Petit Nevis. Continuing to Paget Farm, you will come to the **Banana Patch Studio** of Sam and Donna McDowell, creators of scrimshaw and shell art. Their studio is open by appointment only, ☎ 784-458-3865. The road rides down to the water, where a concrete tower stands and several brightly painted speedboats lie waiting. This is Bequia's fishery, where you can hire a speedboat to take you to Mustique, Petit Nevis or any of the surrounding islands.

Paget Farm is the main community on Bequia after Port Elizabeth. It is home to fishermen, whalermen and many people that work in the restaurants, hotels and shops in the harbor. There are some shops that sell provisions and, past the end of the bus route, is **Mr. Gregg's rum shop**, where it is difficult to resist the temptation of a "missile" – 150 proof white rum – and a chat with the local fishermen.

A short walk farther takes you to the small and efficient airport, the ruins of a sugar works, and Paget Farm School. Feeling thirsty? Visit the **First and Last** rum shop beyond the school. It often looks closed, but can open within minutes if you sit on the benches outside. The track beyond leads to a peculiar complex of homes – "wondrously strange" best describes their character and lifestyle.

Moonhole Guest Room

This is **Moonhole**, a series of homes carved from the living rock by the late Tom Johnston. He began this stone-age venture back in 1961. The first house was excavated from the natural arch of a cliff; now over 20 homes exist, contoured to the landscape. With no electricity, comfort is created with cushions and rattan rugs, and furnishings from local stone. Whale bones from neighboring Petit Nevis have been used as a decorative motif. None of the rooms has more than three walls. Lizards and birds travel freely through the windows, which are open to the wind and the occasional storm. Johnston's son and daughter-in-law give tours to visitors for a small fee. To arrange an appointment, ☎ 784-458-3068.

View from Guest Room, Moonhole

You need to get back to Paget Farm before sundown to catch the last bus back to Port Elizabeth. As it gets later, buses run less frequently. Walking can be unpredictable in the dark; with open drains, gullies and gutters; a flashlight comes in really handy.

Behind Port Elizabeth, a road leads to the windward beaches north of Friendship Bay – Hope, Spring, Industry and Park. **Hope Beach** is the most secluded, with heavy surf that deserves the greatest respect. The ruins of the old Hope plantation house are close to the beach and you might run into Jacob, who makes hats and jewelry from flotsam and washed-up coral. The road to Hope has been in poor condition for some time and is not fit for vehicles. The walk is craggy, to say the least.

HIKING TO CINNAMON GARDEN

For too long I'd had the "life's a beach and my job is to party" attitude. My third visit to Bequia was when I decided to quit smoking and start walking. I knew I needed supplies; water is essential and I thought one big bottle was enough. In addition to a small carton of Bajan cherry juice as a reward, I was bound to need a little refreshment to keep body and soul together. I bought two slices of banana bread and some cookies from the Gingerbread. The kind lady there wrapped them in foil for me.

A beach blanket and a towel took up most of the room in my backpack, into which shades, sunscreen and a hat were also stuffed for good measure. After quick hugs from the Guest House staff in case I never saw them again, I set off on my trek. Destination, Cinnamon Garden.

The road leads uphill behind Julie's Guest House for a quarter-mile, where you come to a crossroads. To the right is Hope Beach; straight ahead, Spring is 10 minutes away. The road to the left takes you to Cinnamon Garden. Or should I say the road heading up? Up and up it goes, and even when it goes from side to side it still goes up. Catching my breath several times I was rewarded with wonderful views of the island.

Near the top of the hill you can see a house on the ridge to your right and beyond it, Cinnamon Garden. Take the path toward the house, skirting below it, and the track, in some places overgrown, will bring you to Cinnamon Garden. A telegraph pole on the summit is the marker. It took me an hour, but I stopped frequently; don't forget I'd just quit smoking. On more recent ascents, I've made it in 45 minutes.

The view is even more breathtaking than the climb. Seven miles across the channel to the north looms St. Vincent. Its highest visible point is often masked by clouds, yet on a clear day it is spectacular. The island seems like a huge predator bearing down upon its little neighbors.

Gazing at the channel itself – there's the ferry that's just rounded the point at Hamilton headed for St. Vincent, and in the distance here comes one returning. Yachts pepper the water and a few speedboats buzz around the scene. Cruise ships or far-off tankers trace the horizon. Magnificent frigate and booby birds glide and dive, telling you where the fish are.

As you look straight down the cliff edge vertigo takes over and balance becomes the only thing between you, thick brush and the bare rocks below. Where's that banana bread? I'd put the backpack in the shade of a tree only a few minutes before. Aaaagh! ANTS!

Walking from Cinnamon Garden down to Spring is almost as hairy as the climb. Just below the telegraph pole is a road leading downhill past a large

Industry Bay Beach

house. It resembles an Olympic skijump. Once you have the momentum going, it's difficult to stop. Follow the road, even when it turns to dirt. Don't be taken in by other roads leading to the left or you'll end up in somebody's garden or doing some serious backtracking. Eventually you reach sea level and walk past what appears to be a farm with cows and goats grazing in the fields. Make a right to go back to town; a left takes you toward **Industry Bay**, the Crescent Beach Hotel, and the Old Hegg Turtle Sanctuary.

A newly paved road leads to **Spring Estate and beach**. The Spring Estate was begun in the 1770s and today there is a hotel on the site. The ruins of the old sugar works have been discreetly transformed into a pottery studio. Mike Goddard has painstakingly preserved a piece of Bequia's history, at the same time making it a useable space. His attention in creating functional pieces of artwork from his kiln is just as impressive. Coconut trees stand sentry over the beach and the smooth road turns farther toward Industry Bay. Drop in at the **Crescent Beach Hotel** for a cold drink or other refreshment. Tired of walking? The owners, Ricky and Dee, have a taxi and can take you to the Turtle Sanctuary on Park Beach, or they can run you back to the harbor.

THE OLD HEGG TURTLE SANCTUARY

It is so pleasing to watch a success story unfold, and all the more so when it is one of conservation. Years ago Brother King was a fisherman working the inter-island trade when a storm blew through and he found himself alone in the sea clinging to a piece of wreckage.

A fisherman heading home at dusk thought he saw something. Later, asleep in bed, he was awakened by a feeling that there was a man out there in the water. And so Brother King was miraculously rescued.

Not long afterwards, in 1995, Brother was camping on the windward side of Bequia when a female hawksbill turtle came ashore. She laid her eggs close to his tent. He was in awe and monitored the scene, from the mother leaving the nest to the day when the first young hatchlings tried to find their way to the ocean.

At this stage, they are most vulnerable, as birds, crabs, dogs and other scavengers are on the lookout for a quick, nutritious meal.

Bequia

Once in the water they become prey to fish, other turtles and sharks. It is estimated that out of 2,500 hatchlings, only one may survive to maturity.

Hatchlings (Lynn McKamey)

Brother King started collecting the hatchlings off the beach. Placing them in large containers, he began by trial and error to find out what these young turtles would eat. He tried lettuce and hibiscus flowers, in addition to fish. Some died, others lived. He pressed on. His wife's protests begging him to come home soon abated. She then was seen crossing the island with bucketloads of fish. Shortly afterwards came protests from the mainland that he was squatting and the owners of the land weren't happy with this so-called turtle farm.

A year later he was releasing turtles that he had nurtured from the beginning. The project achieved political correctness when politicians started showing up at turtle release events. Evidently, the landlords too had second thoughts as the small rubber and galvanized tubs were replaced by larger concrete tanks. No longer was Brother King constantly changing the water by hand; now a pump was in place to regulate the flow.

As the hawksbills reach two to 2½ years, they are released into the sea. Their shells are notched for identification in case they return to their natural nesting area. Patience is involved since turtles take 20-25 years to reach breeding age.

There has been a 50% success rate with the hatchlings, and over 500 turtles have been released to date. The Old Hegg Turtle Sanctuary has come a long way in a short time.

Today there may be weekold hatchlings in one tank, a group of yearlings in another and some large, obviously strong hawksbills waiting for independence day. There is fighting in the tanks, and some turtles get sick or die as a result. In the wild they are solitary and fight to defend their territory. In the Sanctuary it's all there for you to see. This is no sanitized version for the tourists. This is the Caribbean and what you see is real life unfolding.

The Sanctuary is open to the public during daylight hours, seven days a week. With luck, you'll find Brother King there to greet you and tell you about the creatures that have changed his life. Admission is EC$10 per person and donations are very gratefully accepted.

Immediately north of Port Elizabeth is the residential area of **Hamilton**. Follow the road to the end of the point and the site of a 17th-century battery. All these islands were at risk from pirates and privateers, and so a

Fort Hamilton, Bequia

few cannons were positioned in defense of Admiralty Bay. This is as good a picnic place as any; from here you can sit for ages watching ferries and sailboats come and go. It feels like peeking in on another world as it goes about its daily business.

Bequia

■ Scuba Diving

 Having nearly as many sites as St. Vincent, Bequia provides more opportunity to observe large varieties of sealife. Groupers, grunts, jacks, needlefish and sharks can be seen, especially near the smaller uninhabited islands to the south: **Pigeon Island** and **Isle a Quatre**. The *Lireco*, a wreck sunk on purpose for divers in 1986, is home to lobsters at a depth of 85 feet.

Devil's Table, near the entrance to Admiralty Bay, is a frequently visited site good for beginners, while experienced divers enjoy it as a night dive. A handful of sites off the northern coast of the island provide varied diving experiences, but we suggest you go with a local operator, as the currents here can be deceptive and changeable.

Dive Operators

DIVE BEQUIA
☎ 784-458-3504, fax 784-458-3886
www.dive-bequia.com

BEQUIA DIVE ADVENTURES
☎ 784-458-3826
adventures@caribsurf.com, www.bequiadiveadventures.com

FRIENDSHIP DIVERS
☎ 784-458-3422
www.friendshipdivers.com

DIVE PARADISE
☎ 784-458-3563, fax 784-457-3115
diving-in-paradise@caribsurf.com

■ Sailing

Theoretically you could spend all your vacation on Bequia without going in the water. Until the airport was opened in

1991, the only way to get there was by water. It sounds trite to say that there's a big connection between the people and the sea. Some visitors may not appreciate just how deep this connection runs. The strong traditions of boat building, sailing, fishing and whaling still hold.

Racing plays a great part in the Bequia sailing tradition. The **Bequia Easter Regatta** is world-famous in sailing circles and often makes for the busiest weekend in the calendar here. Model boat building is given as much craft and skill as it takes to build large vessels. A major sport now among Bequia boat builders is Sunday model racing on the south side. The races finish on Friendship Bay with food, drink and music drawing a party crowd. In the last few years the boats have been built so big that some entrants believe they are in danger of losing the spirit of the thing.

Bequia Easter Regatta

For information on the Easter Regatta contact: Elaine Ollivierre, Bequia Sailing Club, PO Box 1, Bequia. ☎ 784-458-3086, bsc@caribsurf.com.

Bequia

Sail Operators

GRENADINES ADVENTURE SAILING CO. LTD

☎ 784-458-3917, fax 784-457-3172

quest@bequiasvg.com

The 44-foot yachts *Quest* and *Petrel* offer tours of the Grenadines with skipper and cook.

MYRICK

☎ 784-458-3458, fax 784-457-3420

A 41-foot Gulfstar with crew for day- or longer-term charter.

PELANGI

☎ 784-458-3255, frangi@caribsurf.com

A 44-foot yacht offering day and extended cruises. Special three-day, two night cruise to the Tobago Cays.

PASSION

☎ 784-458-3884, fax 784-457-3015

passion@caribsurf.com

This 60-foot catamaran takes large groups on three different excursions. A day-trip to Mustique, a day-trip to Tobago Cays, the leeward coast of St. Vincent and the Falls of Baleine. Beverages, fishing gear and snorkel gear are included. Lunch is included only on the St. Vincent excursion.

FRIENDSHIP ROSE

☎ 784-458-3661, ☎ 784-456-4709, gaks@ caribsurf.com

This is *the* real thing: an 80-foot schooner built on Bequia in Friendship Bay in the 1960s, she was the main ferry between

Bequia and St. Vincent until the new steel-hulled ferries arrived. She now gracefully glides through the waters on sightseeing tours to Mustique, the Tobago Cays, and St. Vincent's Falls of Baleine at the most northerly point of the island. A trip to Bequia would not be complete without a sail with Captain Calvin Lewis, MBE, on the *Friendship Rose*. Gourmet lunch with a renowned chef onboard to satisfy your palate; you can easily make the choice of sailing with prospective friends, or do as we did, and charter the lovely *Rose* for a special occasion – for us, it was our wedding!

LOST OUR MARBLES

www.gogrenadines.com

Charters come and charters go; perhaps this catamaran, captained and crewed by Neal and Karrie Bongard, will be one that sticks around. Charters are available for four to seven nights and island hopping to all of St. Vincent's Grenadines.

NICOLA III

☎ 784-458-3093

Nicki Hazell provides sailing courses on a 30-foot Pearson. You can learn to sail or improve your skills. Trips can include Mustique or Isle a Quatre with snorkeling.

PUKA

☎ 784-457-4028

Guy and Lara Hadley provide a 51-foot yacht for day cruises that include a three-course lunch, and fishing or snorkeling; or choose a sunset sail with cocktails and snacks.

Bequia

PIRATES ON THE PROWL

Think of pirates and you think of a Caribbean setting. Islands like Jamaica are famous for the likes of Henry Morgan, Calico Jack and Bartholomew Roberts. St. Vincent has played host to its share of pirate legends. Indeed it was here that Blackbeard, the most notorious and sought-after pirate of all time, won fame in the world of piracy.

In November 1717, Blackbeard with Captain Benjamin Hornigold and Stede Bonnet, discovered a 200-ton French slaver, *La Concorde Des Nantes* heading for Martinique. A slaver laden with human cargo and gold dust was no match for two pirate ships loaded with artillery. After two cannon volleys *La Concorde* was boarded by the rogues.

Testimonies by the crew are on record in France giving details of their surrender and subsequent marooning on Bequia. It was the ship Blackbeard was after; the cargo was merely a bonus. He selected some of the French crew to go with him; the cook, three surgeons, a pilot and some carpenters. The pirates then sailed for Martinique to sell the slaves and their old ship.

La Concorde was renamed *Queen Anne's Revenge* and became the new flagship for **Blackbeard** and his men. Seven months later, she sailed into Charleston, South Carolina, thus alerting the British navy of Blackbeard's position. He headed north and ran the ship aground off Beaufort, North Carolina. This provided him with an escape route and more shares in his treasure. Henry Morgan's words, "The fewer we are, the better shares we shall have in the spoils," must have served as a commandment for all pirates.

In recent years the wreck of *Queen Anne's Revenge* is believed found off North Carolina's Topsail Inlet. Studies are underway in Blackbeard's old haunts, including Bequia, to match ballast found at the site of the wreck. Large permanent ballast stones were placed in a ship's hull during construction. Temporary ballast was added or removed to compensate for the loading and unloading of cargo.

Historians know for a fact that Bequia is where the crew of *La Concorde* were put ashore. To discover ballast stone around the island and match it with a particular vessel is quite a feat of archaeology. As you cross the island and notice stones broken from an old wall, remember that it is very likely they were brought here in ships as ballast.

Yacht Services

WALLACE & CO.

PO Box 95, Bequia

☎ 784-458-3360

wallco@caribsurf.com

 Fishing equipment, Penn Senator and Mitchell rods, life vests, flags, buoys, lines and chandlery. Agents for Icom radios. Diving and snorkeling equipment, fish identification books and second-hand book exchange.

BOSUN'S LOCKER

☎ 784-458-3246

bosunslocker@vincysurf.com

Diesel, water and ice supplied. The store behind the Porthole restaurant deals in sailing hardware, maintenance equipment, books, charts, paint and anything else sailors might need.

G.Y.E.

PO Box 79

☎ 784-458-3347, fax 784-458-3696

gye-bequia@caribsurf.com

Yacht supplies and chandlery. Engine and electrical repairs.

LULLEY'S TACKLE SHOP

☎ 784-458-3420, fax 784-458-3797

lulley@caribsurf.com

Penn and Diawa rods, Mustad hooks, lures, bait, snorkel and diving gear, plus a host of other chandlery.

GRENADINE SAILS/NORTH SAILS

☎ 784-457-3507, gsails@cariburf.com

New sails, repairs and alterations, UV covers and awnings.

TURBULENCE SAILS

☎ 784-457-3297

turbsail@caribsurf.com

For new sails, canvas, rigging, installation and repairs.

BEQUIA CANVAS

☎ 784-457-3291

beqcan@caribsurf.com

Diesel generators.

■ Fishing

Water Taxis

Walk into any boutique, restaurant, hotel, tackle shop and marine service store on the island and you'll find a card or flyer advertising independent operators for fishing and sailing. If there isn't one, then the person behind the counter will know someone. Word of mouth still carries a lot of weight here. There are some boats with fighting chairs that come with equipment and refreshments for a full- or a half-day trip. Marlin are the top catch, but you can still thrill to reeling in a tuna, kingfish, bonito or barracuda.

Another option is going to the fisheries at Paget Farm on the south side of the island and negotiating a price with a fisherman there. The boats are 15-foot speedboats with outboard engines and fishing is line and bait. Visit **Lulley's Tackle Shop** in Port Elizabeth if you want to go prepared. The first time we went fishing was with a **water taxi** driver in the late afternoon. We made a mistake by not taking raingear, but after two hours of pulling on a line attached to a simple pole, we felt very proud returning to port with three six-pound bonito.

Fishing Operators

PASSION

☎ 784-458-3884

A 60-foot catarmaran with two fighting chairs and equipment.

C'EST SI BON

☎ 784-458-3218

A 31-foot Bartram handles sportsfishing, snorkeling and tailor-made trips.

MICHAEL'S TOURS

☎ 784-457-3801, 784-458-3782

Sportfishing and day-trips to other islands.

■ Shopping

For its size, Bequia has a large number of gift shops with souvenirs, clothing and artwork. The fact that many artists have chosen to make their home on Bequia has contributed to the diversity of arts and crafts on sale. You can visit some artists' studios and purchase works direct.

The Boathouse, ☎ 784-457-3896, bequiaboathouse@ hotmail.com, in La Pompe, has work by two artists. L.D. Lucy's painting finds the spirits that lie within everything and gives them shape and color, often with bizarre and whimsical results. Kingsley "Prop" King makes model boats that sail;

many are made from coconut husks weighted with lead. Please contact them before visiting.

Lower Bay is the location of **Claude Victorine's Art Studio**, ☎ 784-458-3150, where this French artist has made her home for the past 20 years. She has hand-painted silk pillow covers and crêpe du chine scarves. We admired the paintings of her daughter, Louloune, who produces fantastical works, many with a feline theme.

Spring Studios, ☎ 784-457-3757, produce pottery, garden-ware and ornaments in this tasteful renovation of the old sugar mill on Spring Estate. Mike Goddard welcomes visitors to his workshop and gallery. You'll see his elegant ashtrays in nearly every bar, restaurant and hotel on the island.

Island Things next to the **Anglican Church**, has straw placemats, sailing guides, carvings, jellies and chutneys, rum cakes, candles and small steel drums. **Noah's Arkade** in the Frangipani hotel complex has many locally made souvenirs, as well as books and postcards. Above the Porthole Restaurant is **Local Color**, ☎ 784-458-3202, with a full selection of clothing for the beach and for evening island wear. **Solana's** in Port Elizabeth is like an Aladdin's

Island Things (Lynn McKamey)

Cave of tropical wear, postcards, bug spray, rag dolls and film.

One shop that stands out as the best of its kind in the whole of the Grenadines, and maybe the whole Caribbean, is **Bequia Bookshop**. For regional works of fact and fiction, histories, guides and coffee table books, you can't beat the manager's selection. She also stocks classics from literature, as well as airport novels, children's books, maps, nautical charts, news magazines and postcards. Another specialist store is **Mauvin's Model Boat Shop**, with beautifully crafted miniature, and some not so miniature, models. Eight local craftsmen produce these finely detailed works. Prices range from US$110 to $2,600.

You are spoiled when it comes to groceries. Port Elizabeth has at least five outlets. **Doris' Fresh Food** has every spice imaginable, fancy chocolates, cakes, fresh fruit and vegetables, canned goods, cheeses and nuts. **Knights** has two stores, where you can buy the day-to-day items, frozen foods and wines. **Select**, next to De Bistro, has wines and cheeses and other delicatessen items aimed at the yacht and self-catering market. Slightly out of town on the road to the south side is **Euro Shopper**, ☎ 784-457-3932, with everything you could think of in the way of food and drink. They even offer free delivery service to the jetty. **Shoreline Minimarket**, inside the Porthole Restaurant, offers a good selection of spirits and home-made breads.

In the center of Port Elizabeth is the **Tannis'** store; downstairs is a range of wines, liquor, beers, foodstuffs and things you never knew you needed, like lithium batteries for cameras. Upstairs at Tannis', you can find clothes, shoes, luggage and some haberdashery.

Next door, the **Bayshore Mall** has an ice cream stand, a wine rack, boutiques and the Going Places travel agency.

The **fruit and vegetable market** run by the Rastas takes a while to adjust to. At first you are offered so much produce you think you're being hassled. Don't throw a fit. Pick an item here and there from as many of the vendors as you can, and then everybody will be satisfied. Produce is organically grown in St. Vincent; for freshness and quality it just doesn't get any better! The market is open from 6 am to 6 pm every day, including Christmas.

Sam McDowell and his wife, Donna, produce scrimshaw knives and traditional sailor's valentines from their **Banana Patch Studio**, ☎ 784-458-3865, in Paget Farm.

Bequia

RASTA CULTURE

The Rastafarian culture is world-renowned. Everyone has their own image of what a Rasta is, chiefly from the major influence of reggae music in pop culture from the 1970s onwards. Hair in dreadlocks, heavy bass soundtrack, red-green-gold decoration, and a sweet aroma wisping around them like an aura.

There are deeper sub-texts to be found and only by spending time with these folk can you appreciate who they are and why they live the way they do.

Rastafarians are descendents of Africans brought as slaves to the Caribbean and North America. Christian in faith, they worship God and view Haile Selassie, Emperor of Ethiopia (1891-1975) as his manifestation on Earth. The Bible is their holy text and, in particular, the Old Testament. The story of the Jews' transportation and enslavement in Babylon is viewed as a direct analogy to their own situation in the New World. "Babylon" to them can mean the police, the military or anyone else in a position of authority.

An orthodox Rasta eats neither meat nor fish and takes no alcohol. Vegetarian foods are known as "ital." Fruit, herb drinks and tea are drunk. The Rastafarian will also smoke marijuana, which may leave some people wondering how they can get anything done over the course of a day; though meditation is also a food for the soul. Being in such a tranquil state should indicate that a Rasta is a person of peace.

Inevitably, there are degrees to which a Rasta can lapse from the religion and still be described as such. There are some that drink, some that fight, take other narcotics, steal. Dreadlocks are not compulsory. I know a Rasta who had enormous dreads one year and the next had a military haircut. "What happened," I asked, "did you get a job?" He nodded and burst into great laughter as if he'd been found out.

Rastas without hair are known as "Bald head," and those just starting out with locks anything less than, say, a finger's length, are called "Wiggy." Nicknames are common throughout the Caribbean culture and a Rastaman will use his – "Surge," "Roots," "Big Ras," "Resolve" – more than his birthname.

The fruit and vegetable market in Bequia is run by half a dozen Rastas and they work every day of the year. If you stop and take a look, you'll find an amazing array of produce. At once about three vendors will be at your side and you'll end up with eight bananas, nine oranges, a large lettuce, onions, a papaya and a large melon, coming to about US$10. "But I only came for a lime!" you protest, and speedily three limes are put into your bag and another dollar added to the bill. No problem.

Photography can be a touchy issue where anyone is involved. Where a Rasta is concerned, you could find yourself on the end of a public tongue-lashing that would be an unwelcome addition to your vacation. They are more likely to give their permission to be photographed after you have bought some of their goods. And *please* remember to ask politely. If in time you return to the islands, it's a nice gesture to bring a print for the person in the photo. Your subject may even demand a second sitting, and you'll end up with better pictures and bigger smiles all round.

T-shirt vendors have a covered open-air market by the main jetty with literally walls of cotton for sale. You'll find small stalls dotted around the harbor with ladies selling bread and cakes, fruit and vegetables and homemade jams and sauces, at the best prices on the island.

Shopping hours generally are from 8 am to 5 pm, Monday to Friday, with most places closing by 1 pm on Saturday. There are a few open on a Sunday morning, but they close by noon. If a cruise ship is in, some places extend their opening hours. In off-season, hours are shortened.

■ Where to Eat

Restaurant Directory

COCO'S PLACE, Lower Bay, ☎ 784-458-3463
CRESCENT BEACH INN, Industry, ☎ 784-458-3400
DAWN'S CREOLE CAFE & SNACKETTE, Lower Bay, ☎ 784-458-3154
DAWN'S CREOLE GARDEN, Lower Bay, ☎ 784-458-3154
DE BISTRO, Port Elizabeth, ☎ 784-458-3428
DE REEF, Lower Bay, ☎ 784-458-3447
FERNANDO'S HIDEAWAY, Lower Bay, ☎ 784-458-3758
FRANGIPANI, Admiralty Bay, ☎ 784-458-3255
THE GINGERBREAD, Belmont Walkway, ☎ 784-458-3800
GREEN BOLEY, Belmont Walkway, ☎ 784-458-3247
L'AUBERGE DES GRENADINES, Belmont Walkway, ☎ 784-458-3201
MAC'S PIZZERIA, Admiralty Bay, ☎ 784-458-3474
MARANNE'S ICE CREAM, Belmont Walkway, ☎ 784-458-3041
MOSKITO BEACH BAR & GRILL, Friendship Bay, ☎ 784-458-3222
THE OLD FORT, Mount Pleasant, ☎ 784-458-3440
THE PORT HOLE, Port Elizabeth, ☎ 784-458-3458
TANTIE PEARL'S, Port Elizabeth, ☎ 784-457-3160
WHALEBONER, Admiralty Bay, ☎ 784-458-3233

COCO'S PLACE

Lower Bay
☎ 784-458-3463
US$15-$35 MC, Visa, Amex
Daily, noon until late

Although it opened in the mid-1990s, Coco's still feels new. Painted in Caribbean pastels, built as though standing on stilts, Coco's is recognizable from a good distance. Looking like an attractive place for a meal is half the battle. The cuisine completes the other 50% with no problem. Seafood is understandably what most customers come for and the grilled lobster is a big hit. Another star is The Conch Ting, "a known aphrodisiac cooked in a very special way to enhance its "power." Many people consider Coco's as having the best view on Bequia, as it looks over the entire sweep of Admiralty Bay and the southwest corner of St. Vincent. Live music is staged on Tuesday and Friday, and for most nights in high season a reservation is recommended.

CRESCENT BEACH INN

Industry
☎ 784-458-3400
Under US$15
Daily lunch and dinner

The Crescent Beach Inn provides a perfect spot to lunch on the way to or from the Old Hegg Turtle Sanctuary. Relish hearty sandwiches at lunch and typical West Indian fare at dinner–and

Crescent Beach Inn

plenty. Full Moon barbecues are a long-standing tradition. Look for Ricky's Taxi under the almond tree in Port Elizabeth to carry you to his surfside home and inn for a bit of Bequia hospitality.

DAWN'S CREOLE CAFE & SNACKETTE

Lower Bay

☎ 784-458-3154

Under US$15

On the beach next to De Reef, this is a small but busy little coffee house. Opening early for breakfast, it steals a march on its neighbor.

DAWN'S CREOLE GARDEN

Lower Bay

☎ 784-458-3154

US$15-$25 MC, Visa

Dawn combines the typical West Indian ingredients to produce creole and curried dishes. Nestling below Coco's Place, this is a bit more peaceful than the jumping joint above.

DE BISTRO

Port Elizabeth

☎ 784-458-3428

US$15-$25 MC, Visa

Daily, 8 am-11 pm

A good meeting place in the harbor and great for people-watching. Mitch's De Bistro has a full menu and very often is at full capacity. We particularly favor his barracuda pizza.

DE REEF

Lower Bay

☎ 784-458-3958

US$15-$25 MC, Visa

10 am-late

Beach bar and restaurant serving as the main hub on Lower Bay beach. An assortment of sandwiches, burgers and seafood dishes in a casual atmosphere. Jump ups, usually on alternate Saturday nights, with live music, involve an entrance fee and a lot of people. It starts cooking from 10 pm and simmers until

2 am or later. A great social whirl also on Sundays from lunch-time onwards.

FERNANDO'S HIDEAWAY

Lower Bay

☎ 784-458-3758

US$15-$25

Monday to Saturday

Hidden gem of Bequia's culinary houses, it has an "at home" atmosphere. Nando is a master of local cookery; if you manage to reserve a table for Saturday, you can try his special goat water.

FRANGIPANI

Admiralty Bay

☎ 784-458-3255

US$26-$35 MC, Visa

Daily

We had never eaten here until we came to research this book. For lunch we were impressed with the Mediterranean pasta salad: penne rigate with tomatoes, olives, tuna and mozarella cheese in a fresh basil and parmesan vinaigrette. Dinner crowned the day, with poached kingfish court bouillon served on a bed of couscous, and vegetables.

Frangipani's walkway (Lynn McKamey)

The Frangipani should be proud of its cocktails. This is a favorite spot for green-flash watchers and the crowd only gets bigger after sunset.

Thursday evening attracts many with a barbecue and steel pan music. Sunday evening is another night of live music.

THE GINGERBREAD

Belmont Walkway

☎ 784-458-3800

US$15-$25 MC, Visa

Daily, 7 am-10 pm

Breakfast, lunch and dinner in a cool second-floor restaurant. Our favorite daytime snack is a tuna and cheese toasted sandwich, followed by their mixed-blend juices. Evening meals are a touch more sophisticated, with creole dishes and curry specialties. Crowded in high season during live music nights, and on Saturday and Sunday it is worthwhile reserving a table.

The outdoor Traveler's Tree barbecue takes place daily at The Gingerbread from 11 am to 3 pm, serving kebabs, burgers, steaks and chicken.

The Gingerbread ground-floor café is open from 7 am to 7 pm, with a selection of pastries, sweet breads and cookies – great for picnics and hikes – and juices, tea and coffee.

GREEN BOLEY

Belmont Walkway

☎ 784-458-3247

Under US$15

Daily

Rotis and sandwiches, full meals and snacks, or if you just want a beer and somewhere to gather your thoughts, this is it. At first glance, the Green Boley looks like a funky shack that is a cross between a bar, a café and a beach restaurant. After repeated visits to Bequia, we have come to the conclusion that this is exactly what it is.

L'AUBERGE DES GRENADINES

L'Auberge des Grenadines

Belmont Walkway
☎ 784-458-3201
US$26-$35 MC, Visa, Discover
Daily, noon-10 pm

L'Auberge's enthusiastic owner, Jacques, is determined to vault his establishment into gastronomic orbit. Escargots, mussels, and seafood casserole are some samples from his menu. A live lobster pool means you can meet your dinner. Live music is played on Tuesday and Friday.

GREEN FLASH

It won't be long into your travels to the islands before you hear something about the mysterious green flash. Sitting in a bar at sundown there will inevitably be someone caught in a trance, watching as the sun melts into the sea. In a matter of moments they will either break into a winsome smile or be struck with a loser's

Green Flash at Sunset

frown. You can overhear heated discussions as to whether the green flash stems from an overindulgence of rum punch, optical illusion or reality.

The green flash is a natural phenomenon occurring when conditions are ideal. You must have a direct view of the sun and the sky must be clear of clouds and haze. As the sun begins to set, its light bends

Bequia

and spreads into a spectrum of colors of different wavelengths. It's the same process as light being refracted by a prism. The colors at either end of the spectrum are dispersed more easily than those in the middle, leaving green as the least affected.

As the sun disappears, the colors dissolve one at a time. Red disappears first, followed by orange, yellow, green, blue, indigo and lastly violet. Orange and yellow are absorbed by water vapor, the ozone and oxygen. Then, as the very last segment of the sun goes down, a narrow ribbon of green streaks across the horizon like light in a neon tube. This is the green flash. Blue, indigo and violet are dispersed next, coloring the evening sky.

Perhaps the reason for so many unbelievers is that the flash is so momentary and their attention span is even shorter. It goes without saying that looking directly into the sun at any time is harmful to your eyesight. It is certainly a strain not to blink in the last few seconds of sunlight. According to island lore, the green flash is linked to true love and good fortune. Little wonder that some folks wait for sunset with an almost religious fervor.

MAC'S PIZZERIA

Admiralty Bay

☎ 784-458-3474

US$15-$25 MC, Visa

Daily, 11 am-10 pm

We can't give an unbiased opinion of Mac's because we like it so much. Serving 9- , 13- and 15-inch pizzas with fish, chicken, lobster and many other toppings, you can select your own. Conch fritters and pita bread sandwiches are just two of their snacks. Although we liked the price on a shared 13-inch lobster pizza, we find a nine-inch adequate for two people. This leaves room for dessert, of course. Fruit crumble, double-frosted brownies and Maranne's ice cream compete with the Key Lime pie. It seems the Key lime pie always wins.

THE OLD FORT

Mount Pleasant

☎ 784-458-3440

US$26-$35 MC, Visa

Daily

For a really romantic evening, reserve a table in this hilltop setting with the lights of Mustique twinkling seven miles away. Grilled lobster, catch of the day, piquant appetizers and fresh steamed vegetables from St. Vincent will make this meal a treasured memory. Delicious desserts, such as chocolate

Dining at The Old Fort

mousse, and a choice of fine wines and after-dinner digestifs round off the evening perfectly. You will be tempted to make this a regular haunt.

MOSKITO BEACH BAR & GRILL

Friendship Bay

☎ 784-458-3222

US$15-$25 MC, Visa

Located right on the beach at Friendship Bay. Trade is brisk both day and night. A full range of food is available. Monday nights have an Asian theme; Wednesdays bring lobster barbecue with live music. The bar has swings for seats. One of the better places for a perfect afternoon at the seaside.

MARANNE'S ICE CREAM

Belmont Walkway

☎ 784-458-3041

Delicious homemade ice cream that is worthy of international recognition. Vanilla, vanilla fudge, chocolate, rum & raisin, coconut, passionfruit and banana flavors for EC$5 a scoop. You can also buy by the half gallon. A few restaurants on the island serve it as well. Maranne is thinking of selling the shop, so now we beg: "Maranne, keep making the ice cream, or give us the recipe!"

Bequia

THE PORT HOLE

Port Elizabeth

☎ 784-458-3458

Under US$15 MC, Visa

7:30 am-9 pm, Monday to Saturday

Just as good as any of the fancier places nearby. The Port Hole has its regulars, giving it a pub-like atmosphere. Snacks and full meals in Caribbean and international styles.

TANTIE PEARL'S

Port Elizabeth

☎ 784-457-3160

Lunch, noon-3 pm; dinner, 7 pm-10 pm

US$15-$25

Steamed fish, creole pork chops, West Indian chicken, curried conch, and lobster are the usual entrée choices. Free transport is given from the harbor for parties of four or more. The view over Port Elizabeth is enchanting during an evening meal. Reservations are recommended.

WHALEBONER

Admiralty Bay

☎ 784-458-3233

US$26-$35 MC, Visa

Daily, 8 am-10 pm

 The jawbones of a humpback whale frame the entrance. Fish, rotis and other local dishes for lunch. Dinner we found to be on the expensive side. Monday night's special is barbecue, with live reggae; Wednesday night steel pan music is served as the musical course.

■ Where to Stay

Accommodations Directory

L'AUBERGE DES GRENADINES, Port Elizabeth,
☎/fax 784-458-3201

BLUE TROPIC HOTEL, Friendship Bay, ☎/fax 784-458-3573

CREOLE GARDEN HOTEL, Lower Bay, ☎ 784-458-3154,
fax 784-457-3695

DE REEF APARTMENTS, Lower Bay, ☎ 784-458-3447,
fax 784-457-3103

FRANGIPANI HOTEL, Port Elizabeth, ☎ 784-458-3255,
fax 784-458-3824

FRIENDSHIP BAY HOTEL, Friendship Bay, ☎ 784-458-3222,
fax 784-458-3840

FRIENDSHIP GARDEN APARTMENTS, Friendship Bay,
☎ 784-458-3349, 784-457-3408

GINGERBREAD, Port Elizabeth, ☎ 784-458-3800,
fax 784-458-3907

HIBISCUS APARTMENTS, Union Vale, ☎ 784-458-3316,
fax 784-458-3889

ISLAND INN APARTMENTS, Friendship Bay,
☎ 784-457-3433, fax 784-457-3431

JULIE'S GUEST HOUSE, Port Elizabeth, ☎ 784-458-3304,
fax 784-458-3812

KEEGAN'S GUEST HOUSE, Lower Bay, ☎ 784-458-3530,
fax 784-457-3313

KINGSVILLE APARTMENTS, Lower Bay, ☎ 784-458-3932,
fax 784-458-3000

LOWER BAY GUEST HOUSE, Lower Bay, ☎ 784-458-3675

THE OLD FORT, Mount Pleasant, ☎/fax 784-458-3440

SEA SHELLS HOLIDAY APARTMENTS, Port Elizabeth,
☎/fax 784-458-3656

Bequia

| SPRING ON BEQUIA, Spring, ☎ 784-458-3414, fax 784-457-3305 |
| SUGARAPPLE INN, LaPompe, ☎ 784-457-3148 |
| TAYLOR'S APARTMENTS, La Pompe, ☎ 784-458-3458, fax 784-457-3420 |
| TRAVELLERS INN, Port Elizabeth, ☎ 784-457-3411, fax 784-457-3577 |
| VILLAGE APARTMENTS, Belmont, ☎ 784-458-3883, fax 784-458-3883 |

L'AUBERGE DES GRENADINES

PO Box 14

☎/fax 784-458-3201

www.caribrestaurant.com/aubergetoo.htm,
auberge@caribrestaurant.com

Under US$100 MC, Visa

Host Jacques Therenot and his Vincentian wife, Eileen, offer three rooms with shower, ceiling fan and TV. Although small and basic, L'Auberge is in an excellent location on Admiralty Bay. The restaurant prides itself on gourmet cuisine and has a live lobster pool. Evening entertainment is provided twice weekly.

CREOLE GARDEN HOTEL

Lower Bay
☎ 784-458-3154,
fax 784-457-3695
www.creolegarden.
com, dcreole@
caribsurf.com
Under US$100 MC,
Visa
Five rooms with
shower, floor fan,
and refrigerator and two suites with additional kitchenettes. Lower Bay is the location to "beach" the day away. The after-

noon hike up the almost vertical road makes the beer taste colder, the shower more invigorating and the bed more inviting.

DE REEF APARTMENTS

Lower Bay
☎ 784-458-3447, fax 784-457-3103
dereef@caribsurf.com
Under US$100 No credit cards

Set well back from the beach and road, these 11 apartments are basic in furnishings and suit those wanting little from a vacation save sun, sea and sand.

FRANGIPANI HOTEL

Port Elizabeth
☎ 784-458-3255, fax 784-458-3824
www.frangipanibequia.com, frangi@caribsurf.com
Under US$100-$200 MC, Visa, Amex

The Frangipani, originally a private home, was converted to a hotel over 30 years ago. Of the 15 rooms, those in the house are less expensive than the rooms and suites in the quiet garden be-

hind the house and restaurant; all have showers and ceiling fans. Frangipani is located in the hub of activity as tennis, snorkeling, scuba, restaurants and boutiques are all within a minute's stroll along the waterfront. Designated as "land ho" for many a yachtie, the establishment also holds the distinction of being the birthplace of former Prime Minister, Sir

James F. "Son" Mitchell, and is now managed by his daughter, Sabrina.

FRIENDSHIP BAY HOTEL
Friendship Bay
☎ 784-458-3222, fax 784-458-3840
www.friendshipbayhotel.com
US$100-$300 Breakfast included. MC, Visa

This secluded estate on Friendship Bay offers 27 rooms with shower and ceiling fans. For those desiring to trade sea breezes and the lull of the ocean for air-conditioning, six rooms and the honeymoon suite are available. The **Moskito Beach Bar & Grill** (see page 165) caters all day to the needs of their guests. Activities offered include diving, snorkeling, windsurfing, sailing, tennis and volleyball, for those keen to work off the calories. Prices are slightly higher during Christmas, yet enticing package deals surface throughout the year dependent on the length of stay.

FRIENDSHIP GARDEN APARTMENTS
Friendship Bay
☎ 784-458-3349, fax 784-457-3408
www.friendshipgarden.bequia.net,
friendshipgapt@vincysurf.com
Under US$100-$200

Locally owned and managed, these eight apartments in a quiet garden setting are only a few minutes walk from the beach. Each apartment is spacious, tidy, and rented out by the week at a reasonable price.

THE GINGERBREAD
Port Elizabeth
☎ 784-458-3800, fax 784-458-3907
www.gingerbreadhotel.com,
ginger@caribsurf.com
US$100-$200 MC, Visa

Eight comfortable suites with kitchenette, bathroom and ceiling fan. Four-poster beds in the upper suites, twin beds downstairs. All have balcony or patio views of Admiralty Bay and the Belmont Walkway linking all bay front properties on the "tourist side" of the bay. Several of the original economy rooms are available at a slightly lower rate. The Gingerbread complex is a major gather-

A suite at The Gingerbread
(Lynn McKamey)

ing place on the island; below the restaurant is a busy Internet service and the only travel agent on the island. The café entices those passing by with their sweets, particularly gingerbread, exotic juices and coffees. Tennis is complimentary to guests and a dive shop is situated next door.

HIBISCUS APARTMENTS

Union Vale

☎ 784-458-3889, fax 784-458-3316

hibiscusapts@vincysurf.com

Under US$100 No credit cards

Four self-catering apartments with bath, shower, TV and ceiling fan. It's only a short walk to the harbor.

ISLAND INN APARTMENTS

Friendship Bay

☎ 784-457-3433, fax 784-457-3431

islandinn@vincysurf.com

Under US$100 MC, Visa

Six air-conditioned one- and two-bedroom apartments, with bath, shower, TV, telephone and ceiling fan. The kitchens are fully equipped; laundry and maid service provided.

Bequia

JULIE'S GUEST HOUSE

Port Elizabeth

☎ 784-458-3304, fax 784-458-3812

julies@caribsurf.com

Under US$100 MC, Visa

Julie's has 19 rooms with showers and ceiling fans. Situated in two buildings: one block houses the restaurant, Fancy's Bar, kitchen, and half the rooms set back from Port Elizabeth's main street on what is called, quite obviously, Back Street. The other block faces Front Street and has six guest rooms with a communal balcony overlooking the harbor and the T-shirt market.

Most residents who came to Bequia as tourists started by staying at Julie's. Walking off the ferry jetty, Julie's is the closest accommodations and right in the center of town. Some guests later find another spot on the island – Lower Bay, for those on repeat and extended visits, or Spring Estate for those intent on buying and building. They think of it as graduation.

Other guests keep coming back to Julie's. Is it the bustle and activity of the harbor? The excellent breakfast and three-course West Indian evening meal? The raucous Friday evening gathering of Bequia's expat popula-

tion? Perhaps, but behind it all lies a very special group of people: Julian and Isola MacIntosh, and their large and ever-growing family, work the magic of this place. Now in the hands of their daughter, Shawn, together with her staff, this guest house is a prime example of how welcoming and helpful the people of this country can be. Want to rent a car, learn to sail, catch a flight, order a birthday cake, phone home? Go and see Shawn. If its possible, she'll make it happen. You'll soon feel a part of the family.

KEEGAN'S GUEST HOUSE
Lower Bay
☎ 784-458-3530, fax 784-457-3313
keegansbequia@yahoo.com
Under US$100 MC, Visa

Eleven rooms, with shower and ceiling fan. The rooms in the newer block have air-conditioning. The beach is across the road and you may never get any farther on the island. And that's okay.

KINGSVILLE APARTMENTS
Lower Bay
☎ 784-458-3932, fax 784-458-3000
kingsville@caribsurf.com
Under US$100 No credit cards

Ten attractive air-conditioned cottages set in a lush garden a short walk from the beach. Each equipped with a modern kitchen, bathroom and TV. This is among the better places that have opened in recent years, small and charming.

LOWER BAY GUEST HOUSE
Lower Bay
☎ 784-458-3675
sur-stuefree@yahoo.com
Under US$100 No credit cards

Seven rooms with floor fans and private bathrooms. This is all a true beach bum needs. The guest house has a small restaurant and bar if you aren't lured away by the other eateries around Lower Bay.

Bequia

THE OLD FORT

Mount Pleasant

☎/fax 784-458-3440

www.oldfortbequia.com, otmar@oldfortestates.com

US$100-$300 MC, Visa

Perched on top of Mount Pleasant at one of the highest elevations on the island. The southeastern aspect gives stunning views of Mustique and neighboring islands. Built on the foundations of an 18th-century sugar and indigo plantation estate house, the inn has six rooms with showers and ceiling fans. The local stonework and windows open to the sea breezes give the rooms a cool feeling. This is the first place we've stayed at with live plants in the rooms, making them feel very homey. A superb restaurant, bar, and swimming pool complete the picture. Rubbings of St. Vincent's petroglyphs decorate the stone walls of the restaurant and a small museum cabinet is crammed with curiosities found on the site by Otmar, the creator of The Old Fort.

Nights are quiet and dark with the twinkling lights of Mustique filling the background. Without a doubt, The Old Fort continues the high quality of cuisine and service that has been their standard for the past 20 years.

The Old Fort may be rented out by the week for your exclusive use, with a household staff of five and accommodating up to twelve adults.

SEA SHELLS HOLIDAY APARTMENTS

Port Elizabeth
☎/fax 784-458-3656
www.cwsvg.com
seashellsbq@
vincysurf.com
Under US$100-$200

Dangling between the road and Admiralty Bay below, these two unique and whimsical one- and two-bedroom apartments are convenient to all things Bequia. At the entrance a bus or taxi can easily be had in minutes while the property overlooks the bay giving guests complete privacy.

SPRING ON BEQUIA

Spring
☎ 784-458-3414, fax 784-457-3305
www.springonbequia.com
springonbequia@caribsurf.com
US$100-$200 MC, Visa

Nine rooms in luxurious hillside surroundings on a 225 year old working plantation above Spring Bay. Several rooms have a glass wall looking out across the Atlantic, the ideal way to watch the sun rise. The old mill at the entrance has been beautifully converted into a pottery studio and art gallery. A pool and tennis court entices those wanting to exercise in a quiet private setting. This is a place to escape from adventures for a while and simply relax in the company of mango, papaya, and banana groves. With no phones or TVs, the only music will be the breeze coming off the ocean.

Bequia

SUGARAPPLE INN

LaPompe

☎ 784-457-3148

www.sugarappleinn.com

info@sugarappleinn.com

Under US$100

Eight roomy apartments overlook Friendship Bay. They are complete with kitchenettes, shower, TV, phone, and ceiling fan. Corner jalousie windows open fully allowing sea breezes to cool the rooms. Housekeeping is provided and a heart-shaped pool is shared between the apartments, although the beach is only a five-minute walk downhill. A bus stop is conveniently located outside the apartments making Port Elizabeth easy access for a couple of EC dollars.

TAYLOR'S APARTMENTS

La Pompe

☎ 784-458-3458, fax 784-457-3420

gena@caribsurf.com

Under US$100 No credit cards

Six apartments with bath, shower, kitchens and lounge. The apartment block is condominium-style and dwarfs the neighboring houses. It presents stunning views over the southern Grenadines. There is a 15% discount on stays longer than one week; a 10% discount on dinners at the **Port Hole** restaurant in Port Elizabeth.

TRAVELLERS INN
Port Elizabeth
☎ 784-457-3411, fax 784-457-3577
travellinn@vincysurf.com
Under US$100 No credit cards

Five bedrooms spread over two apartments. Bath, shower, fans and fully equipped kitchenette in both apartments. The balcony has a snooper's view of the whole harbor. Ideal for a large family or group of friends to rent the entire premises.

VILLAGE APARTMENTS
Belmont
☎ 784-457-3026, fax 784-458-3883
tvabqsvg@caribsurf.com
Under US$100 No credit cards

Eight self-contained apartments with air-conditioning at extra cost. Set within a lovely garden, the buildings reminded us of an eastern Mediterranean village. A short walk downhill brings you to Admiralty Bay and Port Elizabeth. Above the apartments, a convenient bus stop connects you to Lower Bay, Friendship Bay and Paget Farm.

Villa Rentals

From small and cozy one- and two-bedroom apartments to cottages, houses and sub-palatial size villas, the choices on Bequia are as broad as on larger islands in the chain. Some are in beachfront locations, others tucked away on hillsides. Because of the volcanic slopes you are assured of a good view from most of the properties. Owners usually offer better deals for longer stays of a month or more.

BEQUIA BEACHFRONT VILLAS
Friendship Bay
☎ 784-457-3423, 800-367-8455
bequia@fortrecovery.com

One-, two-, three-, and four-bedroom villas located right on the beach at Friendship. Prices vary according to size and gener-

Bequia

ally run from $200 per day to over $800 per day. Traditional West Indian architecture with red corrugated tin roof, a gingerbread trim, and modern amenities within. Spacious porches and louvered doors open to the sea.

FLAMINGO & TURTLE POINT VILLAS

Princess Margaret Beach

☎ 246-435-8973, fax 246-435-6583

nina@bequiavillas.com

US$2,700-$3,700 per week.

Two luxurious villa homes above Princess Margaret Beach, an architectural blend of Alpine chalet and West Indian gingerbread. With a group of six family or friends, the cost is not as high as it appears.

LIME HOUSE VILLA

Spring

☎ 784-457-3092

limehouse@caribsurf.com

A comfortable studio and two-bedroom cottage with private pool in hilltop setting on the quiet side of the island.

MIMOSA COTTAGE

Port Elizabeth

☎/fax 784-458-3290

www.mimosa-house.com/contact.asp

Cottage is offered at US$1,800–$2,000 per week, studio for $450–$600 per week. It doesn't get any more real than here! Once a colonial home across the island, the house was carried by ox to its present site. Until recent times it functioned as a silk-screening workshop, the Crab Hole, and now as a delightful guest house. Traditional in design, West Indian hardwood floors and gingerbread trim, the property is located at the quiet end of the Belmont Walkway. Both properties are ideal hideaways in the midst of Bequia life.

MOONHOLE

Paget Farm
☎ 784-458-3068
www.begos.com/
bequiamoonhole.com
moonhole@vincysurf.com

One-of-a-kind villas, carved out of volcanic rock under the watchful eye of the late Tom Johnston, these homes are built of stone, wood, cement, whalebone, and cushions – lots of cushions. Offered at US$1,275 per week, the villa includes a staff for cooking and cleaning. With no electricity, its best to let someone else do the hard work – you're on vacation. This private eccentric community is managed by Johnston's son, Jim, and his wife, Shanna. For the curious but reluctant to commit, call for a tour.

PETIT ALL AWASH

Industry
www.allawash.co.uk, enquiries@allawash.co.uk

Like a treehouse above a sandy beach, this quiet gem sits hidden within an exotic garden with its own salty pool. Traditionally furnished, with louvered doors; you may never leave. Cozy hideaway for two at US$1,000 in winter, slightly less in summer months.

Bequia

SOLANA'S
☎ 784-458-3554,
784-458-3335
solanas@caribsurf.com
Three homes in Lower Bay priced at US$450, $800, and $1,400 weekly.

Typical island cottage

WINDSONG

Spring

☎ 784-457-3092, 44-207 267 72 47 (UK)

www.bequiawindsongvilla.com,
g.samuel@doughtystreet.co.uk

Three-bedroom house accommodates up to eight guests with full time housekeeper. Yellow stucco with white trim villa nestled in gardens with all the convenience of home within, yet retaining its West Indian accents. Pool and verandah overlook Spring Bay. US$1,800 weekly in summer, US$3,400 in winter.

■ After Dark

There's always something happening on Bequia during the evening.

It can be as informal as a trio of local musicians playing at **L'Auberge des Grenadines**, or as international as the **Blues Festival** held at the Plantation House in February during, the height of the season . A full-moon barbecue is held each month at **Crescent Beach Inn** under the stars and swaying palms. On Thursday nights, the **Frangipani's** barbecue is livened with musical entertainment by a local steel band. The lovely sound of the pans can be heard across Admiralty Bay; no one ever seems to mind.

Lower Bay is a hive of evening activity! **Coco's Place** provides music on Tuesday and Fridays. **DeReef** hosts a jump-up every Saturday night in high season featuring a number of Vincentian bands. One of the favorite bands around is

Bequia's own New Direction, guaranteed to pack the place until the wee hours. **Friendship Bay Hotel's Moskito Bar** brings the local string band out on Wednesday nights during the winter months. J. Gool is the singer with a voice hardly needing amplification.

Truly local is **Bedrock** in Port Elizabeth. Music can go on until 3 am in this hot and sweaty club. Most venues along Belmont Walkway will have impromptu music as various local or visiting musicians turn up. You never know who might be playing. One night we walked into a bar to find Led Zeppelin's Robert Plant giving his all with a Bequia rock'n'roll band.

A WORD TO
THE WISE

First timers to St. Vincent & the Grenadines may want to bring a pair of foam earplugs to ensure a good night's sleep as often there is a chorus of late night dogs and roosters.

Mustique

■ Orientation

The second largest of St. Vincent's Grenadines is only three miles long and less than two miles wide. It was given its name by the French, who found it swarming with "moustique" – mosquitos. Sugar played a major part in its history, with seven plantations at the height of production. Yet by 1820 there were only two estates, Cheltenham and Adelphi, with 325 slaves. With the end of slavery, Mustique was all but abandoned. Today, only the sugar works of the Endeavour Estate remain standing, along with its Cotton House. A royal grant in 1835 passed ownership of the island to the Hazell family of St. Vincent. For the next 120 years fewer than 100 people inhabited the island as subsistence farmers and fishermen.

Mustique

Mustique

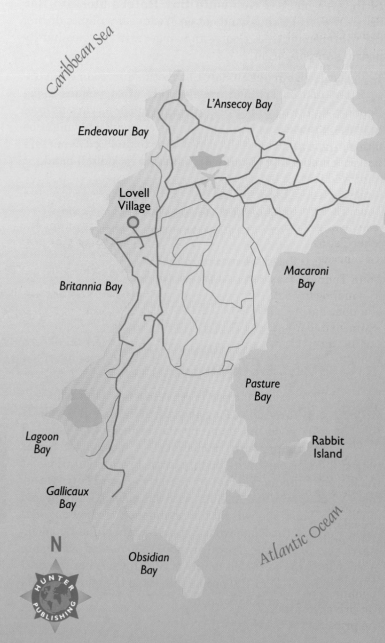

Caribbean Sea

L'Ansecoy Bay

Endeavour Bay

Lovell
Village

Britannia Bay

Macaroni
Bay

Pasture
Bay

Lagoon
Bay

Rabbit
Island

Gallicaux
Bay

N

Atlantic Ocean

Obsidian
Bay

HUNTER
PUBLISHING

NOT TO SCALE

The arrival, in 1958, of an eccentric young Scotsman, Colin Tennant, changed things radically. His family had made their fortune during the Industrial Revolution. An ancestor invented an

View over Mustique (Lynn McKamey)

improved form of bleach and by 1830 his company owned the largest chemical factory in the world. Fifty years later, the Tennant empire had expanded to include mining, steel and railways. Entry into British aristocracy was secured by another Tennant being created the first Lord Glenconnor; his sister married Herbert Asquith, a British Prime Minister.

Colin Tennant traveled to the West Indies to inspect the family's mahogany estate in Trinidad. It had been the settlement of a debt dating back 100 years. He sold the estate and on a whim visited Mustique. Finding a desolate island of scrub and cactus, he purchased the island from the Hazell family for £45,000. In the course of eight years, the island was cultivated into groves of coconut palms and citrus trees. Some 250 acres of cotton were planted, and a dry and lifeless island had begun its transformation into a tropical paradise.

In 1960, Tennant offered his close friend, Princess Margaret, a 10-acre parcel of land as a wedding gift on her marriage to Lord Snowdon. From then on, Mustique was revamped as a private retreat for Tennant's aristocratic friends. Before the decade was out, the airport had opened and the Cotton House welcomed its first guests as an official inn. By the mid-1970s, the island had a reputation for its rich and famous clientele that persists to this day.

Colin Tennant has since taken residence on another Windward island, as The Mustique Company he founded continues to manage the island. Protecting the fragile environment and the privacy of its high-profile owners and guests are among the priorities of the company today.

Mustique

For visitors to Mustique there are rules governing respect for homeowners and their property. Trespassing on private property is not tolerated. Photographing of people or their property is allowed only after obtaining their permission. A discreet, but effective 24-hour mobile security service is on duty.

■ Getting Here

By Air

Barbados is the customary gateway airport for Mustique, although Grenada is an easy flight with the awesome view of flying over the Grenadines and watching the change of hues in the water below as it slides from sapphire to the palest of aquamarines.

The one-hour flight from Barbados costs approximately US$300 roundtrip per person. From Grenada, the flight is only 30 minutes unless the plane calls in on Carriacou, Union Island or Canouan. Even then, expect to be back in the air in a matter of minutes. These quick stops on other Grenadines give credence to the meaning of *puddlejumpers*. From Bequia or Canouan, the flight is approximately seven minutes; Mustique is a mere ten minutes from St. Vincent and twice that from Carriacou and Union Island.

Airlines Serving Mustique	
Grenadine Airways	☎784-456-6793 www.grenadine-airways.com
Mustique Airways	☎ 784-458-4380 fax 784-456-4586 US ☎ 800-526-4789 fax 717-595-8869 www.mustique.com
SVG Air	☎ 784-457-5124, ☎ 784-457-5777, fax 784-457-5077, www.svgair.com

Private charters are available with all the airlines serving Mustique. If seclusion is your intention, or for carrying all your prized toys along, check the airlines for scheduling to meet your needs.

The Mustique Company has a shuttle flight to St. Vincent from Monday through Saturday; to make arrangements, contact the Mustique Airport at ☎ 784-488-8336 or airport@mustique-island.com.

When leaving St. Vincent & the Grenadines, there is a departure tax of EC$40 (US$15) per person. A fixed entry fee for day-visitors to the island is payable either at the airport or with the harbormaster's office if arriving by boat.

By Sea

The ferry **MV *Glenconnor***, makes the 90-minute journey between Mustique and St. Vincent on Monday, Tuesday, Thursday and Friday; leaving Mustique at 7:30am and departing from St. Vincent that afternoon at 2pm. One-way fare is EC$20 and must be purchased at The Mustique Company Office on Mustique or in Kingstown.

For day visits, day charters are possible from Bequia on the wooden schooner *Friendship Rose*, or the catamaran *Passion*. Both return to Bequia before sunset. Local speedboats can be hired at the Paget Farm fishery; they are fairly expensive since they must wait in Mustique for the return journey. Check the St. Vincent tour operators for day trips from the mainland.

For those on private or chartered sailboats, mooring sites are available in Britannia and Endeavour Bays *only*. Tenders may *not* land at any of the beaches.

■ Getting Around

THE MUSTIQUE COMPANY
☎ 784-488-8555
fax 784-456-3510 or 456-4565

 Mountain bikes, scooters, and "mules" (motorized buggies) are all for hire. A local license is required and is available from Immigration at the airport or in Lovell at the police station. It costs EC$50 and you must be over 17 years of age and have a current license from your own country. The speed limit is a sedate 20 mph. Prices go from US$30 per day for a bicycle to US$85 for a mule. A deposit is required.

■ Exploring

 Mustique is a privately owned island, similar to Palm Island and Petit St. Vincent, allowing day-visitors limited access. The island covers 1,395 acres, with the highest point 495 feet above sea level. Mustique has no natural water supply, although tropical plants thrive in these conditions. Bougainvillea, hibiscus, oleander and frangipani give an assortment of blooms, with-

out the need for much nourishment. Mustique's gardeners are masters with these exotic plants, splashing colors around like a palette of rich oils on a dry and taut canvas.

An island tour by taxi is a perfect way to become acquainted with the lay of the land. You'll be surprised at how much has been left in its natural state, giving ideal habitat for birds and reptiles to find food and shelter.

In the Saddle

Pounding along in the surf is the sort of romantic image for which Mustique was created. Island guests can rent mountain bikes or ride horseback from **The Mustique Company**, ☎ 784-488-8555, 488-8316.

On Foot

There are four walking trails. One is in the northeastern corner, winding round Ramier Bay to North Point. This is an excellent place to observe seabirds and hear the elusive mangrove cuckoo in the woodland.

A second trail in the southwestern point of Britannia Bay loops around to Lagoon Bay. This area is hardwood hammock, giving trees the chance to grow in a beach environment; saltwater is converted to freshwater in their root systems. Trees are labelled for identification: black, red, and white mangrove, black torch, manchineel, pencil and walking stick. The holes of land crabs perforate the ground. Hear the iguanas rustling in the bush before you spot them camouflaged against a tree trunk. Herons fish in the lagoon.

Another trail runs inland from Macaroni Beach, full of mangroves and iguana nesting sites.

A fourth trail runs on the windward side from Pasture Bay to Obsidian Bay. Plants twist and bend in contorted shapes sculpted by the wind and seawater. Salt spray burns vegetation, leaving only the hardiest to survive. The manchineel loves it, as do cacti such as prickly pear, Turk's Cap, pipe organ and agave.

Tours

The range of homes is dazzling. An island tour gives an overview of a number of them. Some are as elusive as the mangrove cuckoo, others are very much in your face. For example, that of the most high-profile owner is barely noticeable as it fades away into its surroundings. Another more recent mansion stands out like a giant watershed and is visible from three neighboring islands, making one wonder why Mustique hasn't incorporated a "ridge law" to prohibit buildings that will ruin the scenic value of the area.

Blue Waters, Mustique

Nonetheless, each villa is a work of art and, like all art, the beauty is in the eye of the beholder. You can't help but admire the original houses: the **Cotton House**, constructed from the ruins of an 18th-century coral warehouse and sugar mill; **Blue Waters**, built in plantation house design with thick pastel stucco walls aged by salt and sun. Or there's the guest house, **Firefly**, decked in purpleheart wood and local stone blending into the cliff. And Obsidian, constructed on tiered terracing, truly portrays the West Indian flavor with its elaborate use of gingerbread, latticework and open-ventilation roofing.

As travelers, we don't get an insider's view unless we rent or are guests of a villa owner. But after this preview, two lovely books reveal this island museum of architecture a little closer.

You might say they act as catalogs to the show. *Mustique* and *Mustique II* can be purchased at Basil's Gourmet Shop. They are expensive, but don't assume you can wait until you go home and get them in your local bookstore. You can't. Follow our example, buy an extra tote bag and lug them back as hand luggage. You'll be glad you did.

LOVELL VILLAGE

The small community of Lovell Village was created by Colin Tennant in 1964. Where there had been fishing shacks, he built homes for the dozen local families who chose to remain on the island after it had been sold by the Hazell family. With homes, shared housing units, two stores, two bars, a restaurant, boutique, church, school, library and police station, the community of 150 people are better served per head than some neighboring islands. Walking through the village at lunchtime, it seemed oddly quiet. All the children were in school and, with an employment rate of 100%, the narrow streets were empty.

We stopped to chat with Mrs. Trimmingham at her small boutique, visited with toddlers at the Hilltop Restaurant while lunch was served to a ravenous group of men, and had a cold beer with Harry Osborne, a visiting whalerman from Bequia. No dollar buses roared past, no bass notes boomed from sound systems; this kind of quiet you don't normally experience in the Grenadines.

Then the words of the Honourable Brian Alexander, manager of The Mustique Company, came back to us. He had frankly reminded us that Mustique is a business. Lovell is the village where the workers live; the friendly staff in villas, shops and at the airport make sure that all is run perfectly for the guests. A sign reading, "No boat, no good," was another reminder that behind these silent walls lived Vincentians – Hazells, Lewises, Simmons, and

Mustique

Trimminghams – that had been here when the island was little more than goat pasture and the main activity was fishing. The times have definitely been changing for these families. There was a price to be paid, but, with an educational system and facilities that are the envy of other places in the Caribbean, the glimmer in their eyes can only be promising.

Over a cold beer we wondered what our own hometown would be like with 100% employment and a speed limit of 20 mph.

Bring more film or digital memory cards than you plan on using; unused media is easy to carry home. Film is expensive to buy here, and cards nigh on impossible. The same goes for camera batteries.

The School & Mustique Library

The primary school was donated, designed and built by the late Arne Hasselqvist, the architectural mastermind behind 69 of Mustique's villas, the jetty, airport, boutiques, Basil's Bar and administrative offices. The school opened in 1987 and is financed in part by the homeowners' annual benefit, which provides local children with the best education possible. Some of the world's leading entertainers are numbered among the visiting storytellers.

It's always practical to have a publisher on board when establishing a new colony. Even *The Mayflower* carried a printing press. One of Mustique's homeowners was the sole financier in building and stocking the community library. Over 4,000 books are housed here, with computers as an added facility for staff and patrons. This philanthropist even went so far as to build a two-bedroom cottage as a residence for the librarians. Another fund-raiser has been started to maintain the library's high standard. The library and school stand as testimony that Mustique is not simply a playground for the well-known and well-heeled, as so often portrayed, but is a true community.

■ Scuba Diving

 There are seven sites off Mustique for those interested in starfish instead of stars. Toward the southern end of Britannia Bay is a sheltered reef known as **South Britannia**. Those to the north – **All Awash**, **Pillories** and the wreck of the *Antilles* – can be at the mercy of strong currents, so we suggest you don't try these independently. **House Dive** is perfect for beginners, with its maximum depth of 20 feet, and the wreck of a 65-foot cement boat, *Jonas*, lies off Britannia Bay at a depth of 40 feet. The highlight of Mustique diving must be **Dry Rock**, which is stepped below the surface in tiers between 35 feet and 100 feet, with a multitude of brightly colored fish.

THE WRECK OF THE ANTILLES

On January 8, 1971, the 568-foot French Line passenger vessel, *Antilles,* ran aground off the north shore of Mustique. It had been making its way from Caracas to Barbados when the captain decided to give his passengers a closer look at this island gem.

Just before 4:30 pm, the ship, needing a 30-foot draft, came far too close to land and became perched on the reef, where the water is a mere eight feet deep. It was assumed later that this ruptured the fuel tanks and started a fire below decks.

The crew and some 500 passengers remained blissfully unaware of the rising danger for almost two hours. Indeed, the captain of the stranded ship refused help when it was offered. At sunset it was the locals on Mustique and yachts from the neighboring island of Bequia that alerted them. "You're on fire!"

they shouted from their boats. "Vive La France!" the passengers replied, continuing their cocktail party.

At 6:40 pm, the *Antilles* at last acknowledged her plight with a mayday call. Coast guard and naval craft began making their way to the scene; even the *QE2* was sent from St. Lucia. None would make it to Mustique in time to play an active part in the immediate rescue.

Passengers had been ordered to abandon ship but were put to sea in lifeboats and rafts, with neither oars nor paddles. So began a five-hour operation by yachts and charter vessels from Mustique, Bequia and St. Vincent to save those in the lifeboats drifting aimlessly in the dark and churning sea. The majority were taken to Mustique, but, what seems as strange now as it did then, the captain and officers insisted on being taken to Bequia, seven miles away.

Theories that the accident had been planned by the owners of the cruise ship as an insurance fraud were unsubstantiated at the inquest.

Apart from the burnt husk of the vessel, which remains as a dive site, it is the bravery of those who manned the rescue fleet that is memorable. The squadron of little boats, yachts and charter vessels from Mustique, Bequia and St. Vincent deserves lasting praise.

Dive Operators

MUSTIQUE WATERSPORTS

☎ 784-488-8555, 784-488-8486

watersports@mustique-island.com

An introductory dive is priced at US$55. You can be certified up to Dive Master for US$799 or Rescue Diver for US$440. Children between eight and eleven years can take a "Bubble Maker" course, an introduction to scuba, for US$40.

Snorkeling

Endeavour, **Britannia Bay** and **L'Ansecoy** are highly recommended as snorkeling sites. Check with Mustique Watersports for the best location on any given day. They have
equipment to rent by the half-hour, hour or day for snorkeling,
kayaking, windsurfing, as well as aquafins and surfbikes.
They can also arrange tours to Tobago Cays.

■ Shopping

Shopping on the
island varies
from exciting to
disappointing.
Mustique is so
seductive that
one expects its
few shops to
have merchan-
dise equally as
enticing. While
some fall short in this aspect, Mustique does have **Basil
Charles**, one of the world's greatest shoppers, to act as global
buyer-in-chief of items to bewitch the beautiful people.

Mustique is a private island and residents are pretty serious
about this. When you stay on the island, you get a folder listing

how to contact shops
via the main switch-
board at The
Mustique Company
(shops are not listed
in the SVG tele-
phone book). The
Mustique Company
does not encourage
day-visitors to their
island. Almost all of

the shops are on the beach, the only place where day-visitors and boaters can come ashore.

TREASURE BOUTIQUES: PINK AND PURPLE COTTAGES

There's always a danger that the contents won't match up to the packaging. Perhaps with such attractive buildings it is nigh on impossible to buy merchandise for a place so enchanting. Several times over the years we have stopped in to browse and been unimpressed with the stock. It's not the quality, but the fact that we could buy the very same items on Bequia, St. Vincent, Palm Island, and Grenada. For shoppers staying on Mustique, you will find an assortment of beachwear, Panama hats, light resort clothing, souvenirs and toiletries.

ACROSS FOREVER
☎ 784-456-3407, fax 784-456-5825

Mustique Shops (Lynn McKamey)

This shop is housed in a nondescript building compared to its neighbors, but you'll be thrilled by the travels and selection of the owner, Basil Charles.

We find this assortment of treasures fascinating. Weighty sculptures, furniture and accessories that will be practical as well as conversation pieces in the home. Reasonably priced for what they are and how far they've traveled, these objets-d'art are really intended for local homeowners; if you see something you can't live without, Across Forever will ship wherever your heart desires.

BASIL'S BOUTIQUE

Smaller personal items from the man who brings you Across Forever. Sarongs, swimwear, linen clothing and T-shirts, plus Basil's favorite kaftans in cotton or silk, ranging from US$60 to $115.

Indonesian jewelry to satisfy all budgets, beautiful brass compasses that any mariner will treasure, and complete sets of CDs of the Mustique Blues Festival from 1996 onwards.

BASIL'S GOURMET SHOP

An attempt to cover all bases with a wide variety of wines and biscuits. Oddly enough, this is where you'll find a good book selection, including the two coffee table volumes about Mustique for US$100 apiece. The reasoning must be that good books and good wine make excellent company.

COTTON HOUSE BOUTIQUE

In the restored sugar works of the old plantation, shop for cotton and linen clothing and handpainted swimwear. Handmade jewelry and ceramic kitchenware are available.

SCOTTIE'S BOUTIQUE

Up the hill in Lovell village, Ms. Trimmingham has blue jeans, T-shirts, men's dress shirts, swimwear, sun lotions and moisturizers. She would appreciate your patronage.

Store hours: 9 am-1 pm, and 3-6 pm, Monday to Saturday; 9 am-1 pm on Sunday is the general rule. The exception is Scottie's Boutique which is open until 8 pm, but closed on weekends.

Mustique

■ Where to Eat

Restaurant Directory

BASIL'S BAR & RESTAURANT, Britannia Bay, ☎ 784-488-8350 for reservations, 488-8405
THE COTTON HOUSE, ☎ 784-456-4777
FIREFLY GUEST HOUSE, ☎ 784-488-8414
HILLTOP RESTAURANT, Lovell Village
JOHANNA'S BANANA CAFÉ, Britannia Bay, ☎ 784-456-3522
SWEETIE PIE BAKERY, Britannia Bay

BASIL'S BAR & RESTAURANT

Britannia Bay

☎ 784-488-8350; reservations ☎ 784-488-8405

US$26-$35 MC, Visa; Daily

Assuming you are here just for the day, sandwiches, seafood crêpes, burgers and quiche cost less than you'd think. Don't expect to find celebrities dangling from the ceiling. You will find other star-spotters cultivating a bored, "We're not here just to see *him*," look.

Basil's Bar & Restaurant (Lynn McKamey)

FIREFLY GUEST HOUSE
☎ 784-488-8414, fax 784-456-3514
US$26-$35 MC, Visa
Daily

Dinner in lush surroundings of tropical plants, with the sounds of a piano gently playing, sets the mood for a romantic evening. Firefly boasts the best pizza and pasta on the island, as well as  West Indian cuisine. Reservations are required.

THE COTTON HOUSE
☎ 784-456-4777, fax 784-456-5887
US$26-$35 MC, Visa
Daily

The Cotton House serves breakfast and lunch around the poolside, while candlelit dinners are served on the terrace. Tuesday nights they host a cocktail party for guests and on Saturday night is a beach barbecue with live entertainment. With a widely traveled French chef, you're going to receive only the best of the best. Emmanuel Guemon blends French, Mediterranean, Asian and Caribbean dishes to present a taste that is unique to Mustique. Call for reservations.

Mustique

HILLTOP RESTAURANT

Lovell Village

Under US$15 MC, Visa

Daily

This serves the working populace of Mustique, so you could dub this the people's restaurant. The fare is reasonably priced, the meals delicious and truly West Indian cuisine without any frills. Our lunch consisted of curried chicken served with pasta, mashed potatoes, mixed vegetables and polished off with coconut ice cream.

JOHANNA'S BANANA CAFÉ

Britannia Bay

☎ 784-456-3522

Under US$15 MC, Visa

Daily

Stop in for homemade ice cream after a morning at the beach or perhaps an espresso before heading to your dinghy to sail out from this tropical paradise. Fresh fruit juices and homemade pastries make this a relaxing place to sit beneath the large umbrellas and people-watch along Britannia Bay. If coffee and juice aren't your vacation drink, the café has a bar and can quickly transform that juice into a tropical rum cocktail.

SWEETIE PIE BAKERY

Britannia Bay

Under US$15 MC, Visa

Daily, except Sunday

Early risers can surprise their partner with a quick run down to the bakery at 7:30 am for scrumptious breads and pastries.

■ Where to Stay

Accommodations Directory

FIREFLY GUEST HOUSE, ☎ 784-488-8414, fax 784-488-8514
THE COTTON HOUSE, ☎ 784-488-8449, fax 784-488-8409
MUSTIQUE VILLA RENTALS, ☎ 800-225-4255, 784-488-8000, fax 784-488-9000

FIREFLY GUEST HOUSE

☎ 784-488-8414, fax 784-488-8514

www.fireflymustique.com, stan@fireflymustique.com

US$301-$500 MC, Visa

Firefly is cradled on a hillside overlooking the leeward side of the island and shaded in tropical foliage. The owners, Liz and Stan Clayton, have four exquisite rooms, each with a four-poster king-size bed veiled in white muslin and mahogany and rattan furnishings. Bathrobes and sarongs are included with the room, as are snorkels and masks, a well-stocked mini bar, and an iPod with selected music for your stay. The price is all-inclusive, plus the use of a "mule" (motorized buggy). A series of stone patios surround a two-tiered swimming pool joined by a cascading waterfall. Tennis courts are also on the premises.

Pool & view, Firefly Guest House (Lynn McKamey)

Mustique

The Claytons advertise courtesy roundtrip air service from Barbados for guests staying eight nights or more; offering their guests a hassle-free holiday from the moment they enter the Caribbean. A minimum of 14 nights is required at Christmas, and reservations are usually booked a year in advance.

For those who can afford to indulge on Mustique's terms, Firefly is the social gathering spot come sundown. Exclusive martini and champagne clubs assure this romantic inn can grow quite animated, accompanied by the tree frogs chirping in the background.

THE COTTON HOUSE
☎ 784-488-8449, fax 784-488-8409
www.cottonhouse.net, reservations@cottonhouse.net
US$301-$500 MC, Visa

Built from the remnants of the 18th-century Endeavour plantation warehouse and sugar mill, Oliver Messel's restoration used many of the original features; second and third restorations have been carried out in the last decade. Nine rooms overlook the leeward side, eight terrace rooms and three cottages are at poolside while a two-suite Cotton House Residence is complete with its own private gazebo, swimming pool and several smaller plunge pools. King-sized four-poster beds, draped in white muslin, grace the bedrooms. Cell phones, televisions, and VCRs are provided only at guests' request.

This 5 Star luxury hotel and spa promote relaxation and peace of body and mind. One underlying principle of The Cotton House is "the core of a good night's sleep is getting the pillow right." A Pillow Menu of five choices reads like dessert for the weary. The mini spa has three treatment rooms to serve their guests and offer indulgences such as the ginger rub, papaya body polish, holistic heaven and Cotton House karma. Treatments involve Swedish massage, 60 minutes for US$130; aromatherapy full body massage, 60 minutes for US$140; reflexology, 60 minutes for US$130; hot stone therapy, 90 minutes at US$210. No stone is left unturned in providing comfort.

Hotel bookings are taken for a minimum of three nights; five nights minimum in February; and seven nights maximum at Christmas. Guests may also sail aboard the 50-foot catamaran, *Mustique Mermaid*.

MUSTIQUE VILLA RENTALS
☎ 784-488-8000, 488-8409, 488-9000
In the US ☎ 800-225-4255, 203-602-0300
www.mustique-island.com
villarentals@mustique-island.com
US$301-$500 MC, Visa

For complete privacy, pampering, and breathtaking views, nothing compares with renting a villa on Mustique. Villas are rented by the week and most are booked well over a year in advance. Fees include lodging, household staff of three (cook, maid, and gardener), a start-up supply of food, laundry service, use of the villa's "mule" (golf cart), invitations to the manager's weekly cocktail party, use of the tennis courts and fitness trails. Each villa has spacious grounds and gardens accenting privacy. Terraces with freshwater swimming pools overlook the Caribbean, sister Grenadines, or the Atlantic Ocean.

With 58 luxury villas to choose from, there's plenty of scope in architectural style. One common element connecting the majority of the villas is the architect, the late Arne Hasselqvist. He designed these homes around the personality of the owner and the contours of the island. While the owner's life may read like a fascinating novel, it is the uniqueness of the individual villa that brings a 70% return guest rate.

Mustique

Shogun, obviously Japanese-influenced, is constructed around a central koi pool. Set on 5 acres 300 feet above Britannia Bay, it even has its own 18-hole mini golf course. A double green with nine tees, it is a golfer's dream come true.

Minimum rental periods are seven nights. A surcharge of 7% government tax and an administration fee of 8% is added to bills. Prices differ according to season, and size of villa. As an idea of cost: the least expensive villa rents for US$4,000 per week in low season; airy with cove ceilings and rattan furnishings, elegant and West Indian in design, *Grasshopper*, a four-bedroom villa accommodating eight guests ranges from US$5,000 in low season to US$8,500 during high season. *Yemanja*, an eight-bedroom villa, is available for US$36,000.

These villas are a wonderful extravagance and if you plan to vacation with a large family or group of friends, do the mathematics and you may be pleasantly surprised how the numbers work out on a per-person basis. If price is no object, make a reservation today.

■ After Dark

Guests can enjoy a couple of cocktail parties each week hosted by The Mustique Company and The Cotton House. Other than these and private parties, everything swings at **Basil's Bar and Restaurant**.

Basil is the man when it comes to partying and giving out a good time. Christmas season is the highlight. A fashion show on Christmas Eve precedes the **Christmas Day bash** where Santa makes an appearance. The momentum then builds to the **New Year's Eve Party**, tickets for which are more sought after than backstage passes to concerts by the latest boyband favorites.

No sooner than the decorations are back in storage it's time for the **Mustique Blues Festival**. Held over two weeks from January to February, an assortment of international musicians assemble to riff the night away. Tickets, again, can be quickly sold out on some nights. The festival is recorded and all proceeds go towards the Basil Charles Education Foundation for the local children of Mustique. The man has a big heart and knows he can get everyone involved in the process through entertainment.

Get ready to dance on Wednesday night. A buffet barbecue is followed by a **jump up**. Sunday night has typical West Indian cuisine with the sound of a hot steel band.

Canouan

■ Orientation

 Canouan is like a marker in the sea dividing the northern from the southern Grenadines. Looking south, you can make out the silhouettes of the islands all the way to Grenada. Looking north, you see the other Grenadines, with St. Vincent looming behind them. From the sea, Canouan sticks out of the water like a humpback whale arching into a dive with its dorsal fin suspended in the air.

This plot of about five square miles rises to a hot, dry peak of 855 feet. It takes its name from the Carib word "cannoun," meaning turtle island. Sea turtles feed within the reefs surrounding the windward coast and lay their eggs  in the warm, white sand. No longer are they harassed by fishermen seeking out their nests and eyeing the creatures for the price of their shells. This is not to say that there aren't rogue turtle poachers passing through the reefs, but there's certainly a growing consciousness of preserving sealife.

Canouan

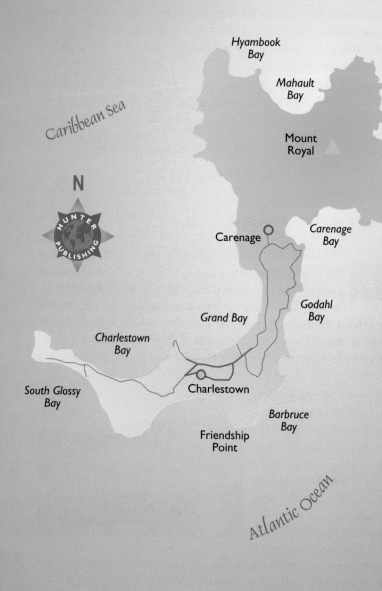

Hyambook Bay

Mahault Bay

Caribbean Sea

N

Mount Royal

Carenage

Carenage Bay

Grand Bay

Godahl Bay

Charlestown Bay

Charlestown

South Glossy Bay

Barbruce Bay

Friendship Point

Atlantic Ocean

1 MILE

1 KM

Canouan had been planted with
sugarcane by early French settlers. When sugar took a tum-
ble, the British owner William
Snagg, an architect, turned to
planting 600 acres of Marie
Galante cotton. His family's estate was in the north of the is-

land where it was dry and the ground often parched – perfect
conditions for cotton. Being resident planters, the Snaggs
built their own cotton gins and produced 30,000 pounds annually. William had two sons: James Frederick Snagg enlarged
the business and built a school, as well as the Anglican Church
at what is now Raffles Resort; the other son, also called William, became Chief Justice of British Guyana, earning a
knighthood.

Following emancipation, James Frederick Snagg brought in a
shipwright, Benjamin George Compton, from Hampshire, England. Fishing and transport were obviously important in the
islands, but it wasn't until 1870 that Compton completed
Canouan's first ship, the 18-ton sloop, *Sir William Snagg*. At
the same time, Bequia was establishing its whaling industry.
A younger Snagg, Henry, together with a Jonathan Lewis,
jumped on the bandwagon and two whale fisheries opened on
Canouan. They remained operative until 1925. Now different
boats were being built – fast, yet quiet, as they slipped through
the sea in pursuit of the great whale. Whale oil was sold to the
New England whaleboats and Canouan began to escape its
total dependence on cotton.

Of equal importance in this history was the passing down of
boat-building skills and the intermarrying of specific families.
Compton had taken on a young Vincentian named William
Mitchell as an apprentice, who married Compton's daughter.
They produced three sons, who spread their skills to three
more islands: St. Vincent, St. Lucia and Dominica. Even today, throughout the Grenadines you find boat builders and
sailors named Mitchell and Compton.

Canouan

This bloodline from Canouan has also produced politicians. In recent years, James Mitchell and Keith Mitchell have been prime ministers of St. Vincent & the Grenadines and Grenada respectively and John Compton has held the same office on St. Lucia.

Canouan remained privately owned by the Snagg family until 1946, when the government bought the island and sold property to the inhabitants. Only recently has it become of interest of foreign investors looking to pump what appears to be an endless supply of money into the island with The Carenage Bay development, now reopening as Raffles Resort.

This has incurred the wrath of the local population. It involved the transformation of the old Anglican Church and the issue of public access to the northern beaches. West Indians are very religious as a people and are guarded as to their hard-earned rights. For a while

there were some unhappy people and angry scenes. To the credit of the developers, they have brought in money and employment, and have built a school and medical clinic. And this is just the beginning.

From an outsider's perspective, it's interesting to watch how islands recover from colonial rule and then fall prey to tourism. Here on Canouan, as elsewhere, it is a sensitive balance that needs to be acknowledged by us as guests. Paradise has two faces. Changes are occurring here faster than local people have ever experienced. As opportunities arise with development, maybe they too can look to the success of their northern neighbors, Bequia and Mustique, and reap similar benefits from the profits of tourism.

■ Getting Here

By Air

If you are flying, the best way to enter is through San Juan, Puerto Rico aboard American Eagle. The last time we booked, the American Airlines agent thought that Eagle had stopped flying into St. Vincent. It has – it now flies to Canouan. "To where?" we were asked. "Canouan" we replied. "How are you spelling that, please?" Sure enough, we managed to convince the employee that her airline did indeed fly to Canouan.

Canouan Airport & Welcome Center (St. Vincent Board of Tourism)

The Eagle's final destination on this flight is Barbados. The other passengers did look stunned as we landed at this wee island after the 2½-hour flight. The thatched roof of the airport makes it look more Polynesian than Caribbean. "Where are we?" passengers asked. The airport's architecture matches that of Raffles Resort, which is no coincidence.

You can also use another gateway into this airport: Barbados, Grenada, St. Lucia or Martinique. All are within one hour's

Canouan

flying time. You might face a layover of a few hours from your main international flight. We have found that less than an hour between connecting flights only adds to the stress factor at the beginning and end of a vacation. **Mustique Airways**, **SVG Air** and **LIAT** are the main inter-island carriers that land at Canouan. You are advised to check their schedules before you book the dates of your main flights; we cannot be more specific than that. The exchange rate of the Eastern Caribbean Dollar stays constant for decades, but the airlines serving these islands change annually.

Airlines Serving Canouan	
Air Martinique	☎ 784-458-4528, 784-458-8888
American Airlines/ American Eagle	☎ 784-456-5555, 800-433-7300, www.aa.com
Grenadine Airways	☎ 784-456-6793, info@grena-dine-airways.com
LIAT	☎ 784-457-1821, 784-458-4841
Mustique Airways	☎ 784-458-4380, 212-202-4087, www.mustique.com
SVG Air	☎ 784-457-5124,800-744-5777 (Caribbean), 800-624-1843 (US & Canada), www.svgair.com

For guests staying at Raffles Resort, there are yet two more options. The first is the "Flight Concierge" program: you are met at the airport in Barbados or St. Lucia and flown via the resort's private plane to Canouan. This is without a doubt, the best option available for sanity and economic reasons. Priced at US$375 per person round-trip, it is only slightly more expensive than flying on an inter-island commercial flight. The second choice for Raffles' clientele is a private seven-seater Cessna Citation II, which may be chartered from as far away as Miami; contact Raffles Resort for pricing.

Taking a lot of equipment for scuba, photography or other some activity? The small inter-island airlines have weight restrictions. It might be worth buying an extra ticket to secure a seat for your gear.

By Sea

Ferry schedules are fairly consistent. Having said that, we did find getting between Canouan and the other islands the most difficult part of the trip to arrange. Either the ferry didn't fit with the flight or vice-versa. Ferries calling in at Canouan are also a bit rugged for the clientele relaxing at Raffles Resort and Tamarind Beach Hotel. Nonetheless, it makes for a genuine island experience. Leaving Canouan we managed to hire a water taxi to take us to Union Island. Returning to Canouan from Bequia we had a delightful adventure when our only choice was to hire the 24-foot *Nicola* to sail us back.

The trusty mailboat, *Barracuda*, does deliver. On Monday and Thursday she leaves St. Vincent at 10:30am, Bequia at 11:45am, arriving at Canouan at 1:15pm. On Tuesday and Friday, she leaves Union Island at 6:30am Mayreau at 7:30am, and arriving at Canouan at 8:30am. Saturdays *Barracuda* leaves St. Vincent 10am, bypasses Bequia, and ar-

MV Barracuda *in port*

rives at Canouan at 2pm. It is always wise to call the day ahead and let them know there are passengers - and then call again the morning you wish to be aboard. ☎ 784-456-5063. Expect to pay EC$25 (US$10) per person for the one way from Canouan to St. Vincent.

Another ferry option is the cargo vessel, MV *Gem Star*, which leaves St. Vincent at 11am on Tuesday and Friday and calls at Canouan then Union Island. It returns from Union Island at 7:30am on Wednesday and Saturday.

A water taxi from Union Island to Canouan will take about 45 minutes and cost around EC$250 or US$100. The scenery from the small wooden skiff is unbelievable, the company entertaining.

■ Internet & Telephone

 The **Ocean View Inn** has an Internet café open from 8 am to 6 pm daily, except Saturdays. Screen time is EC$10 per hour.

Tamarind Beach Hotel has two booths in reception where you can make international calls and they also have an Internet facility. The Moorings opened a marina adjacent to the hotel in 2003 and a full communications bureau in now up and running.

■ Banking

 If you are heading south into the Grenadines and haven't cashed a travelers check for a while, now is the time to do it. The only bank on Canouan is the **National Commercial Bank** in Charlestown. It is open Monday to Friday from 8 am to 1 pm. On Thursday it opens again from 2:30 to 5 pm.

 In the islands, there is paperwork to be completed, whatever your business. Expect to wait a few minutes for every customer in the line ahead of you. Some tourists assume they can bypass the line. Typically their business is the same as our own, namely cashing a travelers check. Please do not be party to this rudeness. If the line looks too long for you, ask at your hotel if they will make the exchange. You will lose a few EC cents against the bank rate, but you will gain that precious time.

■ Exploring

For a bird's-eye view from Canouan, you need to climb **Mount Royal** at the northern end of the island. At 855 feet above sea level, you can see Bequia, Mustique and St. Vincent to the north. Look to the

south and the blues and greens run like ribbons through the sea. This is the reef system of the Tobago Cays and Mayreau to the west. Union Island is the one with pitons, or fingerlike points, and the dusty silhouette in the distance is Carriacou. Beyond that, Grenada sits on the horizon, looking like a cumulus cloud.

Raffles Spa overlooks Godahl Beach

The scene below you isn't too bad either. Covering 300 acres is the **Raffles & Trump International Golf Club**. Until a hurricane in 1921, Canouan's main village was in this bay. Unfortunately for the inhabitants, the windward side is where storms roll in off the Atlantic. The hurricane destroyed the village, leaving only the Anglican Church, built from English stone in the 1800s, standing in its wake. The new development has breathed life into a forgotten zone.

The windward side is a haven for snorkelers and sea turtles. The **Mile Long Reef**, 200 feet from shore, acts as a barrier from the ocean and continues down the island to Friendship Point. **Godahl Beach** is where the locals swim and it can be quite busy on weekends. If it is early summer, there are probably turtle nests in the sand.

DON'T SIT UNDER THE COCONUT TREE

Cartoons of desert islands always show a stranded sailor under a lone palm tree. It's also a constant symbol of tropical bliss. However welcoming it may seem, a coconut tree demands respect from those seeking shade under the canopy of long, swaying branches. Ripe coconuts fall like miniature missiles from heights of up to 100 feet. Even a falling branch weighing around 20 pounds can do damage. The cluster of nuts around the crown can weigh as much as 50 pounds and can definitely ruin a vacation.

The coconut palm has over 360 different uses. From the leaves, the husk, the shell, the meat, oil and milk we get products as varied as coconut cream, coconut butter, cups, bowls, buttons, hats, houses, shampoos and soaps. Some uses not so obvious are as an agent in the manufacture of glycerin, plasticizers, brake fluid, insecticides, roofing tiles and activated charcoal. It has medicinal functions too as coconut water contains sugar, minerals, amino acids and vitamin C. In World War II, coconut water was used as a substitute for intravenous saline solution. You may want to remember this when you feel dehydrated!

An old legend reads: "*The coconut is God's gift to the lazy man. He sleeps in the shade of the tree, is awakened when a nut falls, drinks the milk and eats some of the meat. He then feeds the rest of the meat to the chickens and cattle, which produce eggs, milk and meat. The leaves provide thatch for the roof and walls of his coconut hut, and are also woven into hats, baskets and mats."* (*Coconuts*, Woodroof, AVI Publishing, 1970).

Legend it may be, but not too far from the truth. Just don't sit under the coconut tree.

On the north shore, **Mahault Bay** is also a nesting place for turtles, and a popular swimming and snorkeling spot for humans. To reach it on land, you must cross the **Raffles Resort**  property. You can circumvent this by hiring a water taxi to carry you. Agree on the price beforehand, and don't pay until you have completed the return journey.

The southern end of Canouan is home to the **airport** and **Glossy Bay**. The road to the airport has a traffic light. If it is red, then a plane is about to land or take off. If the plane is running out of runway, the pilot can either head straight for the water, or turn left. Hence the traffic light. Glossy Bay has one of the finest views in the Grenadines. From here it is only a short hop to the Tobago Cays.

■ Scuba Diving

Canouan has seven popular dive sites, including an artificial wreck, ***Shadow***, sunk in 1994, now teeming with marine life. Two submerged rocks, **Gibraltar** and **Gabby Stone**, offer diving to 90 feet, with coral, groupers and parrotfish. A pair of drift dives to the north, with the promise of turtles around Petit Canouan and well-developed sea fans is **Billy Hole**, a shallow dive of only 65 feet, but on the Atlantic side. And remember, you are within sight of the Tobago Cays!

Dive Operators

CANOUAN DIVING CENTRE

☎ 784-458-8044, fax 784-458-8851

GLOSSY DIVE CLUB

☎ 784-458-8888, fax 784-458-8875

■ Sailing

Sailing in these waters has long been the lure of the Grenadines. When you meet local men with surnames of Snagg, DeRoche, Ollivierre, Compton, and Sargeant on Canouan, you can rest assure these are men with generations of boat-building and sailing in their blood. They know these waters like the back of their hand. When they say the wind is not right, take heed.

For those looking for a little sailing camaraderie on the local level, join in on the **Canouan Regatta** the first week of June. Contact Carlos McLaurean, Commodore of the Canouan Sailing Club, ☎ 784-458-8197.

The Moorings of Clearwater, Florida, has opened a yacht charter on Canouan based on Charles Town Bay. You can choose to do about anything with a valid credit card; hire bareboat or with captain and gourmet chef, learn to sail, participate in regattas, buy into a yacht timeshare. The boats in Canouan are either catamarans or monohulls. Select your meal provisions ahead of time, and everything is delivered to the boat before sailing. More amenities per buck than most resorts offer. While you're planning, you might as well as leave all the plane and hotel reservations in their care as well. Locally you can contact them at ☎ 784-482-0653, 784-482-0655, fax 784-482-0654, moorcan@vincysurf.com. On-line brochures may be found at www.moorings.com or contact the main offices at ☎ 1-800-669-7476, fax 727-530-9747.

■ Shopping

Being relatively new to tourism, Canouan hasn't yet sprouted the boutiques and souvenirs you find flourishing on other islands. T-shirts, hats and toiletries are about the extent of things on offer at present.

Le Petit Bazaar at Tamarind Beach Hotel does have a few items of local craftwork. Raffles Resort will have boutiques more in the line of Palm Beach, and a fully stocked pro-shop for the golfing member of the family. If you are in despair that your partner is going to buy a new set of clubs at this juncture, remind them that Colombian emeralds will be on sale in the airport at Barbados or San Juan and are much easier to pack.

At another place in the scale of things, check out the **All In One Variety Store** prior to making your getaway by yacht. This is a serious rum shop, with groceries and other liquors on sale. **The Tamarind** is the place for ice and that last shower before hoisting sails.

■ Where to Eat

Restaurant Directory

R & C RESTAURANT & BAR, ☎ 784-458-8264
RAFFLES RESORT CANOUAN ISLAND, ☎ 784-458-8000
SILVER LINING RESTAURANT, ☎ 784-482-0348
TAMARIND BEACH HOTEL, ☎ 784-458-8044

R & C RESTAURANT & BAR

☎ 784-458-8264

US$15-$25

Daily, 6 am-late

As good as the more expensive places for local dishes, with an international wine list and lots of cocktails. They will prepare food for yachts and offer to deliver. A water taxi service is available.

RAFFLES RESORT CANOUAN ISLAND

☎ 784-458-8000, 866-589-2450

reservations.canouanisland@raffles.com

For visitors not staying at Raffles who wish to dine there, the Sunset Package is offered after 7pm; two choices are available. The **Raffles Culinary Experience** entails a three-course à la carte dinner at Jambus or the Godahl Beach Bar & Grill with access to Trump Club Privée Casino, all for US$125 per person. The **Raffles Fine Dining Experience** is a fourcourse à la carte dinner at La Piazza or La Varenne with access afterwards to the casino for US$175 per person. Both offer a slight discount for those registered at Tamarind Beach Hotel (see below). Neither package includes alcoholic beverages. Reservations are required in advance.

SILVER LINING RESTAURANT

☎ 784-482-0348

US$15-$25

Hutson and Lisa De Roche have a lovely setting for their restaurant, above Charlestown and overlooking Grand Bay. An excellent place for those seeking a pleasant meal without breaking the bank.

TAMARIND BEACH HOTEL

☎ 784-458-8044

US$26-$35 MC, Visa

Pizzas, pasta, salads, fish and a serious wine and champagne list. We sampled the grilled barracuda in lime juice with breadfruit, tomato, beans and cauliflower. Dining here was nothing less than delightful.

■ Where to Stay

Accommodations Directory

ANCHOR INN, Grand Bay, ☎ 784-458-8568
CRYSTAL APARTMENTS, Grand Bay, ☎ 784-458-8356, fax 784-458-8325
OCEAN VIEW INN, Grand Bay, ☎ 784-482-0477, fax 784-482-0306
RAFFLES RESORT, Carenage Bay, ☎ 784-458-8000, fax 784-458-8885
TAMARIND BEACH HOTEL & YACHT CLUB, Grand Bay, ☎ 784-458-8044, fax 784-458-8851

ANCHOR INN

Grand Bay

☎ 784-458-8568

Under US$100 No credit cards

George and Yvonne de Roche run what is really a guest house. The three rooms upstairs are small, with private bathrooms and ceiling fans. Downstairs is a cozy bar and separate dining room where breakfast is served. We thought it a little over-priced as rooms go, but it's difficult to find anything less expensive on Canouan today. A real West Indian "Mom & Pop" establishment.

CRYSTAL APARTMENTS
Grand Bay
☎ 784-458-8356, fax 784-458-8325
Under US$100 No credit cards

Four apartments with shower, kitchenette, ceiling fan and TV. Set back from the beach behind the Ocean View Inn (see below).

OCEAN VIEW INN
Grand Bay
☎ 784-482-0477, fax 784-482-0306
www.oceanview-can.com, oceanview@vincysurf.com
US$100-$200 Breakfast included. MC, Visa

A locally owned establishment on the beachfront. Six comfortable rooms with shower, ceiling fan, TV and telephone. Owned by Augustin and Luenda Pascal, they provide all modern amenities with Internet access available on the ground floor. Air-conditioned rooms costs slightly higher.

RAFFLES RESORT
Carenage Bay
☎ 784-482-2148, 458-8000, fax 784-482-0004, 458-8885
www.canouan.com, reservations@raffles-canouanisland.com
Over US$500 MC, Visa

An interesting blend of Indonesia and Caribbean, as unique and enticing as the shades of blue surrounding the island itself. You have entered Raffles as soon as the plane touches the island; quickly met by resort staff you are whisked away to a catamaran waiting to sail you into Carenage Bay. 156 luxurious villas and suites ranging from 600 to over 1,300 square feet in size, open to views of Carenage Bay, the encompassing coral reef, and the Atlantic Ocean. Each suite or villa is equipped with Jacuzzi, mini bar, air conditioning, ceiling fans, twice daily housekeeping, and all the things you came to Canouan to escape - phones, computer access, satellite television. Relax on white sand beaches with aquamarine waters, or play golf on a spectacular 18-hole course (Jim Fazio's remodeling of a Roy Case original). Rejuvenate at the renowned **Amrita** spa hovering over the reef; the massage table has a plexiglass floor giving views of tropical fish among the coral, as your body is refreshed by a Ginger Glow body scrub. Whatever your needs, you will be pampered beyond expectation.

Prices start on a par with other SVG and Grenada luxury resorts, and at the high end are comparable with those charged to Mustique's clientele. A ten night minimum stay is required during Christmas season.

TAMARIND BEACH HOTEL & YACHT CLUB

Tamarind's dock

Grand Bay

☎ 784-458-8044, fax 784-458-8851

www.tamarind.com, reservations@tamarind.us

US$200-$500+ MC, Visa

Forty attractive rooms and suites are hidden in lush, tropical foliage on a white sand beach facing the Caribbean Sea. Among the diverse styles of accommodations on Canouan, Tamarind proves to be the most traditionally West Indian. Rooms have pitched ceilings, white muslin netting, light wicker furnishings against dark exotic hardwoods, and folding louvered doors opening towards the sea. Thatched roofs show the allegiance to its sister property, Raffles Resort. While guests may use the spa, golf, and casino at Raffles, Tamarind guests have **The Moorings** yacht charter at their doorstep. Located on the edge of the "real island," guests here are privy to Canouan as a working community, while still enjoying the trappings of luxury.

■ After Dark

The night scene on Canouan depends on your budget. For gamblers the night is yours as **Raffles Resort** hosts **Trump Club Privee** inside the Villa Monte Carlo. For the fortunate few, **Villa Monte Carlo** also has a Grand Ballroom for special events. Villa Monte Carlo sits above Raffles and is illuminated at night in an opulent display.

On Thursday evenings join **Tamarind Beach Hotel** for a West Indian Night and on Saturdays, a beach barbecue. The hotel has two bars kept quite busy in high season as guests mingle with the yachties moored in Grand Bay. This is a good opportunity to catch up on local news around the Grenadines.

Several "happening" rum shops are in the neighborhood of Charlestown. You can tell the mood of a rum shop by the noise level. Loud music and the sound of dominoes slamming on the table indicate an overflow of testosterone (you never see women playing dominoes!). If the rum shop owner is jovial and friendly, this reflects the atmosphere of his establishment. If he's a grouch, then the patrons sit outside, entering only when another round is in order. The more the patrons drink, the less they care about the owner's mood until he makes that last call and shuts down for the night.

To ease into the scene try **R&C Restaurant & Bar** on the hillside just above the Tamarind Beach Hotel. For those wanting some island life away from fellow travelers, join in here; just beware of the white rum.

For others, there's nothing like peace and quiet and a little stargazing. The night sky holds more stars than you've ever dreamt of seeing at home. Around you the sounds from the bush are unfamiliar, but not intimidating. The waves drift back and forth like a mother rocking her small child. At last, Canouan has given you something after dark you hadn't planned on – serenity.

Tobago Cays

■ Orientation

What are the Tobago Cays? A group of small islets surrounded by a large horseshoe reef in some of the most pristine waters of the Caribbean. They were purchased by St. Vincent's government in 1988 and designated a **National Marine Park**. Little has been done specifically to protect them – due, undoubtedly, to a lack of funding. Moorings have been provided, a few leaflets printed, and there has been an effort by local dive operators, yacht charters and sailors to educate both visitors and local fishermen.

It has been left up to the local community with a direct economic connection to the Cays to see that visitors have minimum impact on the reefs, the marine life and these alluring islets. In many

ways they are a microcosm of eco-tourism; whether we truly desire to protect what is precious and endangered on our planet. And it is asking a lot of one small, economically strapped nation to protect this playground of international travelers.

Visiting St. Vincent & the Grenadines just isn't complete without a day-trip to the Tobago Cays. An hour or two of snorkeling and sunbathing will bring sweet enchantment and a yearning to return when you are back in the cold, northern climate. So

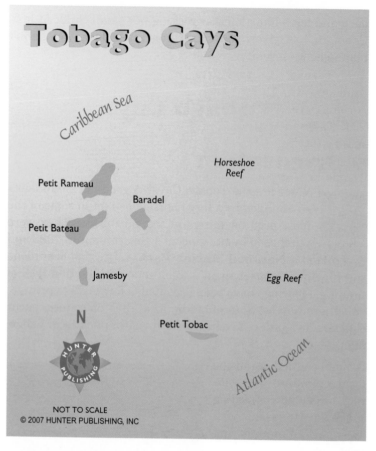

Tobago Cays

Caribbean Sea

Horseshoe Reef

Petit Rameau

Baradel

Petit Bateau

Jamesby

Egg Reef

N

Petit Tobac

Atlantic Ocean

NOT TO SCALE
© 2007 HUNTER PUBLISHING, INC

on with the sunscreen, don a good hat, and grab your snorkel, mask and fins.

By the time your captain comes to round up his flock, your back is probably burnt, your appetite increasing and you're really thirsty. All you leave behind are footprints in the sand, all you carry away are memories.

Sailing or motoring back is often much quieter than the ride out to the Cays. Passengers get lost in their thoughts, in the sound of wind flapping in the sails, or watching the water change color from aquamarine to turquoise to sapphire as it gets deeper. A wave of contentment washes over you. You will sleep well tonight.

■ Getting Here

Just east of Mayreau and south of Canouan, the Cays can only be reached by boat. Taking a water taxi is feasible from any of the southern Grenadines but you'll need to take food and drink, for yourself and

the water taxi driver. From St. Vincent, Bequia or Mustique, it is better to go with one of the tour operators based on those islands. The larger the vessel, the larger the party will be. You could end up on a catamaran with 30 others. Fifteen is an optimum crowd, although for some boats this is their break-even number. Be prepared to be flexible. It is not unheard of for potential passengers to turn up and find the excursion cancelled due to lack of numbers.

Planned excursions worth their salt include lunch on board at the Cays and complimentary drinks throughout the day.

Our preferred operators for day trips to the Cays are:

Friendship Rose, an 80-foot schooner out of Bequia, that helps you indulge your fantasies of life before the mast. The trip, including a light breakfast, lunch, rum punch and soft drinks, costs US$100 per person. ☎ 784-495-0886.

Captain Yannis charters has catamarans sailing from Union Island, visiting Saltwhistle Bay in Mayreau, Tobago Cays and Palm Island. You visit three of the most beautiful beaches in the area in one day. Lunch, rum punch and soft drinks are included at a cost of around US$50 per person. ☎ 784-458-8513.

■ Exploring

Petit Rameau, Petit Bateau, Barabel, Jamesby and Petit Tobaco are the five islets making up the Cays. The sea here has a white, sandy bottom and underwater a wide variety of sealife is at play.

Regardless of your ability in the water, there is something for everyone. The timid snorkeler can easily snorkel off the beach in the shallows. Those with more confidence can swim out deeper; the coral reefs are quite easy to access. For a better look from farther out on the reef, there are plenty of buoys where dinghies can tie up. At either end of Horseshoe Reef there are walls ranging from 30 to 65 feet, with visibility of 100 feet-plus.

See page 248 for Union Island dive operators who cover sites in the Tobago Cays and elsewhere.

The only shade in the Cays is provided by seagrape and almond trees, under which you can stow your pack while you frolic in the surf. Your body will require a lot of fresh water as a result of the sun and the saltwater. Should you forget to bring a cover-up, you'll fry like an egg in a skillet.

DID YOU KNOW?

■ It takes 10-12 years for a cigarette filter to decompose.

■ It takes 10-20 years for a plastic bag to decompose.

■ It takes 50-80 years for a plastic container to decompose.

Reef fish you're likely to see include the **parrotfish**. They are brilliantly colored and have beak-like mouths; you can hear them, too. They scrape algae from the reef and pulverize the coral with their powerful jaws. What they don't need as nutrients passes through them as sand. Yes, that's right, sand. An adult parrotfish can contribute as much as one ton of sand every year to his neighborhood!

The **surgeonfish** is another favorite. The young are yellow in color, the adults are a splendid sea blue. **Damselfish** are the farmers of the reef, being vegetarian. They guard their own areas as if tending gardening plots. If a four-inch-long fish is coming at you and nibbling your mask and fins, it is the bold damselfish. You have to admire their energetic attempt to move you out of their territory.

Giving us sharp reminders that we aren't to touch anything in this underwater world are the triggerfish, trunkfish and porcupine fish.

Triggerfish have spiny needles on their backs, making it virtually impossible to move them from rocks and crevices.

Porcupine fish can transform themselves into a pincushion, similar to their namesake. Anyone who has sampled a porcupine's quill will heed this warning. The **trunkfish** should have been named the armorfish; its body is one armored bony plate. Its lips resemble a supermodel's that have been shot with collagen. The **butterflyfish** is easily discernible by the eye spot near the tail. This is camouflage meant to confuse predators.

Predator fish have evolved three means to catch prey: outrunning, stalking and ambush. Those that pursue and outrun their catch are built for speed and generally hunt in schools; jacks and

snappers are in this group. The stalkers include barracuda and trumpetfish, their bodies long and thin. Having followed their prey at a short distance, they use a few final strokes of their tail to catch up and grab their quarry. The fish that ambush aren't necessarily built for speed and agility through the water. They lie in wait for their unsuspecting dinner to come close, then suck them suddenly into a mouth like a vacuum cleaner. Groupers and scorpionfish belong to this category.

This is only a sampling of life beneath the surface at the Tobago Cays. It's a lot to take in over one visit. Anchoring there for a few days, you have the opportunity to observe the soap opera going on down below. It will make you aware of the fragility of the reef and the need for all visitors to maintain the quality of life here. Should you find something someone else has irresponsibly left behind, please pick it up and dispose of it properly. This is a place where we have to act as our brother's keeper. It is a small price to pay for another good day on our shared planet.

■ Where to Eat

There are no restaurants or cafés on the Tobago Cays. Some vendors sell cold drinks and even lobster, but don't even think of cooking on the beach; campfires are banned.

■ Where to Stay

Not here, unless you're on a yacht! No camping is allowed, except for a few local fishermen. When the day begins to wane, it's time to go back whence you came. Enjoy the return journey.

PARK RULES

■ Enjoy looking at the coral and other sealife, but don't touch animals or plants and by no means remove anything.

■ Always motor slowly around the Cays when in boats and dinghies.

■ Don't speed or create excessive wake with your vessel. Snorkelers and coral heads are all around you.

■ Feel free to use passive watersports equipment in the Cays, such as kayaks and windsurf boards.

■ It is illegal to use motorized watersport craft, such as jetskis and water-skis.

■ Scuba diving is permitted, preferably with a local operator who can maximize your pleasure and safety with their local knowledge.

■ Don't scuba without a dive flag, or in the strong currents without surface support.

■ Use your anchor if aboard a sailboat, but...

Don't anchor, or drag your anchor, near coral, as damage is irreparable. If you are in any doubt as to where you can or cannot anchor, contact the **Tobago Cays Marine Park** in Clifton, Union Island. ☎ 784-485-8191, fax 784-485-8192, tcmp@ caribsurf.com.

Mayreau

■ Orientation

 At only 1½ square miles, or approximately 700 acres, Mayreau is the smallest of the inhabited islands in the Grenadines. A population of 200 inhabitants share some of the most beautiful beaches in the West Indies.

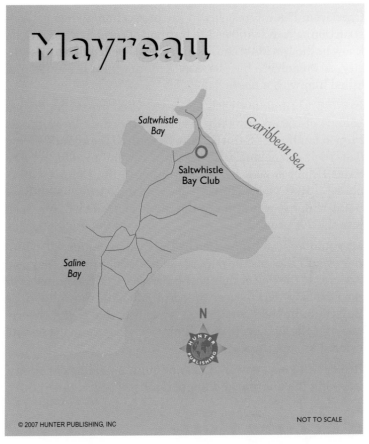

Mayreau

© 2007 HUNTER PUBLISHING, INC

NOT TO SCALE

The first impression from the jetty is that there is nothing here. The road up to the one village is a steep walk. The island is dry and hilly, making agriculture and livestock grazing nearly impossible. Precious rainfall is collected by each family and water conservation is a daily reminder of natural resources. Mayreau is a place where nothing but the sun and sea is taken for granted.

The first European settler was a Monsieur de L'Isle in the 1700s, who was allowed to retain possession even after the British took control. Whether he actually resided on Mayreau is questionable as he is recorded as being a resident of the Tobago Cays, Prune Island (Palm Island), Frigate Island and

Carriacou. His interest lay in the production of lime for construction, which involves the burning of coral in kilns. We do know he died on Mayreau, as his slaves rebelled due to his cruelty. A woman, Nellie Ibo, knocked him from his horse and killed him with a hoe.

In 1776, six tenants with 66 slaves were producing 20,000 pounds of cotton annually. Shortly afterwards, a well-to-do French family, the SaintHillaires, acquired the island, having fled their homeland's burgeoning revolution. One of the Saint-Hillaires was a lady-in-waiting to the Empress Josephine. Her last direct descendant was Jane-Rose Saint-Hillaire, who still ran the island along feudal lines well into the 20th century.

Mayreau was later inherited by the Eustace family of St. Vincent, who still owns the majority of the land. In 1977, they sold 22 acres to the Potter family of Barbados, who commuted over the next two years to clear the scrub and build the Saltwhistle Bay Club. In 1986, another 21 acres was sold to the government for the citizens to have their own village and not be considered as squatters.

Recently, a small power plant was built, providing electricity, silencing the antique and temperamental generators.

■ Getting Here

The nearest airports are on Union Island and Canouan. A water taxi from Union Island costs EC$100 (US$40) and takes 10 minutes. From Canouan, it takes around 40 minutes and costs EC$250 (US$100).

The only ferry service is the mailboat, ***Barracuda***. On Monday and Thursday, it leaves St. Vincent at 10:30 am, Bequia at 11:45 am, and Canouan at 2 pm. On Saturday, it leaves St. Vincent at 10 am and Canouan at 2:30 pm. On Tuesday and Friday, it leaves Union Island at 6:30 am. A one-way ticket to Mayreau costs EC$25 from St. Vincent, EC$20 from Bequia, and EC$15 from Canouan and Union Island.

Make sure you're ready to disembark at the portside exit on arrival; you will literally be dropped off.

It's wise to drink bottled water here. Check the seal of the bottle to make sure it isn't a refill.

■ Money Matters

 Mayreau has no bank. Be sure to cash your travelers checks before leaving one of the other islands. The Saltwhistle Bay Club does accept major credit cards.

■ Exploring

At the top of the island is a picturesque **stone church**. It was built in 1929 by a Belgian monk, who also constructed the fantastically Gothic Catholic Cathedral in Kingstown, St. Vincent. A  former church on this site was built by the Saint-Hillaire family in the early 1800s. One visitor at the turn of the century described it as "nothing better than a garden shed," with a large congregation of ants and birds. The hurricane of 1921 blew it away. The present Catholic church is open for all to visit and worship and stands as the lone representation of Mayreau's history.

For the most part, Mayreau guards its privacy. As is apparent from the deck of a boat, the majority of the island is in its natural wild state. The dry terrain is covered by thorny scrubland, which is a product of hot sun and strong wind. Seemingly hostile, the root systems of the scrub do help prevent soil erosion. Acacia stickers keep people and livestock out of the bush. Cacti such as **Turk's cap**, **prickly pear**, and the tall, slender **organ pipe**, can leave a fierce sting in your fingers. A living remnant of colonial days are the wild **cotton plants** seen on many of these islands, where they flourish in the parched and impoverished soil.

One rose among all the thorns is the **frangipani**, with its waxy-looking flowers of white, yellow, red or pink, and a sweet fragrance. Beware though; its milky sap contains a vicious poison. It is a favorite of the large black and yellow caterpillar who, as a direct result, is also poisonous.

A WORD TO
THE WISE

Most insect repellents lasts three to four hours on your skin. Take care using a repellent with a chemical base, especially DEET, on children. Products made with essential oils of camphor, citronella, lemongrass, clove or eucalyptus can be as effective, less toxic, and more pleasing.

Follow the road from the church down to **Saltwhistle Bay**. The resort here is private but the beach is public. There's plenty of beach to choose from along this perfect horseshoe bay of white sand.

The water is postcard material. Somehow it can strip age and sophistication from all comers, leaving pure and innocent joy radiating from everyone. A narrow strip of sand divides the bay from the Atlantic side. Rough for swimmers, it is an ideal place for fishing and birdwatching. Boobies, terns and pelicans hover and dive as if in Olympic competition.

For snorkeling and scuba diving, **Mayreau Gardens** is an area of reefs located between Mayreau and the Tobago Cays. It is wise to go with a local dive operator from Canouan or Union Island as currents can be tricky. The dive is generally done as a drift dive. For those of you who are "shark people," black tips are known to cruise through and nurse sharks are quite common. See page 178 for details on Union Island dive operators who cover Mayreau.

WHAT COLOR IS THE BEACH?

Have you ever thought what makes a beach a specific color? Between St. Vincent and Grenada you will discover white, pink, gold and black beaches. The color depends upon the rock, the coral or the creature from which it came. The sand in the Tobago Cays is bright white and fine to the touch. On the windward coast of St. Vincent near the volcano, the sand is black and earthy. Grenada's Grand Anse has yellow sand of a gritty texture. How do we account for the differences?

A single grain of sand can be millions of years old. Grains become smaller and smaller by the pounding of the waves. Smoother grains have obviously weathered longer than those that are sharp. Geologists can tell what type of beach the sand comes from just by looking at the color.

In some sand you can find the familiar pink tones of a conch shell, or the whiteness of bleached fishbone. Naturalist Rachel Carson wrote, "Sand is a substance that is beautiful, mysterious, and infinitely variable; each grain on a beach is the result of processes that go back into the shadowy beginnings of life, or the earth itself." What is it that makes us clinch a handful of sand in our fist and slowly let it sift through our fingers until it disappears? We talk of "the sands of time" and use sand in an hour glass, ticking off seconds and belittling its age. By holding it, are we trying to conquer time? We build sand castles and leave footprints on the strand, our own fleeting monuments and signatures. How soon they are washed away and rearranged by the sea.

■ Sailing

GEORGIA

☎/fax 784-458-8594

A 44-foot Irwin available for day-trips, with lunch and drinks included for around US$100 per person. Overnight trips are US$350 per day for the boat. Passengers must bring their own food.

SCOOBY WATER TAXI

☎ 784-458-8079

Thomas Alexander takes snorkeling trips to the Tobago Cays, Palm Island and Mopion; he also offers fishing trips where the catch can be prepared and grilled on the beach. The average cost is US$100 per person per day.

■ Shopping

You can give your pocketbook a rest while visiting Mayreau because shopping in the village is limited to groceries, bottled water and canned goods. It definitely makes you aware of what we consider necessities of life and what we take for granted.

If one of the Windjammers is sitting at anchor in Saline Bay then a few vendors will be offering T-shirts for sale. You'll also find vendors in Saltwhistle Bay with similar stock. The **Saltwhistle Bay Club** has a small boutique with sarongs, T-shirts and regular sundries for those running out of lotions and moisturizers.

■ Where to Eat

Restaurant Directory

DENNIS HIDEAWAY, ☎/fax 784-458-8594
ISLAND PARADISE RESTAURANT & BAR, ☎ 784-458-8941
J&C BAR & RESTAURANT, ☎ 784-458-8558
RIGHTEOUS ROBERTS, ☎ 784-458-8203
SALTWHISTLE BAY CLUB, ☎ 784-458-8444, fax 784-458-8944

Mayreau

J&C BAR & RESTAURANT
☎ 784-458-8558
Under US$15
Daily, 12-3 pm, 6-10 pm

Grilled lobster with garlic sauce, curried conch, and lamb creole sit alongside chicken and fries, fish sandwiches and burgers.

RIGHTEOUS ROBERT
☎ 784-458-8203
US$15-$25 MC, Visa
Daily, 9 am-10 pm

This restaurant has grown a little bit here, a little bit there. Painted in the red, green and gold of Robert's Rastafarian faith, with accompanying music. Lunch and dinner menus are the same, except more expensive in the evening; fish, shrimp, lobster, conch and ribs.

Breakfast was a bit disappointing, cold baked beans are not our cup of tea, but his company was most warming.

SALTWHISTLE BAY CLUB

☎ 784-458-8444, fax 784-458-8944

US$26-$35 MC, Visa

Daily

The thatched dining cabanas are circular and made from local stone so there's no problem eating in wet swimsuits. Lunch features tuna, chicken, lobster, chef's salads, catch of the day or chicken in a basket, all at a good price, considering the upscale nature of the Club.

The evening menu changes daily; on our visit it was smoked mackerel or breaded shrimps for starters; catch of the day, steak, chicken, lamb or pork for main course, and crêpes or ice cream for dessert. As part of our colada crusade we tried the Coco colada, a coconut- and coffee-flavored piña colada. Nowhere else could we find the same sensation.

ISLAND PARADISE RESTAURANT & BAR

☎ 784-458-8941

US$15-$25

Daily, 8 am-10 pm

A comprehensive menu is served throughout the day. The price of dinner includes soup, salad, bread and butter, vegetables and dessert. As a main dish choose from fish creole in white wine sauce, conch in garlic sauce, or lamb chops in red wine. One free dinner is given for every four persons eating. Apart from the upscale Saltwhistle Bay Club, this beats all other restaurants on Mayreau hands-down.

DENNIS HIDEAWAY

☎/fax 784-458-8594

Although not well hidden, the restaurant seems to be open at the whim of its owner. We cannot vouch for it, though we tried stopping in at breakfast and again at lunch. See below.

■ Where to Stay

Accommodations Directory

DENNIS HIDEAWAY, ☎/fax 784-458-8594
RIGHTEOUS ROBERT, ☎ 784-458-8203
SALTWHISTLE BAY CLUB, ☎ 784-458-8444, fax 784-458-8944

DENNIS HIDEAWAY

☎/fax 784-458-8594

Located in the Village, Dennis offers five bedrooms each with a balcony and private bathroom. The rooms are sparse, but tidy. If you are passing through and he's there, you've found a nice, reasonable place to hang your cap.

RIGHTEOUS ROBERT

☎ 784-458-8203

Under US$100 No credit cards

A three-bedroom house with kitchen facilities located in the midst of Mayreau's only community. The cookstove is gas; the advent of power in the recent past might also have brought a refrigerator, for Mayreau is deadpan hot. The battery-operated toilet-roll holder with radio was, at first glance, comic and out of place, but the joke was on us – there was no battery. We would not have felt comfortable had we had to share the house with complete strangers. Rent all three rooms to ensure safety and privacy.

SALTWHISTLE BAY CLUB

☎ 784-458-8444, fax 784-458-8944

www.saltwhistlebay.com, swbinfo@gmx.net

US$201-$500 Breakfast and dinner included MC, Visa

Saltwhistle Bay Club occupies the northern end of Mayreau. Garden suites sit on what is considered by many to be the finest beach in the Grenadines. The rooms are built from local stone and look much like those on Palm Island and Petit St. Vincent, cool, spacious, and luxurious in an understated way. Trees provide blanket coverage and shade from the suites to the beach. Cabanas, seating up to six persons, are threaded around the beachside bar and boutique. This bay is gorgeous with some of the clearest turquoise water in the Caribbean. Private sailboats are welcome and some local charters stop in Saltwhistle Bay on their way to the Tobago Cays and Palm Island. As you sip on a cold drink, or take a relaxing dip in the sea, reflect on those passengers only enjoying an hour or so here while you have as long as you choose.

■ After Dark

 With the coming of electricity, who knows what Mayreau will be like in the night time! The people may crank up the stereos night and day for months on end. They may fall prey to the hypnotic, flickering eye in the corner of the room, more victims for *The Young and the Restless*.

At present, generators provide light in some places on the island. Domino games and pool tournaments are held in the village on most evenings. The sharks have had a lot of practice, so be prepared for a competitive game. With four restaurants and bars, there's sure to be some late night storytelling. The newly paved road makes it much easier to get over to Saltwhistle Bay without stumbling around in the dark. Any rustling you hear in the bush is probably a cow or a donkey. This is when you commend yourself for packing a good flashlight.

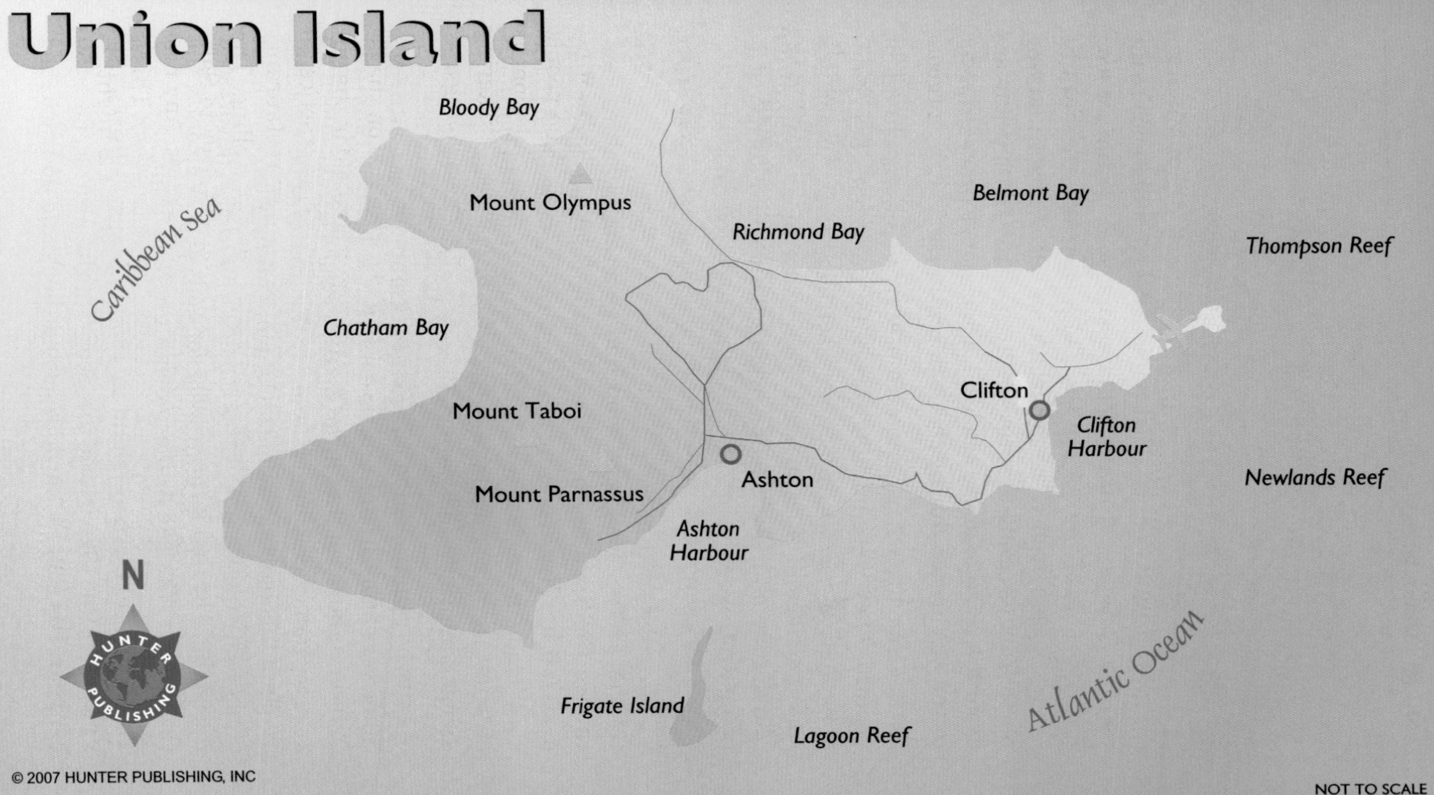
Union Island
Bloody Bay
Mount Olympus
Caribbean Sea
Belmont Bay
Richmond Bay
Thompson Reef
Chatham Bay
Clifton
Mount Taboi
Clifton
Harbour
Ashton
Newlands Reef
Mount Parnassus
Ashton
Harbour
N
HUNTER PUBLISHING
Frigate Island
Lagoon Reef
Atlantic Ocean
© 2007 HUNTER PUBLISHING, INC
NOT TO SCALE

Union Island

■ Orientation

 Union Island is distinguished from a distance by its pitons, **Mounts Parnassus** and **Taboi**, rising sharply out of the sea. On a clear day they can be seen from Fort Charlotte on St. Vincent; sailing north from Grenada they are easily spotted. These peaks are around 1,000 feet above sea level. Their slopes proved ripe for cotton production during the 18th century.

At that time French fishermen from Martinique were frequent visitors. They were hunting turtles for meat and their valuable shell. By 1763, two French settlers, Jean Augier and Antoine Regaud, had arrived. They were most likely from Martinique and Guadeloupe, where the sugar industry was being destroyed by ants. Both turned to cotton and, with 350 slaves between them, grew close to 60,000 pounds of cotton per year.

By the 1800s, the Frenchmen had gone and wealthy merchants, the Span brothers from Bristol, England, had taken over. It is hardly surprising that they were also involved in the slave trade. Records show that their ships traded in the areas of what are now Angola and Cameroon. The Span brothers dabbled in piracy and were victims of it too.

Many who came to Union Island to seek employment with S&J Span were from Bristol, and no doubt felt at home. Clifton and Ashton, suburbs of that large English seaport, have ended up as place names on Union Island. By the time of emancipation, shipbuilding had taken hold on Union. This may have been out of necessity as two hurricanes, in 1817 and 1831, devastated the island. The first large vessel ever built in St. Vincent & the Grenadines was *The Katherine*, built here in 1839.

The Spans sold Union Island in 1850 to Major Collins of St. Vincent. It was then leased to a Scot, Charles Mulzac, for £150 per year. His son, Richard, inherited the island and switched from cotton to whaling after another hurricane in 1898. This was a viable part of Union's economy until the 1920s. Richard's son, Hugh Mulzac, has the distinction of being the first black officer to command a ship in the American navy.

Union Island was eventually purchased by the British Crown in 1910 for £5,000. In 1951, all citizens over the age of 21 were given the vote; five years later the first car, a Land Rover, rolled ashore. In 1972 a secondary school was started and the airport runway was laid soon afterwards. By 1976 there were 12 cars on the island and the first taxi service was up and running. Union Island confronted a new industry with new promises – tourism.

■ Getting Here & Around

Union Island

Union Island is the ideal base for discovering this region. From Union Island, you can visit the Tobago Cays, Palm Island, Petit St. Vincent, Mayreau, Canouan, Carriacou or Petite Martinique for the day and be back on Union in time for dinner.

By Air

Arriving at your gateway airport, Barbados, St. Lucia, Martinique, or Grenada, you must transfer onto an inter-island airline. Once you've chosen the gateway airport, coordinate the connection with the smaller air-

line. When leaving St. Vincent & the Grenadines, there is a departure tax of EC$40 or US$15 per person; any change will be returned in Eastern Caribbean currency.

Airlines Serving Union Island

Air Martinique	☎ 784-458-8826, 784-458-4528
Grenadine Airway	☎784-456-6793, www.grena-dine-airways.com, info@mustique.com
Mustique Airways	☎ 784-458-4380, www.mustique.com
SVG Air	☎ 784-458-8882, 784-457-5777, www.svgair.com

A WORD TO
THE WISE

As of 2002, white rum is not allowed on airplanes, either in hand luggage or in the hold. Sunset's Very Strong Rum from St. Vincent, Jack Iron and Rivers Rum from Grenada are included in this ban as they are highly flammable liquids.

By Sea

If you are adventurous, take the **Osprey Express** from Grenada to either Carriacou or Petite Martinique and then hire a water taxi. This is our preferred method as once we're in the Caribbean, it's time to relax and enjoy the ride.

From Palm Island or Petit St. Vincent, you most probably arrived via Union Island and the management of the resorts will be happy to make arrangements for your transport.

From Mayreau or Canouan, it is feasible to take a water taxi. Canouan to Union Island takes about 45 minutes and costs about US$100. The scenery at waterside is breathtaking. Mayreau to Union Island is only a 10-minute ride and costs around US$40.

From St. Vincent, Bequia, Canouan, and Mayreau, you can travel the mailboat *Barracuda*. Monday and Thursday she departs from St. Vincent at 10:30am, Bequia at 11:45am, Canouan at 2pm,

Union Island Harbor

Mayreau at 3:25pm, and arrives at Union Island at 3:45pm. On Tuesday and Friday, the *Barracuda* leaves Union Island at 6:30am, stopping at Mayreau, Canouan, Bequia, and into St. Vincent around noon. Come Saturday, she leaves St. Vincent at 10am, Canouan at 2:30pm, Mayreau at 3:15pm, and into Union by 4pm. She sails out of Union at 5:30pm and heads directly to St. Vincent, arriving at 10:30pm. It is wise to call St. Vincent before leaving Union Island and have a taxi waiting for you when you arrive; tickets are purchased onboard. This is a commercial port and has all the riff-raff that goes with the territory worldwide, especially late at night. Also make note, the mailboat only stops long enough to unload cargo and let passengers off; be ready when the boat is nearing your destination. Do not assume the vessel will actually cut its engines and let the ramp down – be prepared to hop off.

St. Vincent to Union Island costs EC$30, Bequia to Union Island EC$25, and EC$20 from Canouan. Schedules are always subject to change depending on weather, cargo, holidays or sports events. Its best to alert the main office you are expecting a ride the following day and/or that afternoon. ☎ 784-456-5063.

Another option is the cargo boat, **MV *Gem Star***; leaving St. Vincent at 11am on Tuesdays and Fridays and departing Union Island at 7:30am on Wednesdays and Saturdays and returning to St. Vincent after making one stop at Canouan.

Much smaller, the **MV *Jasper***, leaves Union Island for Carriacou at 6am Monday and Thursday and leaves Carriacou for Union Island at noon on those days. The hour ride is EC$20. Keep in mind you are departing St. Vincent & the Grenadines and entering Grenada's Grenadines; there's the possibility a Customs Officer may be on the jetty for your arrival or departure. If the latter, you'll be expected to pay the EC$40 (US$15) departure tax per person.

Ferry schedules can be erratic during public holidays. They may or may not be running, or may be going somewhere totally off their normal routine. Be prepared to use your creative skills in getting from one island to another. This can be an adventure in itself. Fishermen are generally always on hand and ready to go at a minute's notice.

■ Internet & Telephone

Near the Post Office, above the S&V Grocery is the **Internet Café**, ☎ 784-485-8258, internetcafe@ vincysurf.com. Selling screen time, long distance phone time, and phone cards; they are also the agent for Western Union money transfers. Opening hours are 8 am-5 pm, Monday to Friday, and 8 am-12 pm on Sunday.

Erika's Marine Services, ☎ 784-485-8335, in the Bougainvilla complex, includes e-mail, fax, phone and digital photography.

Charges for international calls are EC$3 per minute within the Caribbean, EC$5 per minute to the USA & Canada, and EC$7 per minute to Europe.

■ Travel Agents

James Travel Service, ☎ 784-485-8306, and **Eagles Travel**, ☎ 784458-8179, both in Clifton, can arrange your onward travel.

■ Taxi Drivers

For an island tour, try **Rose Tours**, ☎ 784-458-8326, youngbuffalo@yahoo.com, or **BJ Taxi**, ☎ 784-458-8989. Benson Joseph is a trustworthy driver/guide for exploring or airport transfers. Any tour should include Fort Hill, a vantage point 450 feet above sea level. This is *the* spot for seeing the chain of islands from St. Vincent to Grenada. The cost for an island excursion is EC$60 per hour. A transfer from Clifton to the airport is EC$5.

■ Car Rental

Car rental is not a big business on Union Island. We handed over the rental fee and were given the keys to a Suzuki. There was no contract, no talk of insurance, and we weren't asked to show a local license, which is statutory in St. Vincent & the Grenadines. This situation will probably change if business increases. For the moment, contact: **Leslie Noel**, ☎ 784-458-8162, or **Charlie Van Hutchinson**, ☎ 784-458-8436.

■ Bike Rental

Bike rental is available from **Erika's Maine Services**, ☎ 784-485-8335, and **T.J. Plaza**, ☎ 485-819-8930.

■ Exploring

Take a ride on one of the half-dozen dollar buses for an overview of the island. You'll be surprised as to how little of the island is paved. Mountain bikers will appreciate this the most as the traffic is minimal and the terrain as varied as the road itself.

From Clifton, head up **Fort Hill**, the peak above the airport. The road looks impassable, but it's not impossible. A few picnic tables are scattered across a shaded pasture. A cannon faces toward Carriacou and another strategically points to the entrance of the harbor. The view from the top is the best in all this island chain. On a clear day, both St. Vincent and Grenada are visible. After the breathtaking scenery careful maneuvering down the rugged hillside feels adventurous.

Continuing over the hill, the hardtop road weaves through grazing lands with houses dotted here and there. We wouldn't recommend that any bushwhacking hikers attempt shortcuts through the scrub; the thorns in the bush are sharp as sea-urchin quills. Past where the pavement ends by the seashore are mangroves, their propped-up root systems sticking out of the water. Large holes in the ground are home to crabs. This is an ideal feeding area for crabs, shrimp and several species of fish that feed on leaf particles. Birders can expect to see kingfishers and herons here, with cattle egrets in the nearby fields.

Richmond Bay is secluded, with good snorkeling, and the **Big Sand Hotel** has a selection of Belgian beers for the connoisseur quaffer.

Another high spot, literally, is the **road leading to the radio/TV tower**. Driving up, we wondered whether the vehicle – a rental car with bald tires – would flip over on the ascent. Coming down seemed worse, especially thinking about potential brake failure. We recommend this adventure be accomplished on foot.

South of Clifton, the road steeps over to **Ashton**, Union Island's second village. If you manage to get past the school cricket field without stopping to watch a game, continue on to **Campbell**, where the houses thin out. A reef system lies in **Ashton Harbour** between Union and Frigate Island. The road pushes toward the southern end of the island, no doubt with future residential development in mind.

CRICKET

Cricket goes with carnival, calypso, and coconut as one of the things that put the "C" into Caribbean. A carnival atmosphere pervades the stadium, with drums and whistles keeping up a hypnotic backbeat punctuated by passing ghetto blasters, transistor radios and vocal offerings of advice and encouragement.

International matches, "Test Matches," against the likes of England, Australia, India, Pakistan, Sri Lanka, South Africa and New Zealand, occur frequently.

Most people can reel off the names of the current national team, show an encyclopedic knowledge of the past, and have ready at hand the names of up-and-coming talent. Cricket is a game that the people of the West Indies have dominated internationally for the last 40 years.

At the local level, teams are divided pretty much by island groups – the Windwards, the Leewards, Trinidad & Tobago, Jamaica, Barbados, etc., who compete in a mixture of one-day and three-day tournaments.

Pass any school and you'll see children with home-made bats and a tennis ball learning their skills. Beach cricket is a popular pastime as well. Although appearing casual, it is just as eagerly contested. If you fancy trying your hand, they will usually allow you to have a bat or a bowl.

Professional cricketers can earn a decent living, particularly in another country. However, today there are bigger fortunes to be made on the soccer pitch and the basketball court. To see a loss of cricketing talent in these islands would be a dent to their national character that would indeed be unthinkable.

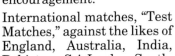

Union Island

Once you have a feel for the land, hire a water taxi to give you the mariner's view. Carry snorkel gear with you for the occasional dip when the captain gives the go-ahead. By boat you can venture onto the wilderness side of the island and picnic on the sandy beach at **Chatham** or **Bloody Bay**. Neither of these beaches have coral reefs. Remember to include your captain on the picnic plan as a courtesy and you'll get more than your money's worth in a tour.

■ Scuba Diving

Two doorstep sites close to Union Island are the reef by Clifton Harbour and Chatham Bay. The **reef at Clifton** extends from 15 feet to 75 feet, but topside has very busy traffic so trust the local operators. **Chatham Bay** is on the western side of Union Island and has a wall dive with lobsters and the possibility of seeing large turtles.

Dive Operators

Union Island's dive operators cover the sites for Palm Island, Petit St. Vincent, Mayreau and the Tobago Cays.

GRENADINES DIVE
Scuba Villa, Clifton
☎ 784-458-8138, fax 784-458-8122
gdive@caribsurf.com

Diving in Palm Island

The closest site is **Grand De Coi**, a circular reef to a depth of 70 feet, with abundant reef fish and coral life.

Diving in Petit St. Vincent

Two sandy islets with reefs prove as delightful to be on as to be below. **Mopion** and **Pinese** have circular reefs with coral walls going down to around 60 feet. Mopion has a small shelter and is a good bet for snorkelers.

Diving in Mayreau

Mayreau Gardens belongs to the Tobago Cays Marine Park and is a drift dive, or series of dives, since it extends down to 120 feet and the currents can be strong. For this beautiful diving location, we suggest you go with a local dive operator as they will get the most out of the area for you. There have been recent instances of independent divers doing untold damage to the reef by carelessness and plain stupidity. Locals single out Mediterranean yachties as the worst offenders.

The *Purini* lies to the west of Mayreau. A World War I gunboat, she lies at a depth of 40 feet and is home to schools of fish and encrusted with coral.

Diving in Tobago Cays

Surrounding the Cays on the eastern side, **Horseshoe Reef** has beautifully clear water down to over 60 feet. It is best to visit with a local guide, as will be evident from places where the reef has died from too much human contact. The number of boats visiting the Cays seems to grow year by year and while it is still an idyllic place to take a day trip and has excellent snorkeling, there will come a time when a limit is imposed. Overcrowding could cause boat rage.

GLENROY ADAMS

On the south side of Clifton is **Grenadines Dive**, the local dive center owned and run by Glenroy Adams. He is a cool and self-assured operator, which must fill his customers and pupils with confidence. As an impressionable youth, he met Johnny Coconut (John Caldwell) of Palm Island and helped him plant trees in the Grenadines. No  doubt this connection fostered Glenroy's love for the environment and his undying drive to conserve its fragile existence.

In 1985, Glenroy left his home on Bequia for the Tobago Cays and Union Island. The Cays at that time had much less boat traffic than today, and lobsters were plentiful and easy to catch in a quick shallow dive. The reefs were full of fish and the beaches strewn with conch shells left behind by generations of fishermen. With Caldwell he began planting palms and seagrape trees to help stop erosion of the beaches, the roots creating a net-like effect beneath the sand. As conch shells fall into the sea, small fish use them as shelter and eventually they break down into their calciate origins.

As the Cays became popular with sailors and divers, so the reefs suffered damage. Anchors scraped and dragged through the coral. People broke off chunks to take as keepsakes. Garbage was frequently dumped in the water. Irresponsibility and ignorance were causing the death of an ancient living organism.

Finally, the St. Vincent & the Grenadines government realized how precious this habitat is, both in terms of its fragility and in attracting the tourist dollar. The Tobago Cays were designated a National Marine Park, but, while Glenroy set out moorings in safe areas, there was nobody to enforce the rules and regulations. It has been left up to people like him, who love the place and depend upon it for their livelihood, to see that the rest of us act as respectful and conscientious guests.

Glenroy focused on what the general public can do to maintain the life of the reef ecosystem. As a start, to sustain a healthy sealife population, we must refuse to buy lobsters out of season. It is prohibited at any time to take lobsters with eggs or those younger than breeding age. The same applies to conch. And turtle is an absolute no-no. Never buy turtle meat nor products made from their shells.

Maybe not as obvious to some of us is that by walking on coral, touching it with our hands or fins accidentally, we are destroying a living organism. Glenroy explained that every shell or calcified bottle in the water has become a home for some small fish. He asked that we respect these homes and not disturb them by picking them up or moving them.

For yachties, there are plenty of moorings away from the reef. Be aware of where your anchor takes hold. He stressed that he found the French and Italian yachties to be by far the worst offenders. We were reminded of how quickly we can be categorized by what our fellow countrymen have done before us. It is our own responsibility to pave the road for others yet to come. Of course, yachties as a whole know not to dump garbage into the sea under any circumstance. It's strange to still find trash floating in the sea. Glenroy even advised not to give garbage to local fishermen or water taxi drivers for disposal. Too often it goes the same way. He suggested taking garbage to one of the following islands: Union Island, Canouan, Bequia or St. Vincent. Another suggestion is to refrain from flushing toilets in the Cays. Look around you at the number of sailboats moored here, and the cruise ships that anchor for the day – and think about it.

While Glenroy was educating us in his busy dive shop, we could hear the cooing and squealing of his young baby in the apartment above. It is apparent that he's not just thinking of the "here and now." He's concerned about the future, the future of his family, of his small country and the future of a large ocean. On this small island far from the madding world of jetports, subway stations and urban sprawl, this man understands the big picture and knows that each and every one of us can make a difference.

Orange cup coral

We highly recommend that divers and snorkelers seek out people like Glenroy Adams to enrich their vacation. It's not just the knowledge of the dive sites, but of the sea itself. We are willing to bet that, at the end of a day with Glenroy, you will walk away wondering what you can do for the Cays, for the marine life, for the next generation.

When you browse in the market or at a stall on the beach, ask the vendor what those earrings are made from; if the answer is black coral or turtle shell, then walk away – you too, have just made a difference.

Union Island Regatta

■ Sailing

The following charter services will pick you up at specified locations once bookings are confirmed.

CAPTAIN YANNIS YACHT CHARTER

☎ 784-458-8513, fax 784-458-8976

www.captainyannis.com, yannis@caribsurf.com

Three 60-foot catamarans and one 60-foot trimaran comprise the fleet that serves up one of the best tours in these islands. The cruise departs to Saltwhistle Bay, Mayreau for snorkeling, visits Tobago Cays for lunch, and drops in on Palm Island before returning to Union. Lasting from 8 am to 4 pm, this cruise is so popular that people fly from St. Lucia, St. Vincent and Grenada to take part and are back at their base by evening.

LEONA

☎ 784-593-5478

Captain Thomas runs private day charters for up to four persons.

■ Yacht Services

UNITECH MARINE SERVICE
Bougainvilla, Clifton
☎ 784-458-8913
unitech@caribsurf.com
Diesel and outboard engine repair, electrical repair and welding are among the services supplied.

ERIKA'S MARINE SERVICES
Bougainvilla, Clifton
☎ 784-485-8335, fax 784-485-8336
erika@caribsurf.com
E-mail and internet, fax and telephone service. Laundry, cash advances, book exchange and bicycle rental.

ANCHORAGE YACHT CLUB
Adjacent to Bougainvilla, Clifton
☎ 784-458-8221, fax 784-458-8365
aycunion@caribsurf.com

AUTHOR PICK

Mooring, laundry service, garbage collection, water, ice and other essentials.

■ Fishing

MORE FRESH
☎ 784-485-8335
Captain Kojak and his speedboat offer fishing, snorkeling, picnics and remote beaches. *More Fresh* will pick up guests at their request.

■ Shopping

Boutiques and supermarkets are the two choices you have on Union Island at the moment. Hotels have their own boutiques and the **Anchorage Yacht Club**, ☎ 784-458-8221, is of top quality. The Italian linen dresses, expensive underwear, old maps and charts, and local history and geography books stand beside the usual beachwear and accessories. **Okaou**, ☎ 784-458-8316, in the Bougainvilla complex, has a colorful array of clothing, post cards, batik and bric-a-brac. In the Clifton Beach Hotel, **Art Shop By The Sea**, has clothes, books, souvenirs, sun creams and disposable cameras.

Visiting **Goatland** can be a journey of discovery. Opposite the post office in Clifton, a narrow entrance reveals a shop selling hand-painted garments and, beyond that, the **Secret Garden Bar**, serving homemade rum punch, cold drinks and snacks. Step far-

Market, Union Island

ther into the labyrinth and you find a gallery of paintings and carvings. A little climb onward and you're on **Rocky Birdland** with a view over Clifton and the sea. The whole experience was concocted by Jutta and her Aussie partner, ☎ 784485-8177.

Two stores with food, drinks and selected delicatessen items that will please the yachties are **Captain Gourmet**, opposite the Clifton Beach Hotel, and the **Little Price Supermarket** at the end of the main jetty; they also stock a selection of wines and local books.

Two **Grand Union** supermarkets lie within a stone's throw of the main jetty; in addition, **Lambi's Supermarket** and the **S&V Grocery** are within a minute's walk. They should have everything you need. Tucked away on Back Street is **Foyle's Supermarket** and opposite is **TJ Plaza**, ☎ 485-819-8930, with sneakers and post cards on display amidst the other produce. The cheapest option for fresh fruit and vegetables is the open-air vendors' market in the center of town.

Looking like a brand-new pin on the main street is **Benji's Mini Mall**. It houses the **Grenadines Gift Shop** for souvenirs and T-shirts; **Cinder's Boutique** for clothes and shoes; and the **Classic Cuts Unisex Hair Salon**.

■ Where to Eat

Restaurant Directory

ANCHORAGE YACHT CLUB, Clifton, ☎ 784-458-8221
CLIFTON BEACH HOTEL RESTAURANT & BAR, Clifton, ☎ 784-458-8235
LAMBI'S RESTAURANT & BAR, Clifton, ☎ 784-458-8549
RODERIGO'S PIZZERIA CAFÉ, Clifton, no telephone
WEST INDIES RESTAURANT, Bougainvillea, Clifton, ☎ 784-458-8311

ANCHORAGE YACHT CLUB
Clifton

☎ 784-458-8221
US$15-$25 MC, Visa
Fresh pastries are delivered most mornings and sandwiches are served until noon when lunch begins. Onion, callaloo, and pumpkin soups, fish, conch, lobster, shrimp and chicken dishes can be had. Dinner is more sumptuous, with large portions for all courses. Leftovers were fed to the nurse sharks, while diners quaked. Their waitstaff makes every meal a pleasure.

CLIFTON BEACH HOTEL RESTAURANT & BAR

Clifton

☎ 784-458-8235

US$15-$25 MC, Visa

Daily 7:30 am-10 pm

The full range of seafood, meats, vegetarian dishes, lunch, snacks and breakfast are served during regular hours. As with most other hotel restaurants, service is confined to regular eating hours, but you can get a little something in-between. Portions are hearty at dinner and dessert is worth saving room for. A barbecue on Saturday night precedes live entertainment. Thankfully, the restaurant doesn't get as crowded as Lambi's next door.

LAMBI'S RESTAURANT & BAR

Clifton

☎ 784-458-8549

US$15-$25 MC, Visa

Popular with sailors, Lambi's is really a large jetty with an enormous dining space and bar. Low-key during the day, the evening buffet is when it springs into life. A host of dishes is provided, including fish, chicken, conch, shark, rice and peas, potatoes, beans and salads. Desserts of cake, mango, ice cream, bananas, watermelon and papaya fill any holes you might have left. Tea and coffee round out the eating frenzy; we opted for a brandy at the bar instead. A five-piece steel pan band play every night. During the high season, Lambi's becomes very crowded with extra entertainment in the shape of exotic dancers and limbo dancing.

RODERIGO'S PIZZERIA CAFE

Clifton

Under US$15

Daily 10 am until late; Sunday, opening in the afternoon (whenever Roderigo gets there!). A brightly painted small building near the airport looks as though it's a locals-only spot. Not so. Roderigo serves excellent pizzas, rotis, vegetarian plates and cold drinks. He is one of the most pleasant Rastas you'll meet.

WEST INDIES RESTAURANT

Bougainvillea, Clifton

☎ 784-458-8311

US$26-$35 MC, Visa

Dishes here are a marriage of Caribbean and traditional French cooking. Continental or cooked breakfast starts the day, lunch is a light affair of salads, omelettes, sandwiches or burgers. Dinner is more elaborate, with the emphasis on seafood. The red snapper was delicious, as was chicken in coconut milk sauce. A charming French couple run the restaurant and bar and have trained and attentive staff.

■ Where to Stay

Accommodations Directory

ANCHORAGE YACHT CLUB, Clifton, ☎ 784-458-8221, fax 784-458-8365
BIGSAND HOTEL, Richmond Bay, ☎ 784-458-8447, fax 784-458-8448
BOUGAINVILLA, Clifton, ☎ 784-458-8878, fax 784-458-8569
CLIFTON BEACH HOTEL, Clifton, ☎ 784-458-8235, fax 784-485-8313
LAMBI'S GUEST HOUSE, Clifton, ☎ 784-458-8549

MARINE VIEW HOTEL & APARTMENTS, Ashton, ☎ 784-458-8400, fax 784-458-8449
ST. JOSEPH'S APARTMENTS, Clifton, ☎ 784-458-8405
SYDNEY'S GUEST HOUSE, Clifton, ☎ 784-458-8320

ANCHORAGE YACHT CLUB HOTEL

Clifton
☎ 784-458-8221, fax 784-458-8365
www.ayc-hotel-grenadines.com
ofc@wyc-hotel-grenadines.com
US$100-$200 MC, Visa

There are 16 rooms of three types. Six rooms above the restaurant and bar are air-conditioned with sizeable bathrooms and balconies overlooking the harbor. Five suites with similar facilities on ground level stretch along the side of the main building. Five tidy and neat bungalows are a little farther away on their own strand of white sand beach and cut off from the happenings of the restaurant and bar, and for that matter, the rest of Clifton. For this reason, the bungalows are priced a bit higher than the rooms.

Tucked away at the northern end of Clifton Beach, this is in an idea place for land and sea adventures. The outdoor dining area is spacious; both daytime snacks and evening meals are of high standard. The staff members are jovial and on the ball. Excursions can be arranged to meet individual whims. A congenial hostess greets guests at the jetty throughout the day. The gift shop has the best selection of items on the island. While the airport is within a stone's throw, the frequent take-offs and landings of puddlejumpers were more entertaining than irritating.

BIGSAND HOTEL

Richmond Bay

☎ 784-485-8447, fax 784-485-8448

www.bigsandhotel.com, info@bigsandhotel.com

US$100-$300 Breakfast included. MC, Visa

Opened in 2002, this apartment hotel features 12 air-conditioned rooms with ceiling fans, fully equipped kitchenettes, and large comfortable sitting areas. Situated on an isolated beach, the management provides airport transport, free watersports equipment and use of mountain bikes. The beach is pristine and gives plenty of scope for snorkeling. Meal plan options are so reasonable you won't use the kitchenettes beyond keeping beverages cold. Bigsand provides an island getaway without emptying the purse.

BOUGAINVILLA

Clifton

☎ 784-458-8678, 458-8678, fax 784-458-8569

www.grenadines.net/union/windandsea.com,
bougainvilla@caribsurf.com

Under US$100 MC, Visa

Five air-conditioned rooms with shower, ceiling fan, TV, and fully equipped kitchenettes. This could be the best deal around if plans are for an extended holiday; weekly rates for a studio apartment in this harbor-side complex cost less than one night in most resorts. An annual rental adds up to only three weeks of their room rate making one wonder how often a room is actually available. For those inclined to rent on a yearly basis, this could be the last great deal in the Caribbean!

The other businesses in this attractive complex - the marine service shop, Erika's laundry and Internet office, and the West Indies Restaurant and bar are extremely professional and welcoming.

CLIFTON BEACH HOTEL

Clifton

☎/fax 784-458-8235, fax 784-458-8313

clifbeachhotel@caribsurf.com

Under US$100 MC, Visa

There are 26 rooms spread over four different sites. This began as a family home; the Adamses started taking in guests and are now in the third generation as innkeepers – hospitality is in their blood. The  main guest house is on the waterfront in the heart of Clifton including a restaurant and bar on the ground floor that literally hangs over the water. While there are several types of rooms available, the most comfortable are the larger ones upstairs with air-conditioning. Captain Yannis Tours departs from the hotel jetty. The Adamses also rent out a cottage at Big Sand beach across the island.

LAMBI'S GUEST HOUSE

Clifton

☎/fax 784-458-8549

Under US$100 MC, Visa

Fourteen rooms with the barest essentials: twin beds, shower and fan at rock-bottom price. For sailors making landfall, a freshwater shower and space larger than a bunk is an entertaining thought. The rooms are located above Lambi's restaurant, bar and supermarket.

MARINE VIEW HOTEL & APARTMENTS
Ashton

☎ 784-458-8400, fax 784-458-8449

marineview@vincysurf.com

Under US$100 No credit cards

Eight fully furnished apartments with kitchens. Some are air-conditioned. This is an attractive modern block and slightly out-of-the-way, but accessible by dollar bus.

ST. JOSEPH'S APARTMENTS
Clifton

☎ 784-458-8405

www.unionisland.com

frandrew@caribsurf.com

Under US$100 MC, Visa

One two-bedroom cottage and two one-bedroom apartments with shared kitchen. Located just outside Clifton, they are managed by the Roman Catholic Church.

SUNNY GRENADINES BEACH HOTEL
Clifton

☎ 784-458-8327, fax 784-458-8398

sungrenhotel@vincysurf.com

Under US$100 MC, Visa, Discover

There are 14 rooms, some with air-conditioning. All have showers, TV and refrigerators. The lackluster staff somewhat grudgingly showed us a room; their attitude would not tempt us to stay. The beach location next to the Grenadines Dive shop is a major plus. The place is up for sale so the future may prove brighter.

SYDNEY'S GUEST HOUSE
Clifton

☎ 784-458-8320

Under US$100 No credit cards

Three rooms with floor fans, two sharing a bathroom, and all sharing a fully equipped kitchen. The balcony lends a view across the airport runway and the beach beyond. Could be fun for a handful of divers; no flights after the sun sets.

■ After Dark

Clifton's waterfront is the center of its nightlife. The **Anchorage Yacht Club's restaurant** has live music during dinner hours, which can get lively as the night progresses. Beside the restaurant is a pool containing a

The Anchorage

dozen nurse sharks, quite a sobering presence.

The **West Indies Restaurant** at Bougainvilla should definitely be checked out for entertainment during high season. **Clifton Beach Hotel** has live music on Saturday night following their delicious barbecue dinner. Next door at **Lambi's Restaurant and Bar**; you can hear a steel band every night no matter what the season. Here also, you can find one or two local sharks carousing at the bar.

For a truly local experience, head out on to the street to any one of Clifton's rum shops. **Roderigo's Pizza** has reggae music as the main soundtrack, and even the bar at the airport con-tains a collage of

Leaving Union Island

local personalities long on stories and loud with laughter.

Union Island

Palm Island

■ Orientation

Palm Island has a single resort on it, but day-trippers can visit certain parts of the island. The modern story of Palm Island began when John Caldwell leased the mosquito-infested swampland formerly known as Prune Island from the government. The 135-acre plot with four low hills at the perimeter was surrounded by white sand beaches and circled by coral reefs. It had been used as a leper colony way back in time, and then planted with cotton like so many of its neighbors. The government bought the island in 1910 and proposed building salt ponds after World War II. The 1960s saw the entry of individuals converting islands to resorts: Mustique, Young Island and Petit St. Vincent. So when John Caldwell approached the government in 1966 with the notion of starting a hotel and providing employment, a deal was struck. He was given a 99-year lease for US$99. Thus ended Prune Island and John Caldwell; so began Palm Island and "Johnny Coconut."

The task of filling in the swampy areas, ridding the land of crabs and mosquitos, and laying out an airstrip to fly in materials was completed in 18 months. The Palm Island Beach Club was opened by a man of more vision than money. He planted coconut trees here, there and everywhere, up and down the island chain, earning the nickname Johnny Coconut. To finance the resort, he and his wife subdivided a portion of the island into lots. Seventeen private homes now sit alongside the resort.

Johnny Coconut is no longer with us, yet his legacy now lies in the hands of an expert management company. Improvements are being made, honing to a fine pitch what previously passed for perfection. Irrigation through desalinization will green up the island's interior. This policy is not expansionist for the sake of profit. The goal is continuing refinement of a little piece of paradise.

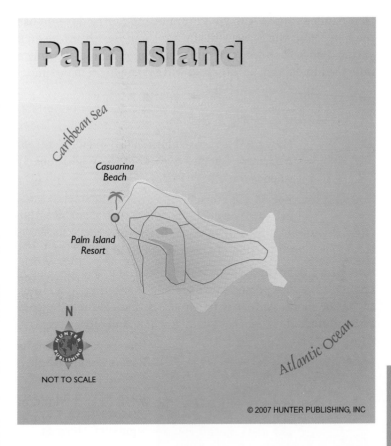

Palm Island

Caribbean Sea

Casuarina Beach

Palm Island Resort

N

NOT TO SCALE

Atlantic Ocean

© 2007 HUNTER PUBLISHING, INC

■ Getting Here

Palm Island's airstrip has now gone. Guests usually arrive via Union Island's airport and are brought by boat. As with the other smaller islands, you begin by choosing an international gateway into the Caribbean: Grenada, Barbados or San Juan, and then transferring to a puddlejumper that lands at St. Vincent, Canouan or Union Island.

Non-resident guests can visit Palm Island for the day and use the beach and the Sunset Restaurant and Bar. If you're on a yacht, then just show up. If you're on Union Island, it's only a mile to Palm Island; a water taxi will get you there in no time.

■ Exploring

How hard is it to explore the island's 130 acres? Not hard if you're a guest of the resort, nearly impossible otherwise.

For day-visitors, limits are established as soon as you set foot on the jetty. Signs reading "Resort Guests Only" will veer you in the direction where you can enjoy a good portion of **Casuarina Beach**.

The white sand and clear water make you feel privileged enough to be here. After a swim, some snorkeling, and lounging in the shade, you can call in at the **Sunset Beach Restaurant**. Lunch and some cold drinks will round off the trip.

Guests of Palm Island Resort have a playground laid out before them. Five white sand beaches with kayaks, windsurf boards or Sunfish sailboats for activity are available when you need something to do. Head for the windward side for solitude; hammocks are positioned along this stretch. You won't be quite alone, as a number of large **iguanas** live here. They are quick to scurry off into the undergrowth when approached. These reptiles are facing hard times due to man's interest in them as a food source and an aphrodisiac. The ocean current is strong on the windward side, but the beach is a great place to search for shells. Nature trails are signposted, leading to the top of Palm's small hills. As well as the view, you can check out the Tobago Cays to the north; if it looks too busy for you, then go another day.

You can play tennis, lounge by a freshwater pool or try the nine-hole golf course. The course is in its infancy, but irrigation will green it up a few years down the road. Mountain bikes are available for more vigorous exercise. Should the weather play havoc with outdoor activities, you can always visit the fitness center to burn off energy or play some table tennis.

Scuba diving, snorkeling, sailing and fishing can be coordinated by the resort with operators from Union Island. See page 178 for details. For those seeking day or night activities off-island, simply make your wishes known.

DIVEART DOC

We admit to loving the artwork coming out of this region.

On Union Island, we kept running into what were apparently photographs of underwater scenes. A grouper's brilliant orange face stared at us as if waiting to suck us in. It did. We were impressed and made inquiries. We were told it was a poster and thought little more about it.

Within days we were in reception at the Palm Island Resort and two more of these large posters caught our attention. Sea turtles swimming with a backdrop of coral and parrotfish and angel fish larger than life made us feel as though we were in an aquarium with the fish looking in on us. The manager explained they were paintings produced on Palm Island.

We were taken unexpectedly to the studio and home of Patrick Chevailler. Virginia, his wife, unrolled the giclées. These are top quality prints on canvas with all the color and intensity of an original. Signed and numbered by the artist, they are produced in limited editions of 75. Another hole was punched in the credit card.

Patrick's father was a painter in Bordeaux, France. Instead of following in his footsteps, Patrick studied medicine, becoming a general practitioner, which took him to Guadeloupe in the 1970s. When he did pick up a paintbrush, it was to imitate images from the age of sail. This he did well until a friend commissioned him to do an eight-by-four-foot underwater scene. By this time, he and his family had settled on Palm Island.

Forced by the scale of the work to paint outdoors, he drew enthusiasm from passing guests and requests for smaller works.

His life turned from being a medical doctor with a painting hobby, to being an artist available for medical emergencies. This new profession feeds another passion – diving. For his work to convey such detail and realism, he has had to advance his skills as an underwater photographer and researcher. His canvas is large, although his work is minute in its attention to detail. He estimates each oil painting takes between 20 and 80 hours of work. We watched him on a work-in-progress. He growled as the oil slid from the hairs of his brush, his head shaking in disagreement with what he had chosen from the palette.

As we walked back to the jetty, I was afraid to turn around in case the house with the wrap-around verandah had disappeared. The next morning we passed the orange grouper again and I could swear it was laughing.

■ Shopping

Like other one-resort islands, shopping is limited, but interesting.

The **Palm Island Boutique** has swimwear, cotton shirts, dresses and some warmer apparel meant for colder climates. CDs of local artists such as Bequia's New Direction are on sale, along with books on the flora and fauna. You may want to check out the island's library; other than Laluna on Grenada, this is the best book exchange we've come across.

Sunscreens and lotions, aloe vera and all those little things you forgot to pack are here at your fingertips. Postcards and prints, knickknacks and trinkets wait for the souvenir-seeker with credit card in hand.

DIVEART isn't really a shop, but a studio. Check with reception about work of the resident artist, Patrick Chevailler. Original oil paintings start at US$400, giclées – top quality prints on canvas – are US$200, and posters begin at US$40. For more information, visit www.artandsea.com.

■ Where to Eat

SUNSET RESTAURANT
Under US$15 MC, Visa
Daily from 10 am-10 pm
This is the beach bar and restaurant of the Palm Island Resort. Chowder, sandwiches, hot dogs and burgers for lunch; chicken, steak or lobster for dinner. We thought the prices for both lunch and dinner a bargain. This is perfect for those who are just visiting on a day-trip.

ROYAL PALM RESTAURANT

☎ 784-458-8824

All-inclusive

The restaurant complements the feeling of relaxed exclusivity you get from the resort. For those without fame and wealth, and that's the majority of us, a meal here can give a glimpse of life in the platinum lane. The menu changes daily, but you can be assured of quality from the selection. If you've never been a fan of cold soups, the cream of cucumber should make a convert of you. Local specialities and international dishes are served in harmonious combination. Casual elegance is the standard. For visitors, correct attire is required in the restaurant at all times, and reservations are necessary.

■ Where to Stay

PALM ISLAND RESORT

☎ 784-458-8824, 800-858-4618
fax 784-458-8804, 954-481-1661

www.palmislandresorts.com, res@eliteislandresort.com

US$300-$500+ All-inclusive. MC, Visa

This is an easy one. This private island is a single resort, a perfect hideaway for those wanting peace and tranquility, but with all the creature comforts.

With 37 air-conditioned rooms and suites, a maximum of 80 guests are allowed on the island. No children under the age of sixteen. Rooms are spacious and luxurious. Interior design is refreshingly West Indian, from cathedral ceilings to terra cotta tile floors. Beds are king-size and inviting, furnishings are mostly rattan with comfortable cushions. Fresh exotic flowers add an extra touch to the tropical artwork hung on the stone walls.

The 75 staff members are friendly and acknowledge each guest by name. The atmosphere is pleasantly informal with a home-away-from-home feel, contributing to the large return rate.

Palm Island is one of the few resorts in these islands to include all gratuity, taxes, and service charges into the room fee; there are no outlandish surprises on departure.

■ After Dark

On Palm Island you don't have to worry about bright lights, cars speeding past, planes coming in to land or just about anything except the nightly chorus of tree frogs and insects. The sound of the sea on the shore will wash away your stress, sending you to slumber. Here you are assured of a good night's sleep.

The two bars stay open until the last drinker leaves. A few yachties may be over in the **Sunset Beach Bar** sharing stories and there's always room for one more. On Wednesday evening guests are invited to the **Manager's Punch Party**. This is the perfect opportunity to meet the other guests on the island; you won't be thought of as antisocial if you don't attend.

Every week the resort holds a beach barbecue with a live calypso band. A jump up follows for those in the mood to dance. Should island fever steal up on you, Union Island is only a mile away.

Palm Island

Petit St. Vincent

■ Orientation

Petit St. Vincent Resort, the only place to stay on the island, was one of the first to open in the Caribbean and is ranked highly as a classic. When Jamaica was still virgin territory to all-inclusives, Hiltons, and Ritz-Carltons, Petit St. Vincent Resort was opening its doors to those who desired remoteness, with the benefit of turquoise waters, coral reefs and white sand beaches. What better place to escape corporate life or begin a new life in wedded bliss?

Going ashore, it feels as though you've arrived at someone's home. You're likely to be met by one of the five yellow Labs in residence. Polite "Guests Only" signs give quiet direction to day-visitors, steering them to the restaurant and main buildings and away from the cottages and other private amenities.

Petit St. Vincent, or PSV as it is locally known, is only 113 acres in size and the most southerly of St. Vincent's Grenadines, being 40 miles from the mainland. It's only  half a mile from Petite Martinique, the northernmost of Grenada's Grenadines. Finding any history of this little place is difficult. Information is gleaned from a sea of documents on other islands, mixed with an equal amount of hearsay.

It is known that the French inhabited the island in the 1700s, many traveling to Petite Martinique to socialize and to attend church. At some point in the 1800s, the entire island was given to the Catholic Church. A Father Aquart raised livestock on Petit St. Vincent for 20 years until drought finished off the animals in 1913. The church then leased the land to Arthur Ollivierre, a cotton planter from Petite Martinique, with the firm understanding that the cedar trees would remain untouched and the undesirable mangrove and manchineels were to be cleared away. Boat building was in its prime and the cedar trees would have come in very handy. The Ollivierre family were whalers, fishermen and shipwrights. Father Aquart had obvious foresight regarding conservation, perhaps from witnessing logging on surrounding islands. Nonetheless, the land lease went through and Petit St. Vincent was finally sold to Ollivierre's widow in 1926.

Lilie Bethel, Arthur Ollivierre's daughter, inherited Petit St. Vincent and kept it in the family for the next 40 years. Then a pair of likeable sailors arrived on a beautiful, mahogany-lined, 77-foot schooner. They had sailed their way from New York to Bermuda, and on to Grenada with the intention of selling charters on their impressive sailboat. As fortune would have it, their first charter was to an American, H.W. Nichols, who was intent on buying a deserted Caribbean island.

Nichols sent out the two sailors, Haze Richardson and Doug Terman, as scouts. After anchoring off Petit St. Vincent, they found Mrs. Bethel on Petite Martinique. At first she wasn't interested in selling her island. But their persistence and charm went a long way and she finally agreed to sell the island for US$33,000. In 1966, Nichols, Terman and Richardson laid plans to build a small, exclusive hotel.

As opening day drew closer, Nichols persuaded Richardson to stay on as temporary manager. He consented and today he and his wife, Lynn, are not only the managing force, but the owners of Petit St. Vincent. Even so, we're sure the five Labradors have quite a lot to say about the way things are handled.

■ Getting Here

 It isn't as hard as it might appear to get to this secluded island. Working backwards makes it simpler. You have to get here by water.

A water taxi from Petite Martinique takes five minutes, the *Osprey Express* ferry links Petite Martinique with Carriacou and Grenada. Grenada is an international airline gateway into this region.

A water taxi, or Petit St. Vincent's own 42-foot motor launch, can bring you over from Union Island in about 25 minutes. Union Island's airport is served by inter-island carriers that link with international flights from Grenada, Barbados, San Juan via Canouan Island, St. Lucia and Martinique.

■ Exploring

Day-visitors are limited to the beautiful white sand beach, the restaurant, bar and boutique. But this can use up all the cash you may have with you.

Guests can use the unique fit-ness trail devised by the management to meet a beginner's needs as well as those of an athlete. There are 20 stations within the self-guided trail, where you exercise the three essentials: stretching, muscle toning and cardiovascular conditioning.

Amblers and ramblers can easily walk the two-mile perimeter of Petit St. Vincent in about one hour.

Two off-island gems are **Mopion** and **Punaise** – small sand-bars surrounded by reefs. Mopion has a thatched umbrella for shade. Petit St. Vincent can provide transport and a packed lunch to these excellent snorkeling locations.

Beach Trees

So you're on the beach scouting out the shade. Perhaps you want to hang your pack on a limb. There are three trees you should be acquainted with before spreading out that beach towel.

We'll start with the friendly trees – the almond and the seagrape.

The **almond** is a large, bushy tree that tolerates sand and sea spray. This makes them ideal shady spots along the seaside. Being fast growers, they are often planted where other trees

have been lost by storm, waves or erosion. Their dark green leaves are eight inches long and turn red before dropping. The almond produces both an edible fruit and nut. The nuts are encased in a hard outer shell. It's fun to watch children beating the shell with a rock to tease out the tasty nut.

The **seagrape tree** grows on windward and leeward coasts. On the windward side, they take on a windblown shape, leaning into a cliffside or twisted into scraggly sculptures. On the leeward side, they grow straight and grand as the almond trees. Bunches of grapes turn from green to purple as they ripen. Although edible, they are extremely sour. To differentiate the seagrape from the almond when not in fruit, examine the leaves. The seagrape leaf is large, stiff and round, six to eight inches wide. Children use the leaf as a plate, or cup it to use as a shovel when playing in the sand.

The bad boy on the block is the **manchineel tree**. Busy beaches where it grows generally have signs alerting visitors. Its sap is so toxic the Caribs used it on their arrows as poison. Cars parked underneath a manchineel tree have had paint stripped as a consequence. The irritation it causes to human skin is severe and could mean an unexpected visit to the hospital. In case you come into contact with the milky sap or are scratched by one of its branches, head into the surf and scrub the area with seawater before applying aloe vera. Blistering can also result as a consequence of sitting on some of the freshly fallen leaves.

You can recognize the manchineel by its greyish bark and droopy leaves. They are two to four inches long, green in color, and elliptical in shape. They have a fold along the middle and there is a pin-sized raised dot at the junction with the stalk; this is the nasty gland. Manchineel is the only tree in these islands to have this gland. It also produces a beautiful shiny green apple, fatal if eaten. Remember Snow White? Hands off.

All these trees can reach a height of 30 to 40 feet on the leeward coasts. If in doubt, ask for advice before setting out your blanket on the beach.

■ Adventures

For scuba and snorkeling adventures, see page 248 for details on Union Island operators who cover the sites here as well. Sailing and deep sea fishing can be arranged. Other watersports equipment is available. A tennis court supplies land-based exertion, in addition to the exercise trail described above.

The best hours to photograph are before noon and late afternoon. The mid-day sun will rob you of the rich Caribbean colors.

■ Shopping

It was nice to visit the boutique at the resort, as it clearly hadn't been targeted by the same souvenir sellers as every other hotel shop in the region. Their buyer is obviously quite discerning. Had we been shopping seriously, we could have wiped out half of our Christmas list. Books, postcards, lotions and T-shirts are what you'd expect. There was also a pleasing selection of clothes for him and her at less than exorbitant prices. Well-chosen arts and crafts from around the islands made browsing a pleasure, rather than giving the feeling we'd seen it all before. We rate this as one of the top three boutiques in St. Vincent & the Grenadines.

■ Where to Eat

As a guest at the resort, prepare for some tantalizing culinary experiences. Meals can be brought to your cottage, to your stronghold on the beach, or you can join other guests in the restaurant. The menu changes daily, but starters could include stuffed avocado with shrimp, eggplant Martinique, or Caesar salad with grilled chicken. Entrées range from broiled barracuda with champagne buerre blanc, pecan-crusted trout with creamy lemon sauce, to grilled lamb chop with honey dijon mustard and mint sauce. Desert island desserts are crêpes Cointreau chocolate, coconut Bavarian cream, baba au rum, or fresh fruit.

Yachties moored by Petit St. Vincent or guests of Palm Island can make dinner reservations. The set price is EC$140 per person (US$54) plus taxes and gratuity. Saturday night brings a beach barbecue for resident-guests only, with a lively steel band. Lunch, of course, is lighter, with a buffet priced at EC$75 per person. Day-visitors must make reservations beforehand.

■ Where to Stay

PETIT ST. VINCENT RESORT

Petit St. Vincent
☎ 784-458-8801, 954-963-7401, 1-800-654-9326
fax 784-458-8428, 954-963-7402
www.psvresort.com, info@psvresort.com
Over US$500 All-inclusive except drinks & scuba; MC, Visa

There are 22 cottages with a maximum of 44 guests on the island at any one time. The staff-to-guest ratio is two-to-one. All cottages open towards the sea, the majority in elevated positions, although a couple sit right on the beach. The buildings on PSV are all local "bluebitch" stone with purpleheart woodwork. Each cottage has a sitting room, two queen-size beds, dressing room, bathroom, and patio. What they don't have is television, phones or keys. Room service is unique; outside each cottage is a bamboo flagpole. Raise the yellow flag and leave your written request in the mailbox for collection. Staff rings a bell to alert you of delivery. Raising the red flag means "leave me alone."

Now, where's that lottery ticket?

Grenada

N

Sugar Loaf
Green Island
Sandy Island

Levera Beach
Leaper's Hill
Sauteurs
Morne Fendue
Bathway Beach

Duquesne Bay

Mt. Rich Amerindian Remains

Mt. Rose

Lake Antoine

Mt. St. Catherine
2,757 ft/840 m

Victoria

Hermitage

Paraclete

Gouyave

Dunfermline

Dougaldston Estate

Grenville

Fedon's Camp

Concord

Mt. Qua Qua
2,372 ft/723 m

Marquis Falls

Concord Falls

St. Margaret

Grand Etang

Seven Sisters Falls

Flamingo Bay

Annandale Falls

Mt. Sinai
2,306 ft/703 m

Crochu

Grand Mal Bay

Perdmon-temps

St. David's

Crochu Harbour

St. Pauls

St. George's

Richmond Hill

La Sagesse Bay

Morne Rouge

Grand Anse

Westerhall Point

Caribbean Sea

Point Salines

True Blue Bay

Prickly Bay

Hog Island

Clark's Court Bay

Calivigny Island

Lance aux Epines

2 MILES
2 KM

© 2007 HUNTER PUBLISHING, INC

Grenada

Orientation

Grenada is universally referred to as the "Spice Island." Once you've walked through the interior, seen the Market Square or eaten at any of the delectable restaurants, you'll find this reputation rings true. Nutmeg reigns, cocoa follows like an heir to the throne, accompanied by an attendant medley of spices and herbs – clove, cinnamon, allspice, bay leaf, and ginger. The scents and flavors are a culinary tease.

You'll recognize some from sprinklings upon savory dishes and desserts, but perhaps you've never seen the trees, the bushes or the roots that are their source. On one small island you can trace a speck of aromatic dust from its origin to its gathering, sorting, processing and exporting.

Yet Grenada is actually comprised of three islands – Grenada, Carriacou and Petite Martinique – and some 20 smaller cays and islets. And if the land isn't enough to heighten the senses, just look out from the coastline into crystal clear, turquoise waters to see them shimmering and sparkling like diamonds in the sunlight. Are you sure there are no mermaids singing in these waters? Study Canute Calliste's paintings of his native Carriacou, and you might be persuaded. Take the plunge off Petite Martinique with mask and snorkel, find fish dancing through the coral gardens and you'll be convinced it is all here for your own personal enjoyment.

Grenada dove

The character of a nation can be gauged by its people. It's the smile that first catches your attention. Then, as eyes make contact, it's in their glistening, as if behind them there lies a secret. A secret they want to share. A secret called Grenada. Can you hear its voice?

Bird song, conch call, booming bass from a passing bus. Let the symphony begin and the story unfold. Grenada has beckoned you to discover with all of your senses, with all of your desire for adventure.

When to Go

December through April is the high season for tourism, when you can expect little rain and temperatures in the mid-80s. From June to November is the rainy season, with temperatures similar to the high season, but more humid. This is also the hurricane season, with September as the highest-risk month.

Getting Here

■ By Air

Air Jamaica has direct flights from New York's JFK on Tuesday, Wednesday, Friday and Saturday; departure flights to JFK are the same days.

Air Canada flies direct on Sunday from Toronto, returning the same day.

If not flying direct, it is best to choose a hub airport like San Juan, Barbados or Trinidad; all have daily flights to and from Grenada.

American Eagle flies from San Juan, Puerto Rico daily, with an early morning departure from Grenada to San Juan.

LIAT and **Caribbean Star** fly round-trip daily from Barbados, St. Vincent and Trinidad.

Grenada

Airlines Serving Grenada	
Air Jamaica	☎ 800-523-5585; www.airjamaica.com
Air Canada	☎ 866-529-2079, www.aircanadavacations.com
American Eagle	Reservations, ☎ 473-444-2222 Flight information, ☎ 473-444-5151 Port Salines Airport, ☎ 473-444-2121, www.aa.com
Caribbean Star	☎ 800-744-7827 within Caribbean ☎ 866-864-6272 US and Canada
LIAT	☎ 473-440-5428, 473-440-2796, 473-440-2797 airport office, ☎ 473-444-4121, www.liatairline.com

> *So many suitcases and bags look alike; colored duct tape or ribbon makes them easier to identify.*

■ By Sea

Cruise Ships

 The new cruise terminal at Melville Street has increased the number of cruise ships visiting the island. Previously St. George's deep harbor allowed ships to dock beside The Carenage, and some still do. Taxis wait at both places ready to whisk passengers to beaches, plantation houses and gardens. If traveling by boat is your preference, you can choose from the largest tall ships, prestigious liners, historic schooners or comfortable sailboats. Whatever you decide, the experience will be saturated with sunshine, pristine water and tropical scenery.

CUNARD – US & CANADA

24303 Town Center Drive, Suite 200

Valencia, California 91355

☎ 1-800-7-CUNARD

www.cunard.com

CUNARD - UK

Mountbatten House

Grosvenor Square

Southampton S015 2BF

☎ 845 071 0300, fax 023 8022 5843

www.cunard.co.uk

Queen Mary 2 drops in on St. George's, Grenada as part of Cunard's Caribbean Adventure and Caribbean Celebration programs.

View of cruise ship from Fort George

PRINCESS CRUISES

24844 Avenue Rockefeller
Santa Clarita, CA 91355
☎ 1–800-PRINCESS

www.princess.com

Vessels from the Princess Cruises fleet make stops in Grenada as part of their seven-day and fourteen-day itineraries. Ports of departure are Fort Lauderdale and San Juan, Puerto Rico.

WINDJAMMER BAREFOOT CRUISES

PO Box 190120
Miami, Florida 33119
☎ 1-800-327-2601,
305-672-6453, fax
305-674-1219

www.windjammer.com

Starting and finishing in Grenada, two ships operate extensive cruises visiting St. Vin-

SV Mandalay

cent & the Grenadines: **SV *Mandalay*** sails a two-week cruise, and **SV *Yankee Clipper*** completes a one-week passage, both from October through May. For family reunions or groups, you can charter the entire SV *Yankee Clipper*.

EASYCRUISE

The Rotunda
42/43 Gloucester Crescent
London NW1 7DL, England
☎ 44-1895-651191

www.easycruise.com

Like their European counterpart, easyJet, an airline offering cheap oneway flights across that continent, easyCruise have hop-on/hop-off cruise deals visiting Grenada regularly through the winter season. A two-night minimum booking is the only stipulation. This affordable, no-frills type of cruising is aimed at the young and those with flexible vacation plans.

FRED OLSEN LINE

White Horse Road, Suffolk, IP1 5LL, England
☎ 44-1473-292200, fax 44-1473-292201
http://www.fredolsen.co.uk

Visits Grenada during the winter season on the *Balmoral*, *Braemar* or the *Boudicca*, or cruise on the *Star Flyer*, *Star Clipper* or *Royal Clipper* on various itineraries.

CLUB MED CRUISES

75 Valencia Avenue
Coral Gables, FL 33134
☎ 1-888-932-2582
www.clubmed.com

Club Med fields some impressive state-of-the-art ships with five 164-foot masts and computer-monitored sails. They call on Grenada and St. Vincent & the Grenadines from November through April.

SEA CLOUD CRUISES, INC.

32-40 North Dean Street
Englewood, NJ 07631
☎ 1-888-732-2568
www.seacloud.com

The legendary tall ship *Sea Cloud* and her sister *Sea Cloud II* make seven-day voyages, calling in on Grenada and Bequia, during the height of the winter season.

SEA DREAM YACHT CLUB

2601 South Bayshore Drive, PH 1B
Miami, Florida 33133
☎ 800-707-4911, 305-631-6100, fax 305-631-6110
☎ UK 0800 783 1373
www.seadreamyachtclub.com

Sea Dream and *Sea Dream II* visit Union Island and Bequia as part of their itineraries.

SILVERSEA CRUISES

110 East Broward Blvd
Fort Lauderdale, FL 33301
☎ 877-760-9052, fax
954-522-4499

www.silversea.com

Silver Shadow and *Silver Wind* include Grenada and Bequia in their Caribbean program.

P&O CRUISES HEAD OFFICE
Richmond House
Terminus Terrace
Southampton SO14 3PN, England
☎ 0845 678 0014 United Kingdom
www.pocruises.com

Another notable cruise line pays court to this part of the world with representatives from its fleet such as *Arcadia* and *Oceana*.

DID YOU KNOW?

A vessel not registered in the United States does not have to comply with US Coast Guard regulations, regardless of the nationality of owner or passengers.

Practicalities

■ Customs & Duties

You can carry 200 cigarettes and one liter of spirits into Grenada.

Returning to the USA, you can bring back US$600 worth of goods; one liter of spirits, 200 cigarettes and 200 cigars.

Returning to Canada, you can bring in C$300 worth of goods; 200 cigarettes, 50 cigars, 200 grams of tobacco and 40 imperial ounces of alcohol.

A WORD TO
THE WISE

Set aside your departure tax in your passport from day one, and you won't be scrambling for money at the airport. Expect to pay EC$50 (US$20) per person as you exit the country.

■ Embassy

The US Embassy is located in Lance aux Epines and can be reached at ☎ 473-444-1173. The British High Commission is at Box 132, Granby Street (opposite the Old Library), Kingstown SV, ☎ 784-457-1701, fax 784-456-2750.

■ Tipping

Always check your bills to see if the 8% government tax and 10% service charge have been added. In a restaurant, for example, this might mean your waiter or waitress will get all or only a share of the tip. If you wish to show your further appreciation for good service, feel free to do so. Any local guide giving you a tour of gardens, forts, nutmeg processing stations and the like, will also appreciate a tip. This goes for taxi drivers and anyone who has taken you on an extended tour. Remember how you treat others will influence them in how they treat the next traveler.

■ Medical Services

Grenada is well served with medical facilities. **St. George's Hospital**, ☎ 473-440-2051, is on the point below Fort George. The **Princess Alice Hospital** is in Grenville, ☎ 473-442-7251, 7252. Close to Fort Frederick is the **St. Augustine's Private Hospital**,

☎ 473-440-6173, with 18 beds and an outpatient unit. The Grand Anse Shopping Centre also has a 24-hour emergency service in the **Black Rock Medical Clinic**, ☎ 473-444-4855. Carriacou and Petite Martinique are served by the **Princess Royal Hospital**, ☎ 473-443-7400.

■ Communications

Internet

Internet cafes across Grenada sell on-line time in blocks of 15 or 30 minutes. Costs vary from place to place, with the terminals at the Post Office working out most economical. Java Kool in The Carenage is one of the more established places, a few doors along from The Carenage Café, the original cyber café of St. George's. Opening hours can be hit and miss; try during normal business hours to avoid disappointment.

Hotels have caught on to the demand for electronic communication by installing Internet rooms and selling screen time. Some of the larger hotels provide access if you have your laptop with you. On-line time will be added to your final room bill. Log on by dialing ☎ 908-4843-638.

The market will be expanding no doubt. By the time you've finished reading this sentence, a new Internet facility has probably just opened.

Telephone

 To call the USA, Canada or other Caribbean countries, ☎ 1 + area code + number.

To call the UK, ☎ 011 + 44 + area code + number.

For all other countries, ☎ 011 + country code + area code + number.

To reach the operator, ☎ 0; for directory inquiries, ☎ 411.

For a collect call to the USA, ☎ 1-800-225-5872.

Credit card calling is available on all phones; ☎ 111 for instructions in English. Prepaid phone cards are sold at many outlets in denominations of EC$20, $30, $50 and $75.

Cell phones that function on a TDMA digital network can be used in Grenada. Calls are charged to your American Express or MasterCard.

For local calls within Grenada, Carriacou and Petite Martinique omit the area code 473. We have included it throughout for your convenience while making reservations from outside Grenada.

Postal Services

✉ The main post office in St. George's is by the cruise ship terminal, behind the Board of Tourism offices and Customs and Immigration. Apart from postal services and the Internet facility, they sell postcards, stationery, scotch tape and duct tape. All the parishes have a post office. Opening hours are 8 am-4 pm, Monday to Friday. Stamps for postcards cost EC$1.

■ Banks

Banking hours are 8 am-3 pm, Monday to Thursday, and 8 am-5 pm on Friday. **National Commercial Bank (NCB)**, **Barclays Bank** and **Scotia Bank** all have branches on Grenada. Hillsborough in Carriacou has NCB and Barclays.

■ Electricity

Voltage is 220 volts. Sockets are the British type, with three square pins.

US standard 110 volt appliances work with a transformer.

Make sure you have an adapter for any equipment before you leave home. It's difficult to buy adapters in the islands, although some of the larger hotels have them already installed for your convenience. But don't count on one being available; carry what you need.

Getting Married

It is possible to get married in Grenada, with a bit of red tape thrown in among the rice, confetti and wedding cake. Hotels that specialize in wedding packages often do the legal work for you, but you should be aware of requirements and documents needed.

First, you must be resident on Grenada for at least three working days (excluding weekends and public holidays) before you can apply for a marriage license. It should take another two days until you receive it, a bit longer if either of you is divorced. You must have in your possession: valid passports, birth certificates, Decree Absolute if one or both parties are divorced, or legal proof of single status in the form of a letter saying that you haven't been married before, a death certificate if either party has been widowed, Deed Poll proof if there has been a change of name, written consent from a parent if either party is under 21, and all papers must be in English.

If all of the above apply to you, you certainly have led an interesting life.

In addition to the legal paperwork, the typical wedding package supplies the honeymoon suite, cake, a bottle of champagne, finger food or hors d'oeuvres, a photographer (who'll provide you with the prints and negatives or digital equivalent), bride's bouquet, buttonhole and a decorated setting for the service itself.

Contact the **Grenada Board of Tourism** for further information. ☎ 473-440-2279, gbt@caribsurf.com.

Holidays & Festivals

 Wondering about the right time to visit Grenada? There are public holidays, celebrations and special events throughout the year.

Where contact information is not given below, details can be obtained from the **Grenada Board of Tourism** at ☎ 473-440-2279, fax 473-440-6637, www.grenadagrenadines.com or by e-mail at gbt@caribsurf.com.

January

New Year's Day – January 1.

Grenada International Triathlon, two days; ☎ 473-440-3343.

Grenada Sailing Festival, two days; Grenada Yacht Club, ☎ 473-440-3050.

Spice Island Billfish Tournament, three days; ☎ 473-440-3327.

February

Carriacou Carnival, two days; ☎ 473-443-7948.

Independence Day, February 7, Grenada, Carriacou and Petite Martinique.

True Blue Indigo Yacht Race; ☎ 473-440-3050.

March

St. Patrick's Day Fiesta, March 17, held in Sauteurs; ☎ 473-442-7109.

Carl Schuster Memorial Round Grenada Yacht Race; ☎ 473-440-2508.

April

Good Friday

Easter Monday

Easter Dinghy Races

Grenada Powerboat Regatta

Petite Martinique Regatta

Gouyave Regatta, two days.

Kite Flying Competition, in Carriacou and Belmont.

St. Mark's Day Festival, in Victoria.

May

Labor Day – May 1.

La Source Grand Anse Yacht Race; ☎ 473-440-3050.

Whit Monday

Spice Island Jazz Festival, weeklong music festival with international musicians in St. George's.

Corpus Christi Outfitter's International Cup South Coast Yacht Race; ☎ 473-440-2508 – May 30.

June

Fisherman's Birthday, Gouyave – June 29.

July

Carriacou Regatta, a week of racing and festivities; ☎ 473-443-7930.

August

CARICOM Day, the first Monday of the month, the entire Caribbean celebrates emancipation.

Rainbow City Festival, Grenville's annual shindig, is an informal street dance.

Grenada's Carnival, Spice Mas, is a week of parades, music and good cheer all round; ☎ 473-440-0621, www.spicemas.com.

October

Thanksgiving Day, recognition of intervention by the United States and allies in 1983 – October 25.

November

Island Fantasy, Grenada's Horticultural Society Flower Show.

Grand Anse Dinghy Races, Grenada Yacht Club; ☎ 473-440-3050.

December

End of Hurricane Season Regatta, Grenada Yacht Club; ☎ 473-440-3050.

Carriacou Parang Festival, a traditional Christmas celebration unique to the island of Carriacou. See page 420 under Carriacou for more information; ☎ 473-443-7948.

Christmas Day – December 25.

Boxing Day – December 26.

New Year's Eve, midnight marathon in Grenville, ☎ 473-442-6660 – December 31.

Carnival in Grenada

 Thanks to the mixture of French and African influences in the Caribbean, we have Carnival today. It has in its time been a moveable feast. Originally it was a festival before the start of Lent in which the upper classes, dressed in their finery, took the major part. It became mixed with the slaves' celebration of the end of the sugar harvest, called Canboulay. Today it is a week-long party and to witness it as an observer you catch a thrill of communal enjoyment, but to take part is to ride the wave of Mas joy.

Carnival has its different characters, the most gruesome of which must be the "Jab-Jab" or "Jab Molassi." Covered with molasses, grease, oil or tar, and with clothes and helmet made from junk, pots and pans, "Jab-Jab" is intended to look devilish. "Shortknee" is dressed in baggy pants and throws white powder at the crowd; it started as the custom for these characters to wear flour on their dark faces to imitate the white people of the day. "Shortknee" is represented by groups of people dressed identically. Another group is the "Wild Indians," again all costumed alike. Carriacou even has Shakespeare Mas where individuals dress appropriately and quote from the Bard of Avon. Much heckling is given to those who fluff their lines.

Calypso has always been the cutting edge of protest and demonstration within Carnival. Satirical songs still have some bite and it's not unusual for a calypsonian to have his song banned if it gets too close to the bone. "The Mighty Sparrow" is no doubt the most lauded Grenadian calypsonian. Slinger Francisco dominated the scene from the mid-1950s for 30 years, often being crowned Calypso King. More recently, Papa Jerry from Crochu has been the most controversial calypsonian. His song "Mo' Fire" was banned in 2001; the authorities feared it would incite arson. The crowd quickly dubbed him "The Fireman."

As with Carnival in other islands, there is a daily theme to the festivities, with prizes for the best band, best costume and best calypso song. Grenada comes alive in song and costume as Carnival takes to the streets in late July and early August.

Island History

■ Caribs' Leap

 The Caribs in Grenada first came into contact with European outsiders in 1609 when a group of British settlers arrived. Their ship delivered them to the ridge overlooking La Sagesse Bay, then continued on to Trinidad. When it returned months later, all but the hardiest had perished at the hands of the Caribs, who refused to give over a piece of their island. The survivors returned to London defeated. Grenada was left alone for another 30 years until the Governor of the French side of St. Kitts, de Poincy, and his men tried to settle, posing as fishermen. They were outnumbered by the Caribs and forced to flee.

In 1650, Jacques Dyel du Parquet purchased Martinique, St. Lucia, Grenada and the Grenadines from the bankrupt *Compagnie des Isles d'Amérique*. For some unknown reason he was accepted by the Caribs and actually welcomed to the island. He brought settlers, waived their taxes and gave them provisions for three months. Du Parquet shipped to Grenada what was perhaps its first pre-fab building for his own residence. Other commodities packed aboard were presents for the Caribs: Madeira wine, linens, iron tools and glass beads. Work began on building a fortified community.

Du Parquet arrived on June 20, 1650, and with 200 settlers Fort Annunciation was completed within a week. This was later known as Port St. Louis and stood by the Lagoon, below where the ruins of the Islander Hotel are today. The chief of all the Carib clans informed du Parquet that if they intended on settling, he would have to be rewarded. And so the trade was made. An island for "a number of axes, bill hooks, knives, glass beads, mirrors and other articles of haberdashery." And not forgetting his two quarts of brandy.

Du Parquet had no intention of being a permanent settler himself. He installed his cousin, le Comte, as governor and returned to Martinique. Eight months later, the natives grew restless. They began to single out and kill settlers found hunting in the woods far from the fort. We can only assume that they had become disenchanted with their deal or perhaps they had run out of brandy.

Reinforcements were called for on both sides. Du Parquet came back from Martinique with 300 troops. Carib warriors arrived from Dominica and St. Vincent. Eight hundred Caribs laid siege to Port St. Louis. As they approached in their ochre war paint, their arrows dipped in poisonous manchineel sap, they were met with cannon blasts and gunfire. Less than 200 Caribs survived the barrage and fled to the mountains, with the French in hot pursuit. When they reached the Carib village, they destroyed it and killed another 80 warriors. About 40 escaped and headed north, again with the French breathing down their necks.

 There was nowhere left to run. As a French priest, Père Labat, recorded at the time, "on the edge of a steep cliff washed by the sea, they threw themselves over it and perished to a man." They chose to leap rather than surrender. This was how *Le Morne des Sauteurs* – Leapers' Hill – got its name.

It was thought all the Caribs had been driven from Grenada, but there were still some hiding out in the interior. Skirmishes with the French continued on other islands and within two years a decree was issue by the Carib nations, "To arms! To every white man death!"

On Grenada, the Caribs carried out guerilla warfare against the French. Anyone straying too far from the fort was dead. Le Comte gathered 250 settlers for a final push; they killed and dismembered all natives regardless of age or gender. They hunted in the hills and scoured the seashore for canoes – no one would live to tell the tale. After this massacre, Governor le Comte, while trying to save a man at sea, fell overboard himself and drowned.

■ Slavery

We don't delve too deeply into this side of Caribbean history. First, you are on vacation, and the subject is far too depressing to be read on the beach or before retiring from a lovely day in the rainforest.

Secondly, this period is one that West Indians on the whole are just beginning to feel comfortable thinking and talking about. Until recently, this grueling past was avoided with a begrudging silence.

If you are interested in this aspect of man's inhumanity to man, we encourage you to seek out books such as Hugh Thomas' *The Slave Trade* (Macmillan, 1998), Robin Blackburn's *The Making Of New World Slavery* (Verso, 1998), James Walvin's *Britain's Slave Empire* (Tempus, 2000), or the intriguing tale from a 17th-century slaver's journal, *The Diligent* (Basic Books, 2002) by Robert Harris.

But Grenada would not be the island we know today without this hideous history. Many of the people that make Grenada the wonderful place it is are direct descendants of the unfortunates.

■ Fedon's Rebellion

Julien Fedon, mastermind and leader of the rebellion on Grenada from 1794 to 1796, was the son of a white French jeweler and a free black woman from Martinique. They settled in St. Mark's parish, where Julien was born. Nothing else is known of him until he married Marie Rose Cavelan, a free black woman in 1780.

Three things about him would have infuriated the British planter society of the time: he was a free colored, his ancestry was French , and his faith was Catholic. Later, he would have a fourth strike against him as he became one of the largest landowners on Grenada.

In 1787, Marie Rose's legal status was questioned by the authorities. It was customary to hold suspects for up to six weeks in prison until proof of their free status was supplied. One of the two justices of the peace who signed her release was Dr. John Hay, later spared as a hostage by Fedon during the rebellion.

Julien pledged allegiance to the English **King George III**, but followed the example of the French Revolution by granting freedom to many of the slaves from his 450-acre estate, Belvidere. Shortly afterwards, the English placed restrictions on the movement of non-whites irrespective of their wealth or class. Catholics were denied freedom of worship, confessions and burials were disallowed and their marriages annulled.

The possible spark that lit the fuse was that Julien Fedon had been charged an outrageous sum to purchase the Belvidere Estate from James Campbell. In today's market the price would be over US$1 million. To add insult to injury, Campbell illegally mortgaged the estate to an English firm that knew nothing of Fedon's purchase.

One of the main characters of the French Revolution now entered the picture. Victor Hugues, a henchman of Robespierre's reign of terror, was sent by the new French regime to recapture Martinique and Guadeloupe from the English. He brought his guillotine with him and long lines of English were led to decapitation on those islands. To Fedon he offered "ideological, diplomatic, and military assistance."

In the early hours of March 2nd 1795, Fedon, with a band of 150 free colored men and slaves attacked the village of Marquis. After looting, they moved towards Belvidere, stopping only to take hostage the British estate holders, managers, and overseers. While this was happening on the windward coast, a second rebellious party was in progress at Gouyave on the leeward side.

Lieutenant Governor Ninian Home, much despised by the suppressed French citizens, was with friends at his Paraclete Estate just north of Grenville. Hearing of the rebellion, they rode north to Sauteurs and boarded a sloop for St. George's. Halfway there, they were intercepted by Fedon's men at Gouyave and taken hostage. Fifty-one men were kept hidden in Fedon's camp on Mount Vauclain until they were executed a month later. Only Dr. Hay and two others were spared and transported to Guadeloupe.

Capture of Governor Home *(Eric Johnn)*

While this was occurring on Grenada, the British faced similar insurrections on St. Vincent and farther up the Caribbean chain. Reinforcements could not be spared elsewhere. Meanwhile, the troops on Grenada were succumbing to malaria and other tropical maladies. Before long, Fedon held all of Grenada under his control except for St. George's.

Eventually, a British fleet gathered at Carriacou and by sheer force of numbers the rebels were pushed back into the hills. Fifty-nine were caught; 38 were quickly tried and hanged in the market square. The remainder were taken to trial and banished, never to return to the island. Fedon and a few of his close officers managed to evade capture.

The last days of Julien Fedon remain a mystery. Years later James Campbell, perhaps feeling the burden of the rebellion weighing upon his shoulders, admitted that he had cheated Fedon and his wife in the purchase of Belvidere Estate.

Until independence in 1974, Fedon was considered a madman in the eyes of his countrymen. It was Maurice Bishop (see page 306 for more about him) who first looked upon him as a hero who stood up against slavery and colonial rule.

Grenada

■ Emancipation

 While the transportation of slaves on British ships was outlawed in 1807, slavery was not abolished until 1834. Then the British government was faced with a big problem. How to work out a way by which the existing planters and economy could survive and at the same time release thousands upon thousands of people who now had freedom, but little means of fending for themselves. It was decided to contract each former slave to a four-year apprenticeship.

Emancipation would lessen the slave's workload, guarantee a small amount of cloth, a hat and a blanket annually, and an amount of salted fish every week. They could not be forced to work longer than a nine-hour shift or to work on weekends. They would be given 14 days annual leave, plus public holidays.

Needless to say, the planters weren't happy about emancipation. They depended on people to work their fields and they had just lost their human property. Grenadian planters threatened independence from Great Britain. The new class of former slaves seemed free, but in effect, were free in name only. Under the apprenticeship scheme, absence from work for two days or more meant up to two weeks in prison. Five days absence meant a month in prison and up to 30 lashes. Carelessness at work could mean an enforced 15 hours labor and women could be put in the public stocks from dawn to dusk. This new regime understandably drew ill will from the apprentices and, of course, was open to abuse by the planters.

The British government attempted to compensate the planters for the loss of their workforce. A field hand or domestic servant could bring between £20 to £34. A skilled tradesman could fetch £41. The slaves on the other hand received only the apprenticeship, with the grand promise of freedom after the four years ahead of them. In 1834, Grenada had 18,316 apprentices.

The loss of enforced labor affected the crops as well as the planters. Sugar lost its importance and was replaced by cocoa. Over the next 30 years, the number of sugar plantations dwindled by 30%, while the number producing cocoa doubled.

The new freemen and women weren't keen to hang around the plantations, although many did remain in agriculture. Others took up carpentry or masonry; others became blacksmiths, wheelwrights, or took their living

Cocoa tree

from the sea. Women tended to stay in domestic service as washerwomen and seamstresses.

Cocoa pod

Within five years, the labor shortage intensified until workers were brought in from Malta. Most of these abandoned their contracts, forcing the planters to look to Portuguese indentured servants from Madiera. In 1857 Indians from Calcutta and Madras arrived on five-year contracts. Nobody wanted to work the white man's cane for any extended time. Within 20 years, many of the sugar estates on Grenada were abandoned.

Cocoa, nutmeg, coffee and tobacco were more viable products for the remaining estates. Before long, coffee and tobacco would decline and cocoa and nutmeg would carry Grenada through the 20th and into the 21st century.

HURRICANE JANET

In September 1955, a storm was brewing and blowing across the Atlantic. It reached hurricane force as it closed in on Barbados. Hurricane Janet, it was reported, would hit Barbados and then head west directly for St. Vincent. Everyone hunkered down. Everyone except those living on Grenada, Carriacou, and Petite Martinique. It was common knowledge that these islands were below the hurricane belt and a storm of that force had never been witnessed in living memory.

Midday on September 22nd, Hurricane Janet veered sharply off course from the normal path and headed south – straight for Grenada. High winds and torrential rains started as the day came to a close. As the sun went down, the power on the islands went out and winds exceeded 130 mph. The eye of the storm was crossing the 20-mile channel between Grenada and Carriacou – meaning the small islands of Carriacou and Petite Martinique, as well as St. Patrick's parish in northern Grenada, were getting slammed.

When the sun rose the next morning, the islands were devastated. In St. George's, the pier and customs warehouse, together with its contents, had vanished. Debris floated about The Carenage; at the bottom of the harbor lay the 820-foot-long pier. In the island's interior, 75% of the nutmeg plantations were destroyed. The towering trees planted in 1843 were uprooted. The cocoa trees, many nestling under the canopy of nutmegs, took a serious blow, as did the coconut groves. Grenada's banana industry disappeared overnight.

Landslides occurred island-wide and thousands were left homeless. Almost 50 years later there are still scars left across the landscape. The habitat of the mona monkeys in Grand Etang has never recovered. Old plantations abandoned long before the storm have sunk lower into the ground. On the other hand, The Carenage shows no wear or tear from the hurricane, homes have been rebuilt, and the nutmeg, cocoa and banana plants flourish once again.

■ Invasion of 1983

After World War II many colonies of Great Britain sought independence and Grenada was no exception. It was not until 1951 that universal sufferage (one person/one vote) was granted and representative government began. Independence came on February 7, 1974, and is now celebrated annually with a public holiday.

Prior to independence, power alternated between the **Grenada United Labour Party** (GULP) with Eric Gairy as leader, and the **Grenada National Party** (GNP) under Herbert Blaize. Gairy, a fervent unionist, was popular with the rural workers and peasant farmers, while Blaize's majority rested with the urban professional class.

By the late 1970s, Gairy had held government for three consecutive terms and the man had become a despotic ruler focused on personal wealth and making laws to silence his opposition. He did this literally by putting a ban on the use of public address systems without a permit, and enforcing a newspaper act preventing publication without a deposit of $20,000.

In the early 1970s, a coalition of protest groups organized a new party, the **New Jewel Movement** (NJM), led by London-trained lawyer, **Maurice Bishop**. Agitation grew as 22 nurses seeking better conditions were arrested. The police shooting of a man in Grenville, and of Bishop's father, Rupert, by government forces at a meeting in St. George's, worsened the situation. Finally, the detention of Bishop and some of his followers created an atmosphere ripe for revolt.

In 1979, Gairy left Grenada to visit the USA; Bishop took the opportunity to stage a bloodless coup and the NJM took power.

The USA refused to acknowledge political relations with Grenada and Bishop was soon courted by Castro in Cuba and the Soviet bloc countries of that time. Grenada received aid from these allies and work began on a new international airport at Port Salines. Hundreds of Cuban workers, all of whom were military reservists, were based there to help in the construction.

In 1983, Bishop became the victim of a coup from an ultra-left wing faction within his own government. His deputy, Bernard Coard, maneuvered himself into power by placing Bishop under house arrest and putting the country under virtual military rule. Bishop's supporters stormed his residence, set him free and he then led the crowd to Army Headquarters at Fort George. Violence broke out and, as a result, Bishop and five other ministers were shot dead. Grenada

Assasination of Maurice Bishop *(Canute Calliste)*

was placed under a 24-hour "shoot on sight" curfew for the next four days.

Other Eastern Caribbean countries called for an end to the strife and started invasion plans in conjunction with the United States. A three-day operation, "Urgent Fury," began on October 25, 1983. It was no pushover. The number of Cuban "airport workers" had recently been increased to 1,100 and all were assisting the Grenadian forces.

America's involvement was ostensibly to rescue 700 medical students on the islands. During bombing at Fort Frederick, the mental hospital next door was also hit. Both forces suffered casualties. After the success of the invasion, an interim government was established and democracy returned to the island. Port Salines Airport was completed with funds from the United States and Great Britain. What had been considered a potential launch pad for attacks upon American interests is now a major gateway into the Eastern Caribbean for squadrons of tourists.

■ Hurricane Ivan

Only the elders on Grenada could remember when a strong wind could blow across from Africa and wreak total havoc on their lush and tidy island. Children heard the tales at school, or when the wind shook their homes threatening to curl a weak corner of the tin roof, surely

Ivan blows across Grenada

grandfather or great tante (aunt) would reminisce aloud about Hurricane Janet on those stormy nights. By 2004 it was once again believed that Grenada lay safely below the hurricane belt. When the foreign sailboats slid into the harbor and furled their sails, battened down their hatches, and were left to rock alone on their moorings from June until November, the islands to the north were under strict weather watch. While the rest of the Caribbean Basin was on alert, Grenada, she was safe.

That was, until a tropical wave was sighted southwest of the Cape Verde Islands on the second of September. The next day this tropical wave had gained the momentum of a tropical storm – with a name. Two days later this new storm, Ivan, grew to hurricane force located 1,150 miles west of Tobago. But 21st-century Grenada was safe, everyone knew these storms hit north of this tropical paradise, until...

On Monday, September 6th, 2004, Ivan intensified off Barbados and the weather bureau suggested Grenada could possibly be right in the path of this Texas-size hurricane. Monday was the first day of the new school year for the children; it was a day they all looked forward to. Twenty-four hours later, Ivan had grown into a Category 4 hurricane and made a direct hit on the island with 140 mph winds; there were no schools left on the island. The capitol took the brunt of the storm as homes, businesses, hotels and historic buildings were completely destroyed.

To the rest of the world, Grenada had gone silent. No word came from the island. A British destroyer, the first on the scene, broadcasted the horrific devastation: Of Grenada's 90,000 residents, 60,000 were left homeless. Homes, schools, churches, government buildings, shops, hotels, were all flattened, as were the banana fields, the nutmeg, cocoa, and mango trees. The seaport was damaged, airport control tower cut down, no electricity, and no potable water to be found on the island.

From the British warship, Prime Minister Keith Mitchell, now amongst his island's homeless, encouraged Grenadians: "... we must take the trials and we must deal with them with love, patience, and fortitude and as we move forward to rebuild this beautiful country, I wish us to do so with one love, one unity, one peace."

As if speaking to all communities across the globe, people and relief organizations set out collecting chain saws and generators to clear the way into the interior and get electricity restored. Individuals gathered clothes, household items and toiletries, seeds and tools to attempt to give Grenada back her roots. While massive transports were in the making, the small island of Dominica was the first on the scene with a tanker of potable water. Ferries from St. Vincent & the Grenadines' arrived carrying canned and fresh foods. Trinidad was there, and the other Caribbean islands, answering Mitchell's words as though they had been from their own heads of state. Red Cross organizations across the world quickly responded with emergency shelters and medical supplies and UNICEF moved in to help children under the emotional and physical stress of enduring the sudden loss of everything they knew as secure.

But what mankind could not repair were the country's most valuable natural resource and the prime source of their economy: the nutmeg trees. Only nature will be able to heal this wound. Recovery for the nutmeg tree is predicted at seven years before it begins to produce fruit.

Two days after Ivan crossed over Grenada the storm reached 165 mph, a Category 5 hurricane, and headed directly towards Jamaica. Two more days and Ivan's winds increased to 170 mph as it swept 30 miles off shore Grand Cayman and weakened before striking Gulf Shores, Alabama, as a Category 3 hurricane with 130 mph winds. By September 21st, Ivan was in Atlantic Canada where as a Category 1 hurricane it downed trees and power lines in the interior of Newfoundland and produced fifty-foot waves off her northern coast at Bonavista.

The following day, Ivan was history, having caused US$19.7 billion in damage and claimed 92 lives. Until Hurricane Katrina in 2005, Ivan was the most intense hurricane on record;

it remains the most southerly Category 5 hurricane since records began. After three occasions of the name "Ivan" being used for Atlantic storms, it has now been retired.

In July 2005, Category 1 hurricane Emily crossed northern Grenada, Carriacou, and Petite Martinique, causing landslides, flooding, and felling fruit trees and banana plantations. What's in a name?

■ The Flag

Grenada's flag is bordered in red with six gold stars, plus a seventh in a red circle at the center. The red stands for the courage and vitality of the people. The seven gold stars represent the seven parishes of Grenada. Within, the red border is quartered diagonally: top and bottom in gold, standing for the wisdom and warmth of the people of this sunny place; left and right in green, signifying the land and its vegetation. Displayed on the green quarter to the left is a nutmeg, Grenada's prime commodity, a symbol of the land's bounty in economic terms.

■ Coat of Arms

Grenada's coat of arms was adopted at Independence in 1974 and designed by the College of Arms in London, England. It depicts the island of Grenada with the Grand Etang lake, below which sit a ripe cocoa pod and ripe nutmeg. Above the lake is a shield held by two supporters: on the left an armadillo, on the right a Grenadian dove. Behind these grow a stalk of maize with three flowering cobs and a banana tree with fruit and in flower. These represent just part of the island's flora and fauna.

In the center of the shield is Columbus' ship, *Santa Maria*, on a gold cross. A gold lion on red background is repeated in two of the quarters representing strength. The other two show a green background, with the Madonna Lily resting on the horns of a crescent. This emphasizes the link with the island first being called Conception by Columbus, and thereafter being dedicated to Mary of the Immaculate Conception. The horns of the crescent symbol were inspired by the Murillo painting of the Immaculate Conception.

Above the shield is a royal helm with purple interior and the crest has seven roses representing the seven parishes, standing between two sprays of bougainvillea, Grenada's national flower. Framing the bottom of the island, a flowing scroll bears the motto: *"Ever Conscious Of God We Aspire, Build And Advance As One People."*

PAPA JERRY

You never know who might be sitting next to you. As our Jeep came to a halt at Cabier Ocean Lodge on the windward coast, a young black man accompanied by three dogs appeared from the main building.

He smiled one of those smiles that stops photographers in their tracks, and then asked if we'd like to see the manager, Marion, who is hotel-sitting while the owner, her uncle, was in Europe for a few weeks. She asked if we would like to stay for the night. Would we be needing dinner? Would we like a drink? Yes, yes, yes, we answered, as the sea crashed against the point upon which the hotel sat like a contented Buddha.

In the course of the evening, the four of us became engrossed in conversation. Alan and Marion reminisced about their European homelands, while Jerry, the young Grenadian who had first welcomed us, and I discussed political events. It was amazing how similar our politics were, whether we spoke of Grenada, the United States, Bill Clinton, George Bush or Maurice Bishop. Then, somewhere in the tangle of talk, Jerry revealed that he was a calypsonian. Politics were what his music was about, what caused his heart to burst into song. He was a Grenadian bard, a voice of the people.

I asked to hear his music. Did he have any we could listen to? I never dared ask if he'd sing for us there and then. Yes, he had a CD we could hear. He told us he had been banned from the airwaves during Carnival in 2001 because of his politics. A true calypsonian then. But the purist would say not. His musical offshoot is soca, which combines soul with calypso. Soca emerged in 1978 at the Trinidad Carnival, when Jerry was only six years old.

Jerry grew up in Trinidad and spent his school years going to the pan yards listening to the steel drums. He realized he liked the songs they played, but not necessarily the pans themselves. It was the lyrics that moved him. He credits his high school teacher for recognizing the musician within him. She encouraged him to take up an instrument. His choice of the flute he later found couldn't amplify the energy he felt inside of him. So he started to sing.

Yet calypso wasn't the genre that really shook him, but reggae. He acknowledges the importance of the calypsonian known as "The Mighty Sparrow" and a song from 1979 titled *The Bassman from Hell* as having a powerful effect on him. All the ingredients came together for Jerry with the release of Superblue's *Soca Baptist* in 1980. He began his own career by pleasing the market with soft rock. The calypsonian within was only sleeping, it started knocking loudly by the time he moved back to Grenada.

It was on his native soil that he turned to soca. Listening to his music and hearing his performances, you can hear he's a calypsonian. The soca simply picks up the tempo and sets the man aflame. So hot is Papa Jerry's music that the people call him "The Fireman." True to the roots of calypso, he becomes energized by performing and controls his audience by his magnetism. As a genuine calypsonian, his lyrics are directed towards political figures and injustice on the island. *"Burn fire burn... mo' fire... music is me matches,"* he sings, about victimization of the poor by the authorities.

The last time we saw Papa Jerry he was holding in his arms his baby daughter, Luna, and snuggling up to her mother, Marion. He wasn't "The Fireman" then, but a sensitive Grenadian artist who cares about the world around him.

Getting Around

■ By Car

Driving is on the left. You must have a local license, which costs US$12. Grenadians don't like to dawdle when driving, so if you're touring at a leisurely pace, pull over and let them pass. You will notice that drivers tend to give a short blast on the horn when approaching blind corners and hairpin bends. We advise you to do the same; it'll feel automatic by the end of the trip.

Car Rental

Most rental companies have 4x4 Japanese-style Jeeps as the standard vehicle and you'll definitely need one for the terrain of the island. Choose one with air-conditioning for extra comfort, and a hard top. Soft tops are fun, but easier to break into – and remember, you're responsible for the car. You need to purchase a local license to drive in Grenada and Carriacou. Many operators can provide the license, or you can obtain one at the licensing department in the police station on The Carenage. Licenses cost US$12 and you must present your current license from home and be at least 25 years old to rent a vehicle. Motor insurance is usually offered by the rental agency in the contract and a Collision Damage Waver (CDW) costs US$12 per day; this should considerably reduce any accident costs. Some smaller rental operators don't offer any insurance, let alone the CDW, so do check the form you are signing. Don't assume your home car insurance company, or credit card policy, will cover you in Grenada.

A deposit is generally required in the form of a credit card number. Keep a copy of the operator's phone numbers in the car at all times in case of an emergency. The average price for a Jeep is US$60 per day. Expect gas prices to be EC$11 per gallon (over US$4).

Rental Agencies

 McIntyre Bros. Ltd., ☎ 473-444-3944, fax 473-444-2899, macford@spiceisle.com, deserves top marks. The Jeep we rented was very clean and smooth running. The battery failed us on Bathway Beach (most likely the driver's fault!) and we couldn't have been farther away from the main office – a two-hour journey. The mechanic arrived with a new battery, but was prepared to hand over his brand new vehicle if he couldn't get ours working properly. They are flexible regarding when and where you wish to collect and deliver your vehicle.

Y & R Car Rentals Ltd., ☎ 473-444-4448, fax 473-444-3639, info@y&r.com. We collected a Jeep from the airport office, having just landed on a Sunday. This was a clean car in good running order and gave no hassles. An employee came to collect from The Carenage as we boarded an early ferry to Carriacou.

Gabriel's Rental & Taxi Service, ☎ 473-443-2304, www.gabrental.com. Marcus Gabriel is an independent, efficient operator in Westerhall. His vehicles are in good condition and he will deliver and collect to meet your needs.

Other Rental Options

Indigo Car Rentals, ☎ 473-439-3300, , are at True Blue Bay Resort, Allamanda Hotel, and Airport Road.

Maitland's Motor Rentals, ☎ 473-444-4022, fax 473-440-4119, located opposite the Grenada Grand Beach Resort, has clean looking vehicles.

Hestel Car Rentals, ☎ 473-444-4247, works out of the Flamboyant Hotel.

L & A Car Rental, ☎ 473-444-4984, operate out of the Grand View Hotel, Morne Rouge.

Sanvics 4x4, ☎ 473-444-5227, has its office at the Grenada Grand Beach Resort.

Archie Auto Rentals, ☎ 473-444-2535, www.archierentals.com

MCR Car Rental, ☎ 473-440-5398, , is in Paddocks, near the Lagoon.

C. Thomas & Sons, ☎ 473-444-4384, ctscarent@hotmail.com

David's Car Rentals, ☎ 473-444-3399, , one of the most experienced on the island.

Avis, ☎ 473-440-3936

Dollar, ☎ 473-444-4786

■ By Bicycle

 Grenada is tough cycling territory. We suggest only fit and hardened cyclists should attempt tours or excursions.

The terrain is very hilly, with many hairpin turns, and on-coming traffic can sometimes be exactly that. If you are still keen to take it on and you don't have your own bike, you can rent one. Mountain bikes are rented by **Trailblazers**, ☎ 473-444-5337, trailblazers@grenadajeeptours.com; they also lead day-tours.

Spice Island Trekking, www.ecole-adventures.com, offers seven-day packages of cycling and hiking, also including Carriacou. They supply bikes, helmets, lunches, refreshments and entrance fees.

Carriacou is a little more bicycle-friendly, but doesn't exclude the inclines. Mountain bikes can be hired from **Wild Track Cycles**, Hermitage, Tyrrel Bay, Carriacou, ☎ 473-443-6472.

■ By Bus

Dollar buses leave from St. George's Market Square for all parts of the island. This is a very economical way of getting around: the fare to Sauteurs is only EC$6.

■ By Taxi

Many taxi drivers operate day-trips and even extended tours. It is an expensive option but at least you don't have to worry about driving and finding your way. Some taxi drivers are very good local guides. The average price is US$30 per hour. For a recommendation, call the **National Taxi Association**, ☎ 473-440-6850.

■ By Ferry

Osprey *Express Ferry*

The *Osprey* express ferry leaves Grenada for Carriacou and takes 90 minutes. It then proceeds to Petite Martinique, arriving 30 minutes later. Departures are from The Carenage at 9 am and 5:30 pm, Monday to Friday; 9 am on Saturday; and 8 am and 5:30 pm on Sunday. Departures from Carriacou to Grenada are at 6 am and 3:30 pm, Monday to Saturday; and 3:30 pm on Sunday. Departures from Carriacou to Petite Martinique are at 10:30 am and 7 pm, Monday to Friday; at 10:30 am on Saturday; and at 9:30 am and 7 pm on Sunday. Departures from Petite Martinique to Carriacou are at 5:30 am and 3 pm, Monday to Saturday; and at 3 pm on Sunday. The fare is EC$70 one-way between Grenada and Carriacou, or EC$140 round-trip. Between Carriacou and Petite Martinique, the fare is EC$20 one-way or EC$40 round-trip.

■ Cruising Permit

To clear in and out of Grenada by sailboat, you need a cruising permit. Permits are valid for one month or until the boat leaves Grenadian waters. Fees are determined by the size of the vessel: under 40 feet is EC$50 (US$19); 40-60 feet is EC$75; 60-80 feet is EC$100; over 80 feet is EC$150.

■ Tour Operators

On your first visit to Grenada you can get a flavor of the island by taking a full- or half-day tour with a guide. This leaves the door open for further excursions if you find an outfit or guide that you like, or it may give you confidence to tackle the island on your own. Full-day tours generally include all entrance fees and lunch. Average prices per person are US$55 for a half-day and US$60-$70 for a full day. First-time hikers should always consider going with a guide, for safety as much as for interpretation of the trail.

The tour operators below caught our interest. Individual guides provide a more intimate service. The larger operators

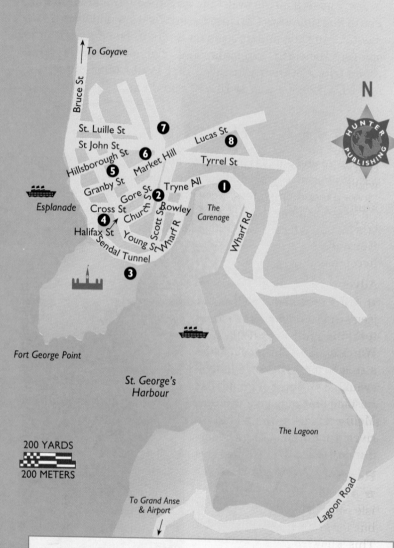

St. George's

To Goyave

Bruce St

N

HUNTER PUBLISHING

St. Luille St
St John St
Hillsborough St
Granby St
Cross St
Halifax St
Sendal Tunnel

Market Hill
Lucas St
Tyrrel St
Tryne All
Gore St
Church St
Scott St
Young St
Wharf R
Bowley

Esplanade

The Carenage

Wharf Rd

7
6
5
2
4
3
1
8

Fort George Point

St. George's Harbour

The Lagoon

200 YARDS
200 METERS

To Grand Anse & Airport

Lagoon Road

1. "Bianca C" Statue
2. St. George's Anglican Church
3. National Library
4. St. Andrew's Presbyterian Kirk
5. Marketplace
6. House of Parliament
7. Roman Catholic Cathedral
8. St. George's Methodist Church

 Cruise Ship Terminal
Fort George

give a wider range of excursions on land, by sea, and in the air, but you will obviously be part of a bigger group. Individual operators are happier offering full-day tours, and quote fees are on a sliding scale, e.g. one person fee is US$110; two or three person fee is US$85; for groups of four or more, the fee is US$65 per person. We have listed the individuals first.

Telfor Bedeau is Grenada's most celebrated hiking and trekking guide, ☎ 473-442-6200.

Dave Tours, ☎/fax 473-444-1596, offers his time at US$25 per hour for groups up to four persons; for larger groups he charges US$45 per hour. Tours can be customized to your wishes.

Mandoo Tours, ☎/fax 473-440-1428, www.granada-tours.com, also has trekking in his repertoire.

Kennedy Tours, ☎ 473-444-1074, www.kennedytours.com Recommended by Princess Cruise Lines.

Adventure Jeep Tours, ☎ 473-444-5337, www.grenada-jeeptours.com has a regular tour that takes in Annandale Waterfalls, Grand Etang Lake, a trek to a sulphur pond and a swim. They lunch at Rosemount and snorkel off Molinere Point. Now offering river tubing also. Tours run Sunday to Friday.

Henry's Safari Tours, ☎ 473-444-5313, safari@spice-isle.com, has a 28-seater mini-bus for groups large and small. This knowledgeable guide has the gamut of Grenada tours in his grasp and provides land assistance to yachties.

Caribbean Horizons, ☎ 473-444-1555, www.caribbeanhorizons.com, pride themselves on quality of service. Evidence of this is a happy volume of repeat clients. Comprehensive tours at competitive prices include land tours, deep sea fishing, and overnight sailing charters. During the summer months they promote a night turtle watch in the north.

EcoTrek, ☎ 473-444-7777, www.ecodiveandtrek.com, is a branch of the EcoDive team. Tours are slanted toward the rainforest and waterfalls, barbecues on desert islands and turtle watching.

Tours weaving history, nature, scents and technology are in the program of **K&J Tours**, ☎/fax 473-440-4227.

Sunsation Tours, ☎ 473-444-1594, www.grenadasunsation.com, has an office in Le Marquis Mall. Their trips visit gardens, forts, rum distilleries and waterfalls. The gardens visited are both private and public. They also offer tours of nutmeg processing plants, spice plantations, as well as full- and half-day, and sunset sails. A speciality tour involves a plane ride to Union Island, and a catamaran sail to Mayreau, the Tobago Cays, and Palm Island. Often these are in conjunction with Captain Yannis Tours of Union Island. But Sunsation's mainstay is *Scaramouche*, an 80-foot wooden Carriacou-built schooner.

Sightseeing

■ St. George's

The French were the first European settlers on Grenada in 1649. Their colony was known as Fort Annunciation, later changed to Port St.Louis. It was situated at the foot of a hill by the mouth of the Lagoon. Atop the hill today are the ruins of the Islander Hotel, featured in the 1957 film *Island in the Sun*. The hotel was bombed during the invasion of 1983. In 1705 the town was moved to its present location and renamed Fort Royal. With the signing of the Treaty of Paris in 1763, the British lay claim to the island and on March 2, 1765, it became officially known as St. George's.

St George's is divided by a ridge separating The Carenage from the Esplanade or Bay Town. You may recognize the word "Carenage" from visits to other islands. It derives from the days when schooners were laid on their side (careened) so their bottoms could be cleaned of barnacles. Of course, you still find boats cleaned in this fashion on some of the Grenadines, but no longer in St. George's. Today The Carenage is the center for businesses, restaurants, boutiques and government offices. The Esplanade is home to smaller businesses, the marketplace and the fish market.

The history of St. George's is punctuated by fire. In 1771, the wooden town of St. George's was destroyed by fire. Governor Leybourne's report tells of the fire breaking out in a French baker's, consuming the town, and causing damage of

On the Carenage, St. George's

over £200,000. It was decided that the town should be rebuilt with stone corners and walls of brick to replace the "paper buildings." This advice was obviously unheeded as four years later the town burned down again. This time damages exceeded £500,000. After this second fire, a law was passed requiring all buildings to be made of stone or brick and to have a tiled roof. Sixteen years later, a ship in the harbor with a cargo of rum caught fire. One third of the town was lost. In 1990, the entire Financial Complex at the end of The Carenage was devoured by flames. This appeared to be the end of the infernos, until July 11th, 2002, when a blaze engulfed a whole block of the old town, including Rudolf's Restaurant.

View from Fort Frederick
(Grenada Board of Tourism)

Begin your tour at The Carenage where the cruise ship passengers disembark. Keep the Fire Station and Police Station on your right and look across to the other side of the water. On the ridge above you can see the Anglican, Catholic and Presbyterian churches that you can visit later in your tour. Halfway around the wharf, there are some British-style telephone booths and the statue, "**Christ of the Deep**." Across the street are cafés, restaurants, souvenir shops and boutiques. Farther around the wharf is the **Nutmeg Restaurant**. A block farther on is the **National Library**, begun in 1846 in what once was a warehouse; its tiled roof arrived on the island as ship's ballast. Be careful of the traffic, as this is where the one-way system takes vehicles to the Sendall Tunnel and the Esplanade at the other end. Behind the library is Monckton Street and the **National Museum**.

GRENADA NATIONAL MUSEUM

The museum was built in 1704 as a French army barracks; when the British took over it became a women's prison. Later it was transformed into a warehouse on the ground floor and upstairs became the Home Hotel. After changing hands, it was known as the Antilles Hotel. The bars on the windows betray its former purpose and the decorative ironwork on the upper balconies gives a clue to its age. It's amazing that it has remained untouched by the fires that have ravaged this city.

The museum was developed in 1976 "to educate the people about Grenada's past and present – the land, fauna and flora, the people; their origins, technology, their festivals, the events that have shaped their lives and determined how they live." Inside, the exhibits are arranged by periods: Pre-Colombian Arawak and Carib artifacts; the Colonial period, with representations of plantation life; and Post-Colonial, beginning with Independence in 1974 and highlights of the Revolution and subsequent coup in which Maurice Bishop was executed.

Our particular favorite in the museum's collection is Empress Josephine's bathtub. Originally from Martinique, Josephine married the son of the local French governor, before becoming the wife of Napoleon Bonaparte. Let us hope the museum will grow as more finds are unearthed during construction work, and more historical records are discovered. Open 9 am-4:30 pm, Monday to Friday; 10 am-1 pm, Saturday. Admission EC$5 for adults, EC$1 for children. ☎ 473-440-3725.

Grenada

Outside the museum, turn left onto Young Street, where you find **Tikal**, the first souvenir shop in Grenada, established in 1959. The road is very steep up to the ridgeline and the intersection with Church Street. Turn left for **St. Andrew's Presbyterian Church**. The church was financed by Scottish Freemasons in 1830; its bell arrived three years later from Glasgow. The adjoining **Knox House** served as the home of the first governors of the island. Uphill past the church is **Fort George**, also housing Police Headquarters. Don't let this daunt you; the Fort is open to the public. A dozen or so cannons and a large mortar point out to sea from the battlements. In the courtyard is a basketball pole and hoop scarred with bullet holes, chilling reminders of the execution in 1983 of Maurice Bishop and others.

Now retrace your steps, cross the Young Street junction and walk up Church Street. On the right is **St. George's Anglican Church**. Built in 1828, it typically occupies the position of an earlier church and is quite modest in appearance. Inside are a small number of memorials to the good and the great. At the back of the nave, a marble monument honors the 48 captives executed on Morne Vauclain by Julien Fedon during his rebellion in 1795. Another touching tribute is to a young gunner and bugler who died in an accident when firing a cannon in memory of the death of Prince Albert, husband of Queen Victoria.

The flags and bunting of **York House** beckon you on. This is where the Grenadian Parliament sits and trials are held. Lawyers in their traditional robes come and go, while sharp-uniformed police officers watch over the scene. Adjacent is the small two-story **Registry**, where some of the country's records are kept. For a small fee and a large amount of patience, applicants can browse through documents, land deeds and records of births, marriages and deaths.

The **Catholic Cathedral** stands opposite. Mostly renovated in 1884, its tower dates from 1818. It is larger and more ornate than its Anglican cousin down the hill. What is impressive from here is the view over The Carenage. If you take any of the streets downhill to the right, you'll reach the **Market Square**.

The square was used as a parade ground from the mid-1700s, later the site for public executions and the buying and selling of slaves. Not only did it have meat and vegetable vendors, but it had a public cage and guillotine at the time of the French Revolution. Notices were posted by slavers announcing their newly arrived cargoes: "William Arnold & Company selling 50

Prime Young Windward Coast Slaves imported in brig *Swift*, Captain Dent from Bance Island." These would appear beside playbills for opera and recitals. An announcement was most likely made here for the hanging of Fedon's rebels. In the southern corner of the square today, a marker commemorates their execution.

As a common courtesy, please ask permission before taking someone's photograph. A polite inquiry often leads to a winning smile and a better picture.

The Market Square nowadays is as full of bustle as ever it was. This is the best place to buy fresh produce at the cheapest prices. The full range of fruits, vegetables and spices are sold by traders underneath their colorful parasols. A few covered buildings allow a quieter and cooler way to browse the stalls in less crowded surroundings.

At the heart of the square is the main dollar **bus terminal** for all routes over the island. This adds to the market's seemingly perpetual cycle of people coming and going. If the lines and numbers of buses feel confusing, they do have a logical system. Just ask any driver which bus is going in your direction.

If you don't fancy the climb up and over to The Carenage, you can always brave the **Sendall Tunnel**. It was dug 340 feet through a rock in 1895 to make carting goods over to the Esplanade easier for the donkeys. Walking from the Esplanade back to The Carenage, the traffic flows against you in this seven-foot-high passage.

Forts

Fort George was built in 1705 to protect the entrance to the harbor. The cannon had a range of 1½ miles. Following the people's revolution of 1979, it was renamed Fort Rupert in honour of Maurice Bishop's father. The fort reverted to its original name after 1983. Admission is free; opening hours are 6 am-5 pm.

Fort Frederick was built in 1779 on Richmond Hill by the French. They had avoided the cannon of Fort George by landing at Molinière and attacking St. George's from inland. Thus they took power and constructed this "backward-facing" fort. Within four years, the British were back in control and named the fort Frederick after a son of George III. It was never used in combat and was finally abandoned in 1850; yet it is still the most intact of Grenada's fortifications. Presently its underground tunnels are being excavated.

At over 700 feet above sea level, Fort Frederick has the best view you'll get of St. George's, Grand Anse, Point Salines and the south coast as far as Westerhall. Opening hours 8 am-4 pm daily, with guides available on weekdays. Admission is US$1.

Fort Matthew lies adjacent to Fort Frederick and is the largest fort on Grenada. It was named after the French Lieutenant-Governor, Edward Matthew. In 1880 the mental hospital was moved here and was bombed by the Americans during the invasion of 1983. It is now vacant, but being restored.

View of Fort George

Fort Adolphus and **Fort Lucas** also occupy Richmond Hill, but are much smaller and for the most part, in ruins.

Mount Cardigan is the ridge between Richmond Hill and The Carenage. A military hospital was built here in 1788. Fire destroyed this and it was rebuilt in 1854, becoming a men's prison in 1880, then the womens' prison in 1901.

The original prison in St. George's was built in 1704 and in 1880 the prisoners transferred to Mount Cardigan. The old prison became the Home Hotel, the present site of Grenada's National Museum.

■ Exploring

Nutmeg

It is impossible to go to Grenada and avoid the nutmeg. The spice is sprinkled on your rum punch, mixed in sauces, an ingredient of pastries and the tree grows profusely throughout the island. *Mysristica fragrans* is the botanical name of this sturdy evergreen that bushes up to a height of 70 feet. Its origins are in Indonesia and Arab traders introduced it to Europe around 600 AD.

Once the Europeans found out where it came from, the race was on to capture the Moluccas islands and monopolize the spice trade. This race is colorfully chronicled in Giles Milton's *Nathaniel's Nutmeg* (Farrar, Straus, & Giroux, 1999).

What was it that made this smelly little kernel so desirable? St. Hildegard stated in 1147 that given a nutmeg on New Year's Day, if carried on your person at all times, it would keep you safe from all ills. In Elizabethan England, it was thought to be the only cure for the plague that wiped out thousands of lives. A small bag of nutmegs would have bought you a house complete with servants. And it proved another incentive for Columbus as he headed west in search of a new passage to the spice islands.

Exactly when the nutmeg arrived in Grenada is a matter of dispute. The La Grenade family believe their ancestor, Louis, was given seeds by a missionary in the late 1700s. Public records state the first nutmegs arrived on the Belvidere Estate of Frank Gurney in 1843. Here lies the motive for historical corruption: Louis La Grenade was a free-colored man of French ancestry in a slave society. Gurney was white and British.

The nutmeg tree prefers a moist, but well-drained soil. You would never guess from the landscape of Grenada that these trees are fussy about their environment. They grow in abundance along the road as you head away from the coast and uphill towards the cooler interior. Their dense foliage provides an excellent canopy for cocoa trees. The fruit of the nutmeg resembles a small peach and appears shortly after the tree has flowered. The flowers are small, yellow and fragrant. As the fruit ripens, it splits open and falls from the tree. If retrieved immediately, the yellow skin can be used in the making of jellies and jams.

Picking up the fruit, you find the nut encased in what looks like a red, waxy lace. This is mace, which is removed by hand and laid out to dry in the sun. As it dries the color darkens and dulls. In 1300s England, one pound of mace would have bought you three sheep. Medicinally, it has been used for a variety of stomach disorders, from diarrhea to indigestion.

Once the mace is removed, there is the dark brown shell that contains the nutmeg. With the shell intact, the spice will keep fresh for up to 30 years. Without the shell, the nutmeg is good for only three years. The shells are used on Grenada to cover walkways and as a mulch around plants to hold in moisture and keep out weeds. At the Nutmeg Oil Distillery in Sauteurs, shells are a source of fuel in the boiler. Burned in barbecue pits, they enhance meat with a spicy flavour.

Bags of nutmegs from the market or spice kits from souvenir shops often include a nutmeg grater. Grate the kernel onto foods or into drinks such as rum punch, the signature drink of Grenada.

Nutmeg Processing Stations

The 7,000 nutmeg farmers on Grenada bring their crop to one of the 16 receiving stations on the island. The farmer receives EC$2 per pound for his nutmegs. At the receiving station, they are examined and any defective ones are discarded. The nutmegs are then transported to one of the three processing stations at Gouyave, Victoria or Grenville. For a small fee, you can visit a processing station and take a tour with one of their knowledgeable guides. It is a labor-intensive industry and, having seen it, you'll wonder how we can afford to buy this precious spice so cheaply. It's amazing how many hands each nutmeg goes through.

The nutmegs are left to dry for six to eight weeks, and the mace is aged from four to six months. Mace is graded into three categories. Prime quality mace is used for culinary seasoning and brings the farmer EC$4 per pound. The second and third grades bring EC$3 per pound and are used in food preservatives and cosmetics respectively.

In Gouyave, the station has been open since 1938 and little has changed on the production line. After drying, the nutmegs are put through the de-shelling machine. This merely cracks the nut, which is then removed by hand. A team of ladies completes this process and sifts out damaged and infected kernels or any that are not yet open.

The defective nutmegs are bagged and sent to the oil distillery in Sauteurs. The good nutmegs are given the water test. Placed in water, nutmegs with a desirable high-oil content will sink. Floaters contain less oil and will be sold to the cosmetic and pharmaceutical industries. The wet nutmegs are left to dry for another 24 hours.

The next step for the top-grade nutmegs is sorting by size; 110 small nutmegs will equal one pound in weight, the same as 80 large nutmegs. Each sack for export contains a total of 140 pounds of nutmegs. The gunny sacks are sewn on the premises close to where the tour ends. Here is the small print shop where the destinations are stenciled onto the sacks by hand. In the course of one year, Grenada processes between three and four million pounds of nutmegs – roughly one quarter of the world's supply.

Admission fee is EC$2.70 (US$1) per person. Open 8 am-4:30 pm, Monday to Friday. Please remember to tip your guide. If you'd like to photograph, please ask the guide at every stage. The guide will in turn ask the workers if they mind. Don't be offended by a refusal. They are being photographed daily, often without permission or even a simple thank you.

Nutmeg Oil Distillation

Nutmeg oil has been around a lot longer than Grenada's spice industry. It was used by the Egyptians in embalming their pharoahs, considered in India as a treatment for intestinal disorders and was thought by Europeans in the Middle Ages to ward off the plague.

Sauteurs has the island's only oil distillation plant. Here the imperfect nutmegs are sent from the processing stations and distilled for 18 hours. Nutmeg shells are burned as fuel in the furnace. The second-stage boiling takes 24 hours, with filtration removing any impurities. It takes 19 gunny sacks of nutmeg to produce one drum of oil. The oil is then bottled for the local market or exported in the large drums. A total of 24 gallons of oil are produced daily.

The fragrance of the oil is tangy and sharp, yet musky and warming. Used externally, it has proven effective for rheumatism and sore joints and muscles. It is reputed to stimulate both the digestive and circulatory systems, as well as benefiting the heart, regulating menstrual cycles and increasing dream activity. The oil seems to be able to calm and strengthen at the same time.

Today nutmeg oil is widely used in the manufacture of soaps, shower gels and lotions, although its presence may be hidden by other ingredients. The oil is extremely potent and as much as a teaspoonful taken internally may prove fatal. It may also be caustic to the skin if added to bathwater without being diluted in a base oil, such as coconut or olive oil. Overuse can cause delirium, convulsions and induce numbness. Used properly, it can invigorate the mind and has been claimed to be an aphrodisiac. You be the judge. Mix an ounce of coconut or olive oil with 10-15 drops of nutmeg to make a soothing massage oil. Or place in an essential oil diffuser and allow its sensual aroma to fill the air. However you choose to enjoy this warming oil, treat it with respect.

The Distillery is open 8:30 am-4:30 pm, Monday to Friday. There's no set admission fee as yet, but do tip the worker who guides you. US$5 for two people is fair.

Plantations

The role of the plantation is not yet finished in Grenada. There are several estates that can be visited, stayed in or are open for lunch.

Tower House in St. Paul's has large, stone gateposts bearing its name. From St. George's, it is on the left after St. Paul's police station. Gothic in style and built from grey stone and red brick, it is reminiscent of a Scottish castle. The owners have worked very hard to create the sort of formal garden that would not be out of place in an English stately home. This is a must for any garden enthusiast. In addition, it is a working plantation and you can find drying trays of cloves and cocoa beans in the back areas. Admission by appointment only, ☎ 473-440-3243.

Dougaldston Estate

Dougaldston Estate is immediately south of Gouyave. Turn right between the bus stop painted in Air Jamaica livery and the cemetery. Follow the dusty road as it forks left across a small bridge and between two yellow gateposts. The parking area is behind the buildings.

If only walls could talk, you'd learn a lot about the past 300 years since Dougaldston was established in 1700. It was a rebel stronghold during Fedon's Rebellion. The cane fields were swamped in seawater by the wave action produced by the bubbling Lagoon in St. George's in 1867. At one time the estate encompassed 1,000 acres and had 200 laborers. Today, only 24 employees work the estate. It is hard to believe the place is still functioning, as the buildings appear run down, yet it remains the major producer of nutmeg and cloves on the island.

Several people that work in the "boucan" or main building, also give tours. The lady in charge gives a lovely presentation of the spices and can tell you how they are used in foods and as bush medicine. You can sample pimento, cinnamon, bay, clove and nutmeg. In the office, old ledgers dating from the early 1900s line the walls. Outside, large drying racks can be rolled underneath the boucan in bad weather. If there aren't too many other tourists around, ask if you can see the building where cocoa is processed. Spices are sold on the premises. Open 8 am-3:30 pm, Monday to Saturday.

Rosemount Estate is inland from Gouyave. Take the road by the Texaco gas station and turn right at the sign to Waterloo. From Grenville, take the Clozier road north of Birch Grove. It makes an excellent lunchtime venue as you progress up the leeward coast or hike the Grand Etang area. Originally called the Montrose Estate, the name was changed when the British took control of Grenada in the 1760s.

During Fedon's Rebellion, slaves fled from Rosemount to Gouyave, enticed by French ideals of freedom and the fear of the French finding them in service to the British. After peace was restored, it was incorporated into the large sugar estates of Dougaldston and St. Martin. Today it is much smaller in size and the present owners, the Duncans, grow bananas, nutmeg, cocoa and vegetables. The cool breeze on the hillside and stunning flower garden will certainly make you glad you found the place. Behind the restaurant is an old boucan where mace is dried on railracks. Lunch is by reservation only, ☎ 473-444-8069.

Hellvellyn House is to the east of Sauteurs. The house dates from 1941 and was built by Alister Gleam, a self-taught engineer, sailor and electrician. All of the stone came from a local quarry and had been intended for a fort. This is our favorite place for a West Indian lunch and breathtaking views of the Grenadines. From the garden you can see Caribs' Leap in nearby Sauteurs, where the Caribs in 1652 chose death rather than capture by the French. The gardens are beautifully laid out with flowering trees such as frangipani and flamboyant. Fruit trees of golden apple, passion fruit, soursop and papaya border the garden. Taking center stage is a large mahogany, providing shade during the heat of the day. A calabash tree hangs heavy with gourds and air plants that look like part of the tree itself, and not just using it as a host. A stone terrace looks north toward the underwater volcano called Kick 'Em Jenny, the cays called The Sisters, and islands farther up the chain. The present owner is Karen Maaroufi, grand-daughter of Alister Gleam. Together with her husband and willing staff, she will see to it that you feel right at home.

Lunch is served 11 am-3 pm, Monday to Friday, and on Sundays for brunch, by reservation only, as this is a popular spot with tour parties; ☎ 473-442-9252.

Morne Fendue Plantation House is farther east of Sauteurs and on the road to Mount Rich. Sitting on the foundations of a 1700s house, the present building was built in 1908 from a mixture of stone, lime and molasses plaster. There are no steel or concrete walls on the old house. An addition of eight lodging rooms built in 2002 blends in nicely. The gardens are stunning. Trees and shrubs of varied colors and flowering seasons surround the house. Don't be too alarmed by bats flying about; locals hardly seem to notice them and they do keep the mosquito population down.

The house belongs to Dr. Jean Thompson, the medical director of the northern region of Grenada. The previous owner, Betty Mascoll, had made it a favorite stop for visitors, and the house contains many momentos of her life. The guestroom above the entrance was where Princess Margaret slept in the 1950s when she arrived aboard the Royal Yacht *Britannia*. Lunch is by reservation, ☎ 473-442-9330. Dinner and breakfast are available for overnight guests. See page 386 for details.

Belmont Estate spans the communities of Tivoli, Hermitage and Coobarrie in the parishes of St. Patrick and St. Andrew. It was John Aitcheson from Airdrie in Scotland who owned the estate when it was leased to Alexander Campbell in 1770.

Campbell would later lose his life at Fedon's Camp. When Aitcheson died in 1780, the estate was valued at close to US$2.5 million in today's money. Purchased by the Houstoun family of London, England, it remained in their trust until 1944. Then it was sold to the Nyack family, who still own it today. This was something of a landmark as the Nyacks were the first Grenadians of Indian descent to own an estate. Belmont was one of their six plantations on the island. It is quite unusual for an estate to have had only three owners since 1765.

Ruins of the sugarworks stand as a centerpiece for the garden in a working plantation that has turned from sugar to cocoa and nutmeg, with an additional 10 acres of fruit trees. Striving to be organic and working to help build their local communities, Belmont is very active in a number of ways. Summer school programs and the building of a local library are just two of their commitments so far.

Here you can observe the process of what happens to a cocoa bean from harvest to export. Although cocoa is grown on the estate, Belmont also purchases from local farmers and sells directly to the Grenada Cocoa Association. Visitors can inspect not only the cocoa process, but also the making of coconut oil and charcoal, and walk along the nature trails within the estate. As part of their cocoa bean tour, you get a taste of "cocoa tea." A small museum gives a glimpse into the life of the owners, Mr. & Mrs. Nyack, with clothing, furniture, horseracing memorabilia and plantation records. A tasty West Indian lunch is served on the premises. It's essential to call for reservations as Belmont is sure to be busy during the high season. ☎ 473-442-9524.

The main house of **La Sagesse Nature Centre** looks very much like one of the grand estate houses elsewhere on the island. It is younger than the old plantation houses, but its history is no less checkered.

It was built in the 1960s by Lord Brownlow, one of the British aristocracy and cousin of Queen Elizabeth II, as his pied-à-terre in Grenada. He already owned other properties in the Caribbean, notably in Jamaica and St. Lucia. His visits were few and far between, echoing the behavior of absentee landlords of West Indian estates in the previous two centuries. Though he expected his privacy to be respected, he nonetheless installed gates at his property line and refused local people access across his land to the beautiful La Sagesse Bay.

Small wonder that, when the Peoples' Revolution came about in 1979, it began at these gates. A mob stormed through and ransacked the house. It later became a temporary barracks for the Peoples' Army. Lord Brownlow made no efforts to recover his property and the house started to go to ruin.

In the late 1980s American art history specialist, Mike Meranski, was touring Grenada by motorbike and found La Sagesse and a new vocation at the same time. After negotiations, he became the new owner, restaurateur, hotelier and keeper of the La Sagesse Nature Centre.

The most striking feature of the house is the external staircase leading to Mike's personal apartment. It flows from the upper floor, a cascade in pink stone, like a lolling tongue. Many artists have tried to capture the look and feel of La Sagesse on canvas. These paintings are dotted around the main buildings of this delightful place. ☎ 473-444-6458.

Rum Distilleries

Rum distilleries are as much a part of the Grenadian landscape as are the spices. In fact, rum was being made here long before nutmeg arrived. It has been the ruin of many in the past, from the planting of the cane to the drinking of the inebriating brew. A visit to a rum distillery is an enlightening experience for the rum drinker and an enchanting adventure for anyone interested in steam engines or water mills.

Today, there are two rum-producing distilleries, another blending and bottling plant, and a handful of former rum factories in various states of disrepair. Clarke's Court is regarded as producing the best rum on the island by those in the south; Rivers Rum has its followers in the northeast.

Clarke's Court is in the Woburn area of St. David's parish. Approaching from either direction, you can see the cane fields. If you're not familiar with sugar cane, it is a tall, slender stalk growing straight up to a height of six or seven feet. The leaves are sharp and can easily slash through clothing or skin.

Large trucks transport the cane from the fields to the distillery. They are weighed upon arrival before unloading. The cane is then fed onto a conveyor belt, bringing it inside the building, where steam-powered knives strip the cane. The stalks are then crushed, squeezing out the juice. The waste cane is thrown into boilers as fuel.

The remaining juice is mixed with white lime and water in heated tanks. The lime and sediment sink to the bottom and the juice is extracted through evaporation into another tank. The product at this stage is a sugar syrup, to which yeast is added. Fermentation takes three days, at which time it is

12% alcohol. This mixture is distilled to a 96% alcohol content and then blended down to a 69% solution. It rests in holding tanks for six weeks, before being tested by government inspectors, and is then bottled for consumption.

Much of the machinery in the distillery is British-made. The weighbridge was built by H. Pooley & Son in 1935, the boilers made by Mirrlees Watson & Co. of Glasgow, and other workings from Birmingham and London. Engineering museums in Great Britain would cherish these pieces and perhaps be surprised that they are still in use and producing 40,000 gallons of rum every year.

Clarke's Court makes 11 different products from the sugar cane. Top of the line is a white rum, but personally we recommend the Spicy Rum, aged for four years, or the Camerhogne Spice Liqueur that tastes similar to Bailey's Irish Creme. Judge for yourself in the tasting reception area at the end of the tour. Open 8 am-4 pm, Monday to Friday. Admission fee is EC$5 per person.

Located close to Lake Antoine in St. Patrick's parish is the **Rivers Rum Distillery**. Watching the rum-making process here could kill or cure an alcoholic. Dating back to 1785, this is the oldest rum distillery still working in the Caribbean. Their one and only product is a white rum that can compete with the most potent rums of the West Indies.

The Rivers Rum process of distilling is totally different from Clarke's Court, which is 150 years more advanced. Just seeing the buildings takes you back two centuries. This is no reproduction – it's the real thing. Sugar cane is fed into a three-roller press by hand. The press is turned by a huge water wheel. You can see the juice dripping from the press, and the crushed cane is sent through a second time. The juice flows down toward the boiling house, where it is cooked in large bath-size coppers (pots). Cane residue is used as fuel for the fire simmering below them. The juice looks less and less appealing as it is moved from copper to copper in giant-size ladles. Lime is added to assist fermentation and to help get rid of impurities. Bats fly inside the boiling house and no doubt are the prime providers of those impurities. Then again, that could be the magic ingredient, for all we know!

After several hours, the liquid is drained to fermentation tanks where yeast is added. The journey from cane to rum takes 12 days. Twelve tons of sugar cane are used every day, producing 1,000 gallons of juice, which in turn makes 90 gallons of rum. That might seem a small number, but bear in mind that it is around 150 proof. A little goes a long way. The aroma alone can knock your socks off. None of the rum is made for export; it all serves the local market. Some say it can still be smelled on the breath the day after it is drunk.

You are encouraged to try it yourself at the end of the tour. Don't mind the workers watching your expressions as you gasp for breath. Only the fearless will walk away with a bottle in hand. Open 8 am-5 pm, Monday to Friday, and 10 am-4 pm on Saturday. Admission fee is EC$5, or US$2 per person. Please remember to tip your guide.

Westerhall Distillery is in St. David's parish not far from La Sagesse. They produce Westerhall Plantation Rum, which is sealed with wax over the cork, and each label contains a hand-written batch number. They also bottle the notorious Jack Iron of Carriacou. Carriacou's famous fire-water is now produced in Trinidad and shipped to Westerhall to be bottled. Westerhall was established in 1800 by the Williams family. It is possible to tour the premises. For information contact, ☎ 473-443-5857.

Dunfermline Rum Distillery, in St. Andrew's parish, was sleeping when we visited. Vegetation had taken root in the cane crusher, yet water still passes through the water wheel. The building appears as though it could easily be brought back to life by an entrepreneur with an interest. Located within a few miles of the Rivers Rum estate, it has easy access. The Dunfermline estate of 300 acres started production in 1797 and we hope hasn't seen its last days.

GRENADA CHOCOLATE COMPANY

Grenada Chocolate Company is situated in St. Patrick's parish. Drive up the hill behind the Hermitage police station and the building is easily found by the colorful painting of cocoa pods along the front wall. This recognizable logo is featured on the wrapping of the chocolate bars and on the company van.

If you want to learn the art of making fine chocolate, this is the place to come. Despite Grenada producing cocoa pods for centuries, the beans were always exported to European factories, where the finished product was manufactured. Mott Green, a hip American, decided to put this right and start making chocolate on its home turf. In partnership with a Grenadian cocoa farmer and an American buddy, he set up shop. This cottage industry has the same feel to it as Ben & Jerry's Ice Cream did before it became too large to be controlled by two funky Vermonters.

Green tried to learn the process from existing chocolate companies, but they were peevish about a new kid on the block. After much searching, he found some old chocolate-making machinery and, along with some machines he built from scratch, the production line was ready to cook. The factory is fascinating and also ecologically sound, as all equipment is run by solar power.

Because of its size the factory can accommodate only a handful of visitors at a time. The aroma is deliciously wonderful and the sight of a large, brown mass of chocolate being ground into a yummy paste can cause serious salivating. The visit is worth the trip, if only for the stories behind the antique and handmade equipment. The cocoa is fermented on-site, so you can experience every production stage from pod to tasting.Open 9 am-4 pm, Monday to Friday. There is no fee for admission. The chocolate is sold in stores in St. George's and at the airport. You can now order their chocolate on-line at www.grenadachocolate.com.

Bay Gardens

AUTHOR PICK

This is one place that lovers of flowers and plants must not miss when visiting Grenada. This compact, yet extensive collection grows on the site of an old sugar plantation in St. Paul's. Paths covered in nutmeg shells lead through an array of flowering trees and shrubs. The trail is self-guided; signs are posted on individual specimens giving their botanical names as well as their local names. Some are quite humorous – you don't need to stretch your imagination too far to equate "old man's balls" with its visual appearance.

The canopy of tropical foliage covers nearly all seven acres of garden. Huge staghorn ferns grow in the shade of old-growth trees, while smaller plants shelter beneath the ferns. The winding path takes you past screw pines, traveler's trees and bamboo groves. Look for the collection of exotic heliconias, members of the banana family. The orchid section is bountiful, and then suddenly you are at the end of a botanical journey that will leave you wanting more. Cut tropical flowers can be purchased and shipped overseas. ☎ 473-435-4544.

Grenada

KEITH ST. BERNARD

The prime mover behind Bay Gardens was Keith St. Bernard. In his sixties he exuded a quiet yet strongly magnetic appeal normally associated with elder statesmen.

His love of plants began in childhood. He left Grenada to study horticulture at King's College in England. Upon returning home in 1976, together with his brother Lyle, he began clearing land around an old sugar mill. As he worked on this project, the revolution was stirring. Being young, idealistic and ambitious, he was heavily influenced by Maurice Bishop. As tension increased, he found himself indicted for disturbance and thrown into jail. He remained there until the American invasion of 1983.

From then on, his only attempt at reforming his country was through agriculture. He continued a thread of history that survived longer than the Colonial era – namely the exchange of plants and knowledge between the Eastern Caribbean and Kew Gardens in England. This exchange began in the 1760s when Sir Joseph Banks, Director of Kew Gardens, offered prizes to shipowners for transporting healthy exotic plant specimens from the East Indies to the West Indies, as well as to England. Perhaps the best known of these expeditions is **William Bligh's** transportation of breadfruit from the Pacific to the Caribbean. Mangoes too carried a prize, as did cinnamon and other exotics. Gardens were established in the Caribbean and managed by Kew and, oddly enough, the War Office. Interest in, and finance for, far-flung gardens waned with the passing of George III. Many of the gardens withered away as a result.

Captain William Bligh
(Pitcairn Library)

Keith St. Bernard received no government sponsorship, nor was he the paid curator of Bay Gardens, but through his work he cultivated active local interest in the country's agriculture and horticulture. His hope was to train local people to pass on the knowledge of flowers and crops; his fear was of the loss of knowledge such as bush medicine. Keith now tends more heavenly gardens, and we miss him.

His brother, Albert, has taken up the torch, and the light still burns bright at Bay Gardens. Visiting with him we were reminded that when Keith spoke, one felt the heartbeats of people long passed. His eyes carried the twinkle of an aging man who cared for the unborn children of future generations. He was a sage, a man rooted in his homeland and a national treasure.

To reach Bay Gardens, turn off the main road behind St. Paul's Police Station and then take the left fork. The gardens are a half-mile down the narrow road.

Adventures on Land

■ Hiking

The majority of hiking trails begin in the interior at **Grand Etang National Park**. If you've confined yourself to the coast thus far, you will be surprised to discover the diversity of the island when you reach the rainforest.

Lake view, Grand Etang National Park

Driving from St. George's, go through the Sendall Tunnel and past the new fish market on the coast. You may want to stop and inspect the morning's catch. The size of the tuna, wahoo and mahi mahi can be impressive. Continue until you see a cemetery on your right, and turn inland here. The Queens Park stadium will be on your left.

At the roundabout or rotary in Tempe, take the left fork at the Texaco station – you are barely two miles from The Carenage at this point.

The road climbs through Beaulieu, Snug Corner, Constantine, and Vendome. The air gets cooler as you pass these residential areas. Nutmeg trees line the road, incredible ferns, the Grand

Etang fern, hang off the manicured roadside as you wind along and continue to climb. Enormous bamboo stand in the shade of the forest. You are now in the Grand Etang Forest Nursery and only six miles from the bustle of The Carenage. A sign welcomes you to St. Andrews Parish, 1,910 feet above sea level.

Hiking, Grand Etang National Park

The first trail you come to is the **Beauséjour Lookout Trail**, an easy 15-minute stroll. A trailhead sign gives times for hikes to the Lake (15 minutes), Mount Qua Qua (three hours), Fedon's Camp (four hours), and Concord Falls (five hours). Of course this doesn't allow for "oohing," "aahing," photos, or a stopping for a snack during a 10-minute monsoon.

Before heading for any trail go to the **Grand Etang Visitor's Centre**. You must buy an inexpensive pass here that you need to keep with you on your hike. This small investment helps to maintain the trails. There are two snack bars here if you've forgotten to bring supplies. The Visitor's Centre house was traditionally used as a stopover for travelers crossing from one side of the island to the other. Your vehicle may have protested on the way up, but try to imagine walking or riding a horse from St. George's to Grenville. Or worse, carrying a load of Rivers Rum from the distillery to the marketplace in St. George's.

The house has vital information about the trails and a lot of material about the flora and fauna found along them. Even if you aren't the least bit interested in the mona monkey, the armadillo or the snakes, you're bound to come across one of over 300 different types of hummingbird that live on the island. There's information about the various trees that grow in the forest and how to identify them by their bark. On the trails you'll find numbered yellow tags corresponding to the samples; these include *mahoe*, *gommier*, mountain palm and *bois canoe* trees.

At some places on the trails, wooden railings have been installed. Beware of these since some are not as sturdy as they seem. Unless you see new pressure-treated wood, trust your feet and not the railing.

> *Normal hiking boots are too hot and bulky for the Caribbean – invest in some lightweight hiking shoes for good grip.*

HIKING TRAILS ARE GRADED FOR DIFFICULTY FROM 1 TO 10

1 – Very easy, provided you are not handicapped.

2 – Easy.

3 – Up to a mile, with some uphill climbs.

4 – The trail could be up to two miles, but fairly straightforward.

5 – A challenging walk, from two to three miles along estate roads or in the forest.

6 – Easy forest hike or a long estate road walk with slopes and up to four miles.

7 – A forest hike of about four miles with slopes.

8 – A challenging forest hike with long, steep hills. Expect mud. For intermediate-plus hikers and a local guide is recommended.

9 – A difficult forest hike. The trail will be steep, muddy and rough. Maybe some climbing using your hands.

10 – A very difficult forest hike. Steep, muddy, rough and potentially dangerous in places. Expect some scrambling and possible use of ropes. Experienced hikers only.

> *Try the hike right behind the Visitor's*
> *Centre. It's rated as a "1."*

Morne LeBaye Trail is lined with nutmeg shells, though patches of slippery red clay poke through. Marouba trees are covered in Spanish moss. Bamboo and heliconia line the forest. At the top of this easy walk is a picnic table, a defunct lookout tower and a partially covered area that gives little protection from either rain or sun.

The **Grand Etang Shoreline Trail** is the next step up at a level 2. You cross a small pond before reaching the lake, actually the crater of an extinct volcano. Early in the morning or late afternoon, you have a chance of seeing **mona monkeys** in the bam-

Mona monkey

boo groves. This is a good trail for birding too, with species ranging from **hummingbirds** among the flowers to broad-winged **hawks** soaring over the lake.

Confidence gained, you might want to try something a little more taxing. **Mount Qua Qua** is a six-mile round-trip, or from Mount Qua Qua continuing on to Concord Falls it's a 10-mile hike. Although graded 3 and 4 respectively, we would bump them up to 9 and 10 ourselves. If you do attempt these longer hikes, take ample amounts of food and water. Wet weather gear is also recommended, as the interior is nearly always covered in clouds, and rain is likely. The tradewinds alone are reason to have a parka handy, as you will definitely get a chill as you approach the top, especially if you are wet and perspiring.

Again, look out for the slippery red clay. Signs are posted with the letter **Q** and a number. If you've done your homework at the Visitor's Centre, you'll know that most of these refer to types of vegetation, but Q7 marks a potential landslide area – proceed with caution.

Passing Q8, you see a trail leading off to the left; this is the way to Concord Falls. Head straight on if you want to reach the summit of Mt. Qua Qua. The closer to the top you are, the more slippery it gets. At the top, you are 2,372 feet above sea level.

To continue to **Concord Falls** is downhill from here on. The information markers are now labeled with a **C**. C1 is at Mt. Qua Qua. At C3, a trail leads off to the right. A short but steep hike will bring you to **Fedon's Camp**. Imagine yourself a hostage brought from Gouyave or

Concord Falls, Grand Etang

Grenville and forced up the trail at gunpoint. Forty-eight prisoners were murdered at this camp in 1795.

Scarlet Ibis
(Grenada Board of Tourism)

Back on the main trail at C8, you must choose the 10-minute hike down to the lower and middle falls or the left fork to the upper falls. When you reach the parking area by the lower falls, you might be able to hitch a ride down to the village of Concord. If it is earlier than 5 pm and not a Sunday, you can catch a bus back to St. George's.

If time doesn't allow for a Grand Etang hike, the **Morne de Gazo Nature Trail** is closer to St. George's and not as strenuous. It is signposted and begins 1.4 miles past the St. Paul's Police Station.

Grenada

PETROGLYPHS

There are sites listed on Grenada as having petroglyphs or Amerindian remains. These are faces carved into boulders centuries ago. When asked for directions, many local people refer to them as the "Carib Stones" or the "Slave Stones." These carvings go further back in time than the period of slavery or the

Petrogyphs (Karl Eklund)

Caribs. The current belief is that they were made by the Arawaks, who lived on these islands long before the arrival of the Caribs.

Unfortunately, time and weathering are taking their toll on these carvings and many are almost unrecognizable. The best example still in its natural state is just south of Victoria. We gave a ride to two ladies on their way into town to eat lunch with their schoolchildren. In return, they gladly showed us the large boulder by a drainage pipe on the seashore. Two faces are visible; one very handsome in design, the other looking like a happy face logo.

A much-publicized petroglyph outside Sauteurs isn't nearly as visible and river currents have all but worn away the features. It is near the Mount Rich estate on La Fortune River. On the leeward coast at Duquesne Bay, more petroglyphs have been found. Sadly the beach level has risen so you'd have to dig to find them.

Better examples can be found at the Grenada National Museum in St. George's. At this writing, there is far more digging going on in the north than the island has ever experienced. A new resort and golf club are under construction at Levera. We hope that while the dirt is being moved around, more faces and figurines will catch someone's eye and be properly preserved for Grenada's rich cultural heritage.

■ Waterfalls

Travel from St. George's along the Grenville road, heading for the Grand Etang National Park. Between the communities of Constantine and Vendome is an old Methodist church. Here is a fork in the road. Make a left to reach the **Annandale Falls**.

The falls are easy to reach, but you are likely to be hounded by local men of all ages wanting money. The divers will offer to leap off the 40-foot falls and call out your name before hitting the water. They will ask for a mere US$10 for doing this. As you stand stunned by their audacity, they quickly add that they do this so they won't steal from you. You suddenly wonder what's happening back at your vehicle a few hundred yards away. Young children looking for a bit of employment will act as tour guides describing the local flora. There lies a promising vocation, but not with their apparent mentors preying on the tourists. An elderly calypsonian-wannabe with guitar awaits your return to the parking area to sing a song just for you – for a price. The waterfalls are spectacular; the human hounding not so pleasing. If you go with a tour group, the chances of harassment will be less for fear of being reported. We went on our own and were relentlessly pestered. This is the only uncomfortable experience we've ever had in Grenada.

Local police and the Ministry of Tourism are aware of this problem. In reporting this nuisance, you may feel uncomfortable, but if enough reports are registered the chances are greater that it will be dealt with at its source.

Deeper into the interior is **St. Margaret's**, locally known as **Seven Sisters Waterfalls**. Half an hour's hike along a rocky road east of the Grand Etang Park is this series of falls. The trail is steep in places and can be slippery. Another trail winds around, but you are advised to take a guide as it isn't well-marked and crosses private property. Guides can be hired for a minimal cost at the Grand Etang Visitor's Centre and will only enhance the experience.

Royal Mount Carmel Falls, or **Marquis Falls** as they are known locally, are the tallest in Grenada. Only two miles south of Grenville, it is an easy 30-minute hike. The trail takes you through a plantation and if you really want to indulge yourself in this adventure you should call upon Mr. Telfor Bedeau to join you for a reasonable fee. He lives in the area and is the renowned master of hiking and kayaking in Grenada, ☎ 473-442-6200.

Traveling up the leeward coast, the turn off for **Concord Falls** is outside the village of Concord. The road twists and turns and becomes narrower as you drive into the hills. A parking area by the falls is patrolled by a security guard. There are three sets of falls. By the parking area, you can simply enjoy the first falls or swim in the pool 35 feet below them. The middle set of falls is larger and a 45-minute hike above the first. The rocks are slippery and the canopy of nutmeg trees is pleasantly distracting. Although the trail is marked, you may chose to take along a guide – they can be hired at the parking area. Be sure to agree on a price before you set out. The upper set of falls is known as the **Fountainbleu Falls** and is a good deal higher up the trail. For these, a guide, snacks, and water are essential. The cool, clear swimming hole at the base of this 65-foot waterfall will be more than inviting when you arrive.

Tufton Hall Falls are southeast of Victoria. The staff of the Victoria Hotel told us the trail is unmarked and even locals can get lost. Ask at the hotel about an appropriate guide. The town is known for its soccer team, the Hurricanes, so finding someone in good condition shouldn't be a problem.

■ Beaches

All beaches on Grenada are public. This was one item of resentment that helped spark the revolution of 1979; people were being denied access to the sea. While property owners may not want you crossing their land, look

Bathway Beach

around and you will find public access to the beach.

The most celebrated beach is **Grand Anse**. Many hotels look out onto its white sand and obviously it can be quite busy, especially on weekends. Close by is **Morne Rouge Bay**, smaller but no less busy on Saturday and Sunday. Nearer to

Grand Anse Beach

Point Salines and the airport, you see signs to the **Aquarium Restaurant** and the **Beach House Restaurant**. The beaches here are lovely places to snorkel and sunbathe, with the additional attraction of delicious food at both.

True Blue Bay is another option, but bear in mind its popularity with yachties. It's a lively spot in winter months. **Prickly Bay** has its fair share of water traffic, but the beach itself is well-shaded and big enough to find a quiet spot.

Don't be deterred from trying a beach that has been seemingly taken over by a resort. Don't be so bold, however, as to use their chairs and parasols!

Petit Bacaye has a shallow bay, although there is some seagrass. Otherwise the snorkeling around the little cay in the bay is excellent.

La Sagesse Bay is one of our favorites. You can rent beach chairs and equipment from the hotel, or head to the less crowded area to the west.

The eastern side of Grenada is where all the weather comes in. The sea is generally rougher here. It's best to ask advice. If the locals won't swim there, then neither should you.

Plastic sandwich bags should be on your "things to pack" list. Baggies can keep the ants out of your snacks, sand away from your film, postcards and stamps together, your wet swimsuit in your backpack and any of number of uses. They can be washed, re-used and carried back home.

Mangrove trees at Bathway Beach

At the northeastern tip of the island is the 450-acre **Levera National Park**. Here are pristine beaches and outstanding coral reefs. Mangrove swamps will satisfy any birder. From May to September, these beaches are protected due to sea turtles coming ashore to lay their eggs. **Bathway Beach** is in this location also. Huge rocks lie close to the shore and protect a small corridor of water and beach from otherwise pounding surf. A small beach bar serves hot lunches and cold beers. Opposite at the Levera Visitor's Centre are washrooms and public telephones.

■ Golf

Grenada Golf & Country Club is in Golflands. From Grand Anse Road, take the road by Roydon's Guest House. Carry your clubs up the hill and you'll need a rest before you start playing. It's best to take your own vehicle or hire a taxi. We did once persuade a dollar bus to make a detour to the top of the hill for an additional EC$5.

Caddies jostle for your bag. Their fee is EC$20 for nine holes. Carrying even your own Sunday bag is an effort in the heat and a caddy can show you the line on the greens. A fellow hacker described the putting

Golf in Grenada

surfaces here as more like a hairbrush than a pool table. The nine holes can be fun. Aside from the par-three holes, only one hole is of any great length. Several holes cross each other, which adds to the adventure factor. It is easy to make a bad score and blame it on the course. Clubs are available for rent from the clubhouse for EC$40. Boys outside will sell you balls that they will probably find and sell again after your round.

The clubhouse has a large verandah where, over a cold drink from the bar-cum-pro shop, you can witness other hackers perplexed by the turf. Late in the afternoon, members arrive for their daily round and, with the benefit of local knowledge, they effortlessly carve out a good score.

To further humiliate yourself, try taking on your caddy for a game. Some of these guys can hit the ball a country mile. The cost for nine holes is EC$60. ☎ 473-444-4128.

Grenada Grand Beach Hotel and **La Source Resort Hotel** both have a nine-hole pitch-and-putt course for guest use only. Begun in 2002, the course at **Levera Golf & Country Club** in the north of the island is Grenada's first 18-hole course; 473-440-6209.

■ Triathlon

The Grenada Triathlon is gaining stature among the world's iron men and women. Held over a weekend every January, it consists of a number of races. The first day is the individual's race, with a one-kilometre swim, a 20-km bike race and a five-km run. A mini-marathon and junior events are also held. Sunday features the same events for teams of three; in one category, at least one team member must be female; in another, the combined ages of members must be over 100. If you wish to take part contact: **Triathlon Grenada**, PO Box 44, St. George's, Grenada.

■ Hashing

Hashing would not appear out of place as part of military training. This combination of run-and-chase does have its origins in the army as a Monday morning cross-country run to sweat off the excesses of the weekend. Hashing takes place on alternate Saturdays across the island and is meant to be a communal exercise, rather than a competitive race. Any hashers breaking away from the group are liable to be sent astray by "the hares" setting the route. The finish line is very likely to be a rum shop, which shows how the original intention of hashing has been adapted for modern-day results.

Want to hash? Contact **Hash House Harriers**, www.grenadahash.com; Hashmasters, Evan Otway, ☎ 473-440-3669, eotway@hotmail.com.

■ Horseback Riding

Contact **Ernest Pascall**, ☎ 473-440-5368. He is in the St. George's area and is the only one we could find with horses for rent.

Adventures on Water

■ Scuba Diving

The waters around Grenada are teeming with marine life, coral reefs and wrecks that can fulfill the needs of beginners and more experienced divers. There are some 28 dive sites in Grenada alone and most are within a 20-minute boat ride of Grand Anse. Dive depths vary from 20 to 150 feet, with visibility from 30 to 100 feet. Sites include wrecks, walls, reefs and drift dives and all have plenty of sea life.

Seahorse

Coral takes many forms and all are delicate, so please don't touch. Enjoy the beauty of **finger coral**, **sea fans**, **brain coral**, **sponges** and **gorgonians**. Among the varieties of fish you can see are **angelfish**, **parrotfish**, **spotted drum**, **eels**, **barracudas**, **nurse sharks**, **rays**, **groupers**, as well as **lobsters**, **shrimp**, **sea horses** and **sea turtles**.

Bianca C is the largest wreck in the Caribbean at 600 feet long, and one that all divers want to explore. As you drop down to 100 feet, you get only 15 minutes to inspect the vessel, so two trips are in order to discover this gem. Also, because of the depth, it's for experienced divers only. Expect sea turtles, rays, jacks and barracudas.

BIANCA C

Considered the largest wreck in the Caribbean, the *Bianca C* is a highlight of the Grenadian dive experience. She lies at depths of 90 to 160 feet about a mile off the tip of Point Salines.

Bianca C *of the Costa line*

Weighing 18,000 tons, she was built during the 1940s as part of the Italian Costa Steamship Line. She sank in 1961. On October 22nd, having finished one of the regular visits to the island, the captain and 300 crew prepared to depart with 400 passengers aboard. An explosion in the engine room started fires below decks that burned for over 24 hours and claimed the lives of three of the crew.

The Grenada Yacht Club picked up the distress signal and soon a small armada went to the rescue of those on board. Yachts, dinghies and even rowboats supplemented the lifeboats and larger craft that ensured the safety of the remaining passengers and crew.

The captain and officers were the last to leave but, at the end of the two-hour operation, their route to the stern was blocked. Luckily, a rope ladder was found and they too were saved.

Eyewitness reports talk of the hull of the *Bianca C* glowing red and the water around her bubbling. Fearful that she would sink and block the shipping lane, a British frigate, HMS *Londonderry*, was summoned to tow away the stricken vessel. Due to her poor condition and a strong cross-wind, the tow broke and thus she rests in her present position off Point Salines.

The Grenadian people were not only swift in their response to the disaster, but followed up by giving passengers and crew food, clothing and shelter until alternative transportation was arranged.

In return, the Costa Steamship Line presented the people with the bronze statue, "Christ of the Deep," which stands on The Carenage today.

Bass Reef is a five-mile stretch from the harbor of St. George's to Point Salines. The coral is abundant and rich in variety. Close by is the **Three Part Wreck**; at only 40 feet down, it's easy for beginners. Angelfish and rays are likely to be seen here.

Great Anemone (Dive Grenada)

North of St. George's is the **Marine Park** around Molinere Point. Here you can find wall sites such as **Happy Hill**, with shoals of fish, eels and sea fans. **Flamingo Bay**, **Dragon Bay** and **Grand Mal Reef** are all good for beginners, while **Molinere** is a good spot for beginners and a snorkeler's haven. The wreck of the **_Buccaneer_** is 80 feet below the surface and was sunk to create a dive site.

Off Point Salines, near the site of the *Bianca C* is **Whibbles Reef**, a drift dive. **SS _Orinoco_** lies off La Sagesse Bay, where the water is rougher and thus for experienced divers only.

Prices differ for longer courses, specialized courses and night diving. Sometimes a lunch, snacks and soft drinks are included; also some operators will arrange transportation to and from your accommodation.

Average Prices for Diving	
One-tank dive	US$40-$50
Two-tank dive	US$80-$90
One-day Discover Scuba	US$80-$100
Four dives + certification	US$375-$450

Queen Triggerfish (Dive Grenada)

Dive Operators

AQUANAUTS GRENADA
True Blue Bay Resort
☎ 473-444-1126
www.aquanautgrenada.com

AQUANAUTS GRENADA
Blue Horizons Garden Resort & Spice Island Beach Resort
☎ 473-439-2500
www.aquanautgrenada.com

DIVE GRENADA
Flamboyant Hotel
☎ 473-444-1092
www.divegrenada.net

ECODIVE
Coyaba Beach Resort
☎ 473-444-7777
www.ecodiveandtrek.com

ECODIVE
Grenada Grand Beach Resort
☎ 473-444-2133
www.ecodiveandtrek.com

SCUBATECH
Calabash Hotel
☎ 473-439-4346
www.scubatech-grenada.com

■ Deep Sea Fishing

 Fish have been part of the staple diet of these islands ever since they were inhabited. A good many communities still rely on the fishermen to bring home the bonito. Row boats and speedboats are the most common fishing craft today. Two rods and lines stick out amidships like antennae waiting for a bite. A fisherman might let you go out with him and try your luck.

One of the main events on the international deep sea fishing calendar is the **Spice Island Billfish Tournament** held in late January. Some 150 anglers from over a dozen countries participate in as many as 50 boats. During the three-day fishing spree, they expect to catch sailfish, yellow fin tuna, wahoo and the prized marlin. Marlin around these waters can weigh as much as 700 pounds. Substantial prize money can be won for the biggest catch or any new record set. The tournament directors are keen to follow the policy whereby fish are tagged and released. In recent years, having a large percentage of the catch returned to the sea has only enhanced the reputation of this sporting festival. For more information, contact Ian Harford, ☎ 473-443-5477, islandice@spiceisle.com.

A handful of independent operators offer half-day, three-quarter day and full-day fishing packages, which include drinks, snacks and fishing equipment. Expect to pay US$400 for a half-day, US$500 for a three-quarter day and US$600 for a full day. The usual minimum number of paying customers is four, so it works out at about US$125 per person.

The best charter in our opinion is ***Yes Aye*** is a 31-foot craft operating out of True Blue Bay. Contact Gary Clifford, ☎ 473-444-2048, www.yesaye.com.

■ Whale Watching

 Whale watching has intrigued man for centuries; mostly with a view to a kill and the immense profit to be made from whale oil and the many bi-products of the carcass. Only since the 1960s has it become a passive sport to watch these magnificent creatures in their natural habitats. Now whale watching is a booming industry.

As a sport, it does have an element of luck. Nobody can tell you when and where a whale will appear. Much is known of their migratory patterns and habits, but to actually tell a customer that whales will be within sight on a given day is not possible. However, experienced whale-watch operators do know where and when whales are likely to be seen.

How much time will you be at sea? Before booking your whale watch, decide how much time you are willing to be on the water. Trips can last from two hours up to a whole day. Check out the type of boat you'll be on – a large motorized vessel, small fishing boat or sailing boat. This will dictate the clothing you need to take, whether you should carry food and water, and if you have the legs and stomach for the trip. If you are in any doubt, take fresh ginger to ward off a bad tummy. (Or, before leaving home, check your local health food store for ginger in candied or capsule form.) A seasickness patch will prove as effective. These are better alternatives than Dramamine, which will make you drowsy.

A WORD TO
THE WISE

If you do succumb to Noah's nausea, stay outside in the open air. Inside, you will smell engine vapors and the movement of the boat will feel exaggerated. Concentrate on something else – the profile of the island, the flight of seabirds, flying fish skimming the waves. Most people who get seasick forget about it when a whale emerges.

Your captain may or may not know anything about whales. He may be an enthusiastic naturalist or he may be a local fisherman. Many fishermen will know where the whales are, but know nothing about them. If you have ANY questions about safety, ask and be satisfied with the answers before boarding.

Carry extra clothing. The wind on the water may get cool and you may need to escape the direct rays of the sun. A windbreaker or rainjacket is always a good idea on a boat. Be smart in choosing your shoes as boat decks do get slippery.

If you forget the camera, don't sweat it. Unless you are right on top of a whale or have a long lens (300mm), your images of the whale are going to be minute in the great big sea. If you do take a camera, protect it from saltwater and too much exposure to the sun.

Whale watching is for some the ultimate adventure. As a passenger you are not in danger from the whale at anytime aboard a boat. If anyone is threatened, it is generally the whale by a captain who does not give sufficient distance and places the whale in peril. Humpback whales are in the area from January to April, sperm and short-finned whales are resident all year round.

Dolphins are a more common sight. Groups from five to 15 will suddenly appear alongside your boat like motorcycle outriders. This is guaranteed to bring squeals of delight from all aboard. At first sight, they'll probably look smaller than you'd imagined. And so swift are these greyhounds of the sea, that it's not worth fumbling for your camera. Even with your eye at

Grenada

the viewfinder and your finger on the trigger, the chances of catching one in the frame are slim. Be content with the moment. Members of the dolphin family in these waters include the bottlenose, common, striped, spotted, spinner and orca.

Whale Watch Operators

First Impressions Catamaran Chartering, ☎ 473-440-3678, have two catamarans capable of holding up to 35 passengers.

■ Sailing

Sailboats at Carriacou Beach

Sailing is the essence of what these islands have to offer for some. Breezing along downwind and tacking back upwind again in a vessel of any size and shape can be spiritually uplifting. You can feel part of the mariners' cycle stretching through the millennia. Even if you don't know a jib from a topmast, as a passenger you can still experience the wind flapping in the sails and feel the rise and fall of the bow as it cuts through the waves. There's a selection of half-day and full-day excursions under sail from which to choose.

Those skippers and crew that know the ropes well enough will probably want to race. Grenada offers plenty of opportunity for such events. The year kicks off with the **La Source Sailing Regatta** in January, featuring races for both yachts and working boats in various classes. Parties ashore before, during and after the racing enliven the atmosphere. The **True**

Blue Bay Pursuit Race is held in February and April brings the **Easter Regatta** to both Gouyave and Petite Martinique. Carriacou has its own regatta in August, while in December a yacht race celebrates the end of the hurricane season. The Grenada Yacht Club hosts races throughout the calendar. For more information and to find out how to take part, contact **Grenada Yacht Club**, ☎ 473-440-6826, gyc@caribsurf.com.

Just want to be a passenger? Several prepared tours are given by operators. Snorkeling gear, an open bar and lunch included is the norm for full-day sails; drinks and snacks are provided for shorter trips. Expect to pay per person US$70 for a full day, US$50 for a four-hour tour and US$40 for a two-hour sunset cruise.

Sailing Tours

Carib Cats, ☎ 473-444-3222, offer full day sails to Prickly Bay from the Lagoon.

First Impressions Catamaran Chartering, ☎ 473-440-3678, starwindsailing@caribsurf.com, has two catamarans available. You could be one of 15 or 35 passengers on these twin hulls.

Footloose Yacht Charters, ☎ 473-440-7949, footloos@spiceisle.com, does sailing and fishing trips with food, unlimited drinks and onboard entertainment. They come recommended by the Caribbean Travel Organization.

"Bareboat" is the term used to describe a vessel chartered without crew. This operator offers both bareboat and crewed excursions. Prices vary greatly according to the type of boat, excursion and length of charter.

Horizon Yacht Charters, ☎ 473-439-1000, horizonyachts@spiceisle.com, work out of True Blue Bay, with a full service marine facility. Full day charters minimum, US$280 for one to four persons.

Not quite ready to take the helm, but want to learn? The Moorings runs week-long sailing schools. Give them a call in the US, ☎ 800-535-7289.

Yacht Services

Whether chartering a sailboat or cruising in your own yacht, you need to know where to turn should a crisis arise. It might be a torn sail, the dinghy outboard motor has died or the refrigerator is warmer than the deck at high noon. Who are you going to call?

Island Dreams Yacht Services advertises repairs, maintenance, and absentee yacht management. Contact Mark and Anita Sutton, ☎ 473-443-3603, VHF channel 74, mark@islanddreamsgranada.com.

Johnny Sails & Canvas in St. George's is a complete sail, canvas and rigging shop. ☎/fax 473-444-1108, VHF channel 16.

Outfitters International on Lagoon Road in St. George's provides charters, insurance, repairs, charts, chandlery and yacht minding. ☎ 473-440-7949, fax 473-440-6680, VHF channel 16, footloos@spiceisle.com

Grenada Marine in St. David's Harbour, provides bottom painting, repairs and chandlery items, ☎ 473-443-1667, fax 473-443-1668, www.grenadamarine.com.

Grenada Yacht Club has docking and refueling facilities, ☎ 473-440-3050, www.grenadayachtclub.com.

Spice Island Marine is full-service, with haulout, storage and chandlery, ☎ 473-444-4342, www.spiceislandmarine.com.

True Blue Bay Resort & Marina, ☎ 473-443-8783, mail@truebluebay.com, for complete mooring facilities.

Shopping

The place to start is the Market Square. For your fruits and vegetables, herbs and spices, even straw hats, this has the best bargains. Saturday is the busiest day, and it is closed on Sunday.

On Cross Street near the Market Square is the **Yellow Poui Art Gallery**, ☎ 473-440-3001, with paintings, photography, prints, lithographs, maps and sculpture. Most of the artwork is by artists resident in the Caribbean. Over the hill in Young Street is **Tikal**, ☎ 473-440-2310, the oldest tourist shop in Grenada, having opened in 1959. They stock a large and varied selection of local and worldwide arts and crafts, clothing, books, music and souvenirs. It's a personal favorite of ours; we never visit Grenada without calling in at Tikal. Opposite is an alleyway and stairs going up to **Art Fabrik**, ☎ 473-440-0568, with batik clothing for ladies and gentlemen. You can see the batik being hand-printed on the premises. Also on Young Street is **Bains World** for state-of-the-art sports clothing and accessories in an up-to-date building.

On The Carenage below The Nutmeg Restaurant is **Dot's Plaza**, a small boutique carrying clothing, T-shirts and swimwear. The largest store with an enormous range of T-shirts and Grenadian souvenirs assembled under one roof is **Ganzee**; wide aisles and air-conditioning make it easy to browse without feeling cramped or rushed. Smaller, but a charming building in itself is **Figleaf** on the Fire Station side of The Carenage. They have a little biy of everything in terms of souvenirs, some of them unique.

For bookworms and those interested in reading more about Caribbean, and in particular, Grenadian culture and history, **Fedon Books**, should have plenty to whet your reading appetite. Located on HA Blaize Street, near the traffic lights below the Catholic Church.

On the way to Grand Anse is **Arawak Islands**, ☎ 473-444-3577, in Belmont. The building doubles as shop and factory for this thriving cottage industry. They produce soaps, shampoos, perfumes, sauces, jellies, essential oils, incense, candles, insect repellent and also sell spices. Everything is beautifully packaged. Tours are given by the staff, but only small parties please. They are open Monday to Friday, 8:30 am-4:30 pm. Saturdays are by prior appointment only.

Grenada

The **Grand Anse Craft and Spice Market** is next to the tennis courts, where you can find local arts and crafts, spices, jewelry and leather goods. This is where you can get your hair braided or watch some other willing victim. Farther afield in La Sagesse, **St. David's**, the local art and craft market is situated in the grounds of an 18th-century sugar mill.

From La Sagesse, taking the more inland route to St. George's, you pass other shopping opportunites: **Laura's Herb & Spice**, where a tour of the gardens is a must. You should reserve an hour of your time for this tour.

LAURA'S GARDEN

This is an excellent introduction to the flora of the island before you head out into the countryside and rainforest. Guides will lead you around the six acres of gardens identifying orange, nutmeg, cocoa, vanilla, allspice, turmeric and others. They will inform you of the uses of each in cooking, cosmetics or bush medicine. At the end of the tour, ask to peek into the production area, where sorting and packing are done. They have a small counter where a range of their goods – cinnamon, nutmeg, clove and allspice – can be purchased. This is as good a place as the market to get spices, since it is a spice farmers' cooperative. The Garden receives funding from the European Union.

It's located 2½ miles past St. Paul's Police Station, in the community of Perdmontemps. The turnoff for Laura's is on your left, leading uphill and marked by a rather faded sign. Admission costs EC$5 per person. Open 8:30 am-3:30 pm, Monday to Friday.

The **Camerhogne Art Gallery** in St. Paul's shows off carvings, sculpture and furniture by a local craftsman. If he's not open when you call, the Secret Harbour Hotel bar has a magnificent chess set he produced. Finally, De La Grenade's selection of drinks and liqueurs are sold as well as sampled on the premises.

DE LA GRENADE

This family-owned business began in 1967 in the kitchen of the La Grenade home. It was expanded and moved to its present manufacturing plant by Dr. Cecile La Grenade in 1991. The De La Grenade Liqueur goes much further back than this generation, in fact it can be traced to the first La Grenade on record in Grenada.

Captain Louis La Grenade was a free-colored landowner in a time when those words would have been an oxymoron. He was born on the island in 1733, shortly after the British had taken over, and was a mere child when the French came again to repossess it. Throughout his lifespan of 75 years he would know nothing but hostilities on his native soil. Nonetheless, he was a free man, owner of the Mardi Gras estate, and a shipowner trading between the islands. In 1793, he pledged allegiance to the British crown and gave up his Catholic faith for that of the Anglican Church. Within two years he was awarded the rank of captain in the St. George's militia.

According to family legend, Captain La Grenade gave free passage to a Dutch missionary traveling from Banda Island in Indonesia and in return was given some dried nutmeg seeds. This same Dutch man of the cloth also gave him a secret formula for a liqueur as a sign of his gratitude. Like the story, the liqueur has been passed quietly down through the generations. The only hint of the formula they are prepared to reveal is that one of the ingredients is the pericarp, or yellow skin of the nutmeg fruit. This skin, once discarded as worthless, has more recently been used as an ingredient in making jellies, jams and nutmeg syrup.

Grenada

If the legend of Louis La Grenade is true, then it pre-dates the nutmeg brought to Belvidere Estate in 1843. This is more widely acknowledged as the year nutmeg was introduced to the island. History is full of ironies. If Captain La Grenade did have the first nutmegs on his Mardi Gras estate, this robs Belvidere Estate of its claim by half a century. Belvidere was owned in La Grenade's time by Julien Fedon. Although both men were free-coloreds, they fought bitterly on opposite sides during the rebellion.

Louis La Grenade is buried at his family's estate overlooking the production factory of the mysterious liqueur that bears his name.

Vendors' stalls (Karl Eklund)

Back in St. George's by the cruise ship terminal is a tourist gift shop, and a row of stalls where vendors sell spices, herbs and such. If there's no cruise ship in dock, you won't find many vendors.

■ Supermarkets

If you are shopping for food either on land or at sea and are stocking up on provisions, or if you are just getting stuff for a day on the beach, a hike or a picnic, you have a handful of supermarkets in St. George's to choose from.

Real Value is in Spiceland Mall, and **Food Fair** in the Grand Anse Shopping Centre. **Foodland** is on the Lagoon Road; another **Food Fair** is directly below The Nutmeg Restaurant on The Carenage.

Store Hours

Shops and stores open generally from 8:30 am to 4 pm, Monday to Friday, and on Saturday from 9 am to 1 pm. Supermarkets tend to follow these hours, but Food Fair in Grand Anse is open until 7 pm, Monday to Thursday, and until 8 pm on Friday and Saturday. Food Fair below The Nutmeg is open until 9:45 pm on Friday.

ARAWAK ISLANDS

It is hard not to describe Arawak Islands as a cottage industry. It is situated in a 100-year-old house between St. George's and Grand Anse that acts as the main office, gift center and factory, where everything except their jams and sauces are produced. Inside, they are bursting at the seams as each room has many uses. The kitchen doubles as a workshop, where loofahs are bleached, dried and packaged. In a corner a gentleman shrink-wraps spices, while down the hall his brother hand-paints the cotton bags that will hold spices or soaps. The bags are even sewn on the premises. Another room holds giant jars filled with essential oils in which wooden balls soak. Used as air fresheners, they will retain their scent up to six months. Aromas of nutmeg, cinnamon and vanilla fill the air.

What looks like a long established firm only came into being in 1986. There are 12 local people employed and all hands are constantly busy either in production, selling at the front counter, answering the phone or labeling boxes to be shipped out in the afternoon.

One intriguing process is the making of soap. Down in the cellar the soap is cooked for three days, poured into large, wooden trays and dried for three weeks.

Cheese wire is used to cut the blocks into bars. The scraps are put into a meat grinder and made malleable for hand-pressing into balls. Coconut, orange, clove and cinnamon are among the soaps in their line. It's difficult to keep your nose out of a bar of soap while looking at the process. You certainly walk out appreciating the effort put into the production, considering the small price you pay for a bar of soap.

Arawak Islands tries to use Grenadian raw materials wherever possible. They prefer to buy from the spice cooperatives or the small farmers. The next preference is to buy from Caricom countries. Only after these options have been exhausted will they import from outside the Caribbean basin – bottles being a prime example.

Having saturated the local market, they export to St. Vincent & the Grenadines, St. Lucia, Barbados, Trinidad, St. Martin, Nevis and Antigua. Searching for souvenirs? Wanting something authentic and original? With Arawak Islands' products, you carry back a piece of the island. They now offer shipping from their website at www.arawak-islands.com. Open 8:30 am-4:30 pm, Monday to Friday, and on Saturdays by prior appointment only.

Where to Eat

As with accommodation, the majority of places to eat are in the south around St. George's and Grand Anse. This does not mean you should confine yourself to this area. Food of quality is served island-wide. In the north, around Sauteurs, there are at least three excellent places serving lunch. Eating at hotel restaurants can be a hit-and-miss affair. A few hotels we dined at seemed to have a restaurant just so they could say they did, but many hotel restaurants can compete on their own. In general, you'll find value for money at restaurants where Grenadians eat. There is such a variety of good and affordable eating places on Grenada, that we've omitted fast-food outlets. If you want them, they can be found, particularly in the malls around Grand Anse.

Almost Paradise (see page 412)

Though prices in these listings are given in US dollars, menus tend to be priced in Eastern Caribbean dollars. Multiply the US figure by 2½ to get a rough estimate in EC dollars. If you wish to work out the price to three decimal places, then you definitely need this vacation. The scale includes a starter and a main course for one person at dinner – including the 10% service charge and 8% government tax. Drinks and dessert are not included. Breakfast and lunch prices are usually lower than evening fare.

St. George's Harbor View

Restaurant Directory

The Southwest
CALYPSO TERRACE, ☎ 473-439-1924
FLAMBOYANT HOTEL'S BEACHSIDE TERRACE, ☎ 473-444-4247
LA BELLE CREOLE, Blue Horizons Cottage Hotel, ☎ 473-444-4316
LA BOULANGERIE, Le Marquis Mall, ☎ 473-444-1131
LA DOLCE VITA, Morne Rouge Road, ☎ 473-444-3456
LALUNA, Morne Rouge, ☎ 473-439-0001
LE CHATEAU, Le Marquis Mall, ☎ 473-444-2552
MARIPOSA BEACH RESORT, Morne Rouge, ☎ 473-444-3171
OLIVER'S RESTAURANT, Spice Island Beach Resort, Grand Anse, ☎ 473-444-4258
PIRATE'S COVE, Grand View Inn, Morne Rouge, ☎ 473-444-2342

Grand Anse Road, The Lagoon & St. George's
AL PORTOFINO, The Carenage, ☎ 473-435-2966
CARENAGE CAFÉ, The Carenage, ☎ 473-440-8701
CHOPSTIX CHINESE RESTAURANT, Grand Anse Road, ☎ 473-444-7849
COCONUT BEACH, Grand Anse, ☎ 473-444-4644
CREOLE SHACK, The Carenage, ☎ 473-435-7422
DEYNA'S, Melville Street, St. George's, ☎ 473-440-6795
JAVA KOOL INTERNET CAFÉ, The Carenage, ☎ 473-435-5005
PATRICK'S LOCAL HOMESTYLE COOKING, Lagoon Road, ☎ 473-440-0364
THE NUTMEG, The Carenage, ☎ 473-440-2539
TOUT BAGAY, The Carenage, ☎ 473-440-1500

TROPICANA, Lagoon Road, ☎ 473-440-1586

Point Salines, True Blue Bay & Lance Aux Epines

AQUARIUM RESTAURANT, Point Salines, La Source Road,
☎ 473-444-1410

THE BEACH HOUSE RESTAURANT & BAR, Point Salines
Ball's Beach, ☎ 473-444-4455

CASTAWAYS RESTAURANT & BAR, Lance Aux Epines,
☎ 473-444-1250

THE RED CRAB, Lance Aux Epines, ☎ 473-444-4424

RHODES, Calabash Hotel, Lance Aux Epines, ☎ 473-444-4334

TRUE BLUE BAY RESORT, True Blue Bay, ☎ 473-443-8783

The Southeast

ISLAND VIEW RESTAURANT & BAR, Clarke's Court Bay,
Woburn, ☎ 473-443-2054

LA SAGESSE NATURE CENTRE, St. David's, ☎ 473-444-6458

PETIT BACAYE, Westerhall, St. David's, ☎ 473-443-2902

WATER'S EDGE, St. David's, ☎ 473-444-6305

The Leeward Coast

ROSEMOUNT, Gouyave, St. John's, ☎ 809-444-8069

VICTORIA HOTEL, Main Street, Victoria, ☎ 473-444-9367

The North

HELLVELLYN HOUSE, St. Patrick's, ☎ 473-442-9252

MORNE FENDUE PLANTATION HOUSE, St. Patrick's,
☎ 473-442-9330

Airport

LIFTOFF RESTAURANT & BAR, Point Salines Airport,
☎ 473-444-2896

Grenada

■ The Southwest

FLAMBOYANT HOTEL'S BEACHSIDE TERRACE

☎ 473-444-4247

US$26-$35 MC, Visa, Amex, Discover, Diners

Daily, 7:30 am-10:30 pm

A la carte menu all day with varied entertainment in the evenings

Caribbean buffet and crab races on Monday with steel band music on Wednesday night.

CALYPSO TERRACE

☎ 473-439-1924

US$15-$25 MC, Visa

Monday to Saturday, 12 noon-10 pm. Open from 5 pm in off-season.

Situated high on the bluff above Morne Rouge Road, with a fantastic view over Grand Anse and into St. George's. Drinks are a little expensive, but the menu is otherwise competitively priced.

LA BELLE CREOLE

Blue Horizons Cottage Hotel

☎ 473-444-4316

US$26-$35 MC, Visa, Amex, Discover

Daily, 7:30-10 am, 12:30-2:30 pm, 7-9 pm

Pleasant and intimate atmosphere, but disappointing lack of choice on the dinner menu, considering the price.

LA BOULANGERIE
Le Marquis Mall
☎ 473-444-1131
Under US$15
Monday to Saturday, 8 am-9 pm, Sunday, 9 am-9 pm
Bread, cakes and pizzas to eat in or to go in a café setting.

LA DOLCE VITA
Morne Rouge Road
☎ 473-444-3456
US$26-$35 MC, Visa, Amex
Tuesday to Sunday, 5:30-10 pm, dinner from 6:30 pm
Italian dishes warmly recommended by dive staff and a few hoteliers. I found my pasta tasted quite bland, but this won't deter me from giving it a second chance.

LALUNA
Morne Rouge
☎ 473-439-0001
Over US$35 MC, Visa
Daily, 7:30 am-11 pm

Grenada

Laluna Restaurant

The latest hot-spot for the in-crowd appears exclusive; but it does welcome reservations from non-residents. Do you need an excuse to sample haute cuisine in a premier-class setting? Go on, spoil yourself, knock a hole in your credit card. You deserve it.

LE CHATEAU

Le Marquis Mall

☎ 473-444-2552

US$15-$25 MC, Visa

Monday to Saturday,10 am-midnight, Sunday, 6 pm-midnight

Good food and patronized heavily by locals and tourists alike, but the terrible state of the washrooms makes us wonder about the kitchen.

MARIPOSA BEACH RESORT

Morne Rouge

☎ 473-444-3171

US$26-$35 MC, Visa, Amex

Daily, 11 am-10 pm

Enjoy Italian home cooking al fresco by the hotel pool with a view over Morne Rouge Bay. We sampled the simple yet tasty pasta Bolognese. Other dishes include lamb with mint sauce, pork in rum and raisin sauce, and seafood crêpes. The portions were generous and the drinks potent.

OLIVER'S RESTAURANT

Spice Island Beach Resort, Grand Anse

☎ 473-444-4258

US$26-$35 MC, Visa, Amex, Discover, Diners

Daily for dinner, 7-9:30 pm

A rich assortment of local cuisine, with a West Indian buffet on Friday. Entertainment varies throughout the week. The dress code is elegantly casual; no shorts. Reservations are required.

PIRATE'S COVE
Grand View Inn, Morne Rouge
☎ 473-444-2342
US$15-$25 MC, Visa, Amex
Daily, 7-11 pm
Some hotel restaurants seem run of the mill. We're glad to report that this is not one of them. Even though we were staying at the Grand View, it felt as if we'd gone out for dinner. The flambéed shrimps in a succulent rum sauce fulfilled its promise.

■ Grand Anse Road, The Lagoon & St. George's

AL PORTOFINO
The Carenage
☎ 473-435-2966
Over US$35 MC, Visa, Amex
Monday to Saturday, 8 am-10:30 pm, Sunday, 7-10:30 pm
This elegant Italian restaurant overlooks The Carenage and presents a first-rate menu and wine list. Of the home-made pasta dishes, the specialty is Linguine al Portofino.

CARENAGE CAFÉ

View of St. Georges from Carenage

The Carenage
☎ 473-440-8701
Monday to Saturday, 7 am-6 pm
Under US$15 MC, Visa

Breakfasts, beers, omelettes, cocktails, pizzas, ice creams and sandwiches. The first Internet café on The Carenage when it opened a few years ago. A steady flow of business was ensured while people waited for one of two screens. Facing stiff competition from other net-works (one now next door), the café is now relaxing into a daytime eaterie that just happens to have an Internet facility. The sidewalk tables are good for people-watching.

CHOPSTIX CHINESE RESTAURANT
Grand Anse Road
☎ 473-444-7849
Under US$15 MC, Visa
Monday to Saturday, 11:30 am-10 pm, Sunday, 5-10 pm
The best choice for Chinese in our opinion.

COCONUT BEACH
Grand Anse
☎ 473-444-4644
US$15-$25 MC, Visa, Amex, Discover
Wednesday to Monday, 12:30-10 pm

French Creole cuisine in cabana surroundings on the beach lends an informal atmosphere during the day. It attracts both formal and informal diners at night. Specialties are Caribbean chicken, Lambie Calypso, and the coconut pie is a delicious dessert.

CREOLE SHACK
The Carenage
☎ 473-435-7422
Under US$15
Monday to Saturday, 10 am-11 pm

This large restaurant offers a buffet-style cafeteria and bright, colorful decoration. The price of food undercuts anything we've seen by half. The bar makes this a lively nightspot.

DEYNA'S

Melville Street, St. George's

☎ 473-440-6795

Under US$15 MC, Visa

Monday to Saturday, 8 am-9 pm, Sunday, 10 am-4 pm

Salt fish, callaloo, fish cakes, Oil Down, curried mutton and rotis, make this very popular indeed with local people. You won't find many travelers in this local hotspot. If you are in the vicinity of the market square, pop in and give it a try. We guarantee you'll be back.

Oil Down is the process of boiling down vegetables and meat, together with coconut milk. It is the national dish of Grenada, and you will frequently see it on menus.

Grenada

JAVA KOOL INTERNET CAFE

The Carenage

☎ 473-435-5005

Under US$15

Monday to Thursday, 9 am-9 pm, Friday & Saturday, 9 am-10 pm, Sunday,1-8 pm in high season only

Fast snacks for on-line surfers.

PATRICK'S LOCAL HOMESTYLE COOKING

Lagoon Road

☎ 473-440-0364

US$15-$25 MC, Visa

Daily, lunch 12 noon-2 pm, dinner 6 pm-11 pm

This is some of the best Grenadian cooking you'll find. Patrick prepares 20 dishes, such as cod fritters, gingered pork, fried Jacks, stir-fried rabbit, cou cou, and lambie in Creole sauce, along with soup and a dessert. It's worthwhile starving yourself before plunging into this gourmet fest. Reservations are essential.

THE NUTMEG

The Carenage

☎ 473-440-2539

US$15-$25 MC, Visa, Amex

Monday to Saturday, 8 am-11 pm, Sunday, 4-11 pm

A perennial favorite with good views across The Carenage. Only five tables have window seats so choose your time carefully. It is more economical as a breakfast and lunch venue.

TOUT BAGAY

The Carenage

☎ 473-440-1500

Monday to Saturday, 8 am-11 pm, Sunday, 4-11 pm

US$15-$25 MC, Visa

Attractive new venue by the financial district of St. George's. This is becoming a haunt of nearby office staff. Lemon pork steaks, scampi Provençale, chicken carbonara, and nachos grande with fish show its international appeal. We must admit we haven't yet tried the curried goat, a good reason for a future visit.

TROPICANA

Lagoon Road

☎ 473-440-1586

Daily, 11 am-10 pm

Soups, rotis, burgers, a Chinese menu and a take out service. Among the specials are curried mutton, grilled fish, and stewed chicken. It's not unusual to find bones in with the meat in the rotis. Whenever you hear Celine Dion on the sound system you know that the place is popular with local people, and thus recommended for the traveler who wants to blend in.

West Indians adore Celine Dion. It won't be a day before you hear her voice coming out of a rum shop, a boutique or a restaurant serving the local populace.

■ Point Salines, True Blue Bay & Lance Aux Epines

AQUARIUM RESTAURANT

Point Salines, La Source Road
☎ 473-444-1410
aquarium@caribsurf.com
US$26-$35 MC, Visa, Amex
Tuesday to Sunday, 10 am-11 pm

The restaurant is spacious and shady with a soothing waterfall. From the menu: callaloo canneloni, freshwater crayfish in garlic butter, lobster barbecue on Sundays. Try one of their calypso coffees if you're not driving or about to use the kayak and snorkel gear on the premises. Being on the beach with excellent snorkeling, this is a perfect place to hang out for the whole day.

THE BEACH HOUSE RESTAURANT & BAR

Point Salines Ball's Beach
☎ 473-444-4455
e mail beachhouse@caribsurf.com
US$26-$35 MC, Visa
Monday to Saturday, 11 am-10:30 pm

AUTHOR
PICK

The specialties include beef satay in teriyaki and eggplant parmesan appetizers. Delicate coconut pasta, Cajun shrimp, and seafood pot pie are among the signature main dishes. There are daily specials and a large selection of wines. We really enjoyed the food and the hospitality here. If there was a competition for "Best Restaurant on Grenada," this would be among the finalists.

CASTAWAYS RESTAURANT & BAR

Lance Aux Epines

☎ 473-444-1250

US$15-$25

Daily, 6 pm-10:30 pm

Castaways has the atmosphere of an English pub, so it's no surprise that Yorkshire pudding is on the menu. The staff did warn us that the stuffed crab backs were spicy and hot, to their credit and our convenience; more cold drinks were ordered. Live music on Friday night.

THE RED CRAB

Lance Aux Epines

☎ 473-444-4424

US$26-$35 MC, Visa

Monday to Saturday, 6-10:30 pm

With 15 years experience here, the owners are German and Scottish; he supervises all the cooking, she runs the bar. Appetizers include stuffed crab back and shrimp crêpe; for main courses, try lobster Newberg, surf and turf, or veal. The menu pricing is slightly eccentric, but you can't argue with the quality of the food.

RHODES

Calabash Hotel
Lance Aux Epines

☎ 473-444-4334

Over US$35

MC, Visa, Amex

Daily, 7-9:30 pm

This is an upscale experience: white linen, silver service, and dining of metropolitan first-class. Gary Rhodes is one of Britain's TV celebrity chefs so expect the quality to be par excellence. The dining-area terrace is framed by a trellis of flowering thunbergia vine, and the wine list itself is all-embracing. Reservations are advised and it's best to wear something smart.

TRUE BLUE BAY RESORT

True Blue Bay

☎ 473-443-8783

US$26-$35 MC, Visa

Daily, 7:30 am-11 pm

Wide-ranging menu with Caribbean and Mexican specialties. Sunday brings Grenadian-style brunch. Steel pan music on Tuesday. Heartily recommended for food and ambiance.

■ The Southeast

LA SAGESSE NATURE CENTRE

St. David's

☎ 473-444-6458

US$26-$35 MC, Visa, Amex

Daily, 8 am-10 pm

Renowned for its fresh fish dishes, chicken plates, and chocolate mousse. Wherever possible, locally grown fruit and vegetables are used in the cooking. This is another venue where you could come for the whole day or just for dinner. La Sagesse offers a day package with transportation, nature walks and lunch; or an evening package with transport and dinner included. Reservations are advised for dinner.

PETIT BACAYE

Westerhall, St. David's

☎ 473-443-2902

US$15-$25 MC, Visa

Daily, 8 am-10:30 pm

The restaurant is proud of its chef and is worth going that extra mile to visit. Lobster, Oil Down (see page 379), and seafood feature on the dinner menu. Delicious sandwiches, burgers and other snacks can be had for lunch if you intend making a day of it. Reservations are requested for dinner.

WATER'S EDGE RESTAURANT
Bel Air Plantation, St. David's
☎ 473-444-6305
US$26-$35 MC, Visa, Amex
Daily 11 am-10:30 pm

Choosing the freshest, locally grown produce, fish straight from the sea, herbs and spices from the Bel Air garden, and all cooked to perfection, is the recipe for a remarkable dining experience. This is truly a culinary adventure guided under the watchful eye of Susan Fisher and her diligent staff. Reservations are advised since guests from other parts of the island quickly fill empty seats. Pop in to the bar one evening and you'll see what we mean, and no doubt be tempted to make a booking.

ISLAND VIEW RESTAURANT & BAR
Clarke's Court Bay, Woburn
☎ 473-443-5962
US$15-$25
Daily

Downstairs bar with snacks during the day and pool tables. Upstairs restaurant for evening meals.

■ The Leeward Coast

ROSEMOUNT
Gouyave, St. John's
☎ 809-444-8069
Under US$15
Sunday-Friday, 9 am-5 pm, lunch from 12 noon-2:30 pm

Inland from Gouyave, this old plantation house is a perfect setting for lunch if you are on a day-tour or hiking. A three-course set lunch costs EC$40 per person. Callaloo soup is the starter; the main course is a choice of fish, chicken, or a vegetarian alternative with rice and peas, coleslaw, chow mein, plantain, and tossed salad; the dessert is a cocktail of local fruits. Juice is included. They serve no bottled drinks nor alcohol. Reservations for lunch are advised, as some tour companies make stops here. Outside lunch hours, you can drop in for a refreshing drink. The gardens provide another incentive for visiting.

VICTORIA HOTEL
Main Street, Victoria
☎ 473-444-9367
Under US$15 MC, Visa
Daily, for lunch and dinner

Come hungry, as dinner is overwhelming. Locally caught fish (tuna, mahi-mahi, kingfish) is served with vegetables and callaloo soup. For hotel guests, breakfast is another large plate. In the morning you'll hear a conch shell being blown; it's the announcement that the catch of the day has been landed and is on sale at the local fish market.

■ The North

HELLVELLYN HOUSE
St. Patrick's
☎ 473-442-9252
US$15-$25
Monday to Friday, 11 am-3 pm, Sunday brunch, 11 am-3 pm

This is an island gem. We count our blessings that we ever found Hellvellyn and we always look forward to returning. In fact we usually visit two or three times over the course of a vacation.

Soup of the day is followed by a choice of chicken or fish with vegetable dishes served family-style; among desserts we've sampled is soursop ice cream. The homemade bread is like a doughnut without the jelly or sugar. Tables are arranged on a covered patio and around the gorgeous garden with a stunning view of the Grenadines to the north. Reservations are required.

MORNE FENDUE PLANTATION HOUSE

Dining on the terrace at Morne Fendue

St. Patrick's
☎ 473-442-9330
US$15-$25
Daily,
12:15-2:30 pm
Creole cuisine in an Edwardian setting. Pepperpot and callaloo soup, chicken and fish with vegetables fresh from the beautiful garden, as well as fruit punches, round off lunch in this popular venue. Reservations are recommended. If you haven't yet seen any of Grenada's old plantation houses, this is one of the finer examples.

■ And finally...

LIFTOFF RESTAURANT & BAR

Point Salines Airport
☎ 473-444-2896
US$15-$25 MC, Visa, Amex
Daily, 5 am-10 pm.

Last chance to dine in air-conditioned comfort before you go through airport security! Prices are a little high, as they are in most airports. Rotis, burgers, curried chicken, mahi mahi, and red snapper all feature on the menu.

Where to Stay

The main concentration of accommodations is in the south-west between Point Salines and St. George's. This is the ideal location for first-time visitors or if you plan a lot of beach-related activity. The southeast area of St. David's is far enough away if you want to avoid the crowds and bustle; yet it's only 20 minutes from the capital on the dollar bus. The lee-ward and windward coasts, and St. Patrick's parish in the north, have fewer places to stay but therein lies their beauty. They are ideal as touring stops or if you want to get away from it all longer-term.

Prices are per-room, per-night, based on double-occupancy in regular high season. High season runs from early December through mid-April. Some hotels charge extra during the weeks of Christmas and New Year. Off-season is from mid-April through the end of November. Expect a 10% to 15% reduction from many hotels and guest houses at that time. Some estab-lishments give discounts for longer stays. Ask.

Grenada

Accommodations Directory

The Southwest
ALLAMANDA BEACH RESORT, PO Box 1025, St. George's, ☎ 473-444-0095
BLUE HORIZONS COTTAGE HOTEL, PO Box 41, St. George's, ☎ 473-444-4316, fax 473-444-2815
COYABA BEACH RESORT, PO Box 336, St. George's, ☎ 473-444-4129, fax 473-444-4808
THE FLAMBOYANT HOTEL & COTTAGES, PO Box 214, St. George's, ☎ 473-444-4247, fax 473-444-1234
GEM HOLIDAY BEACH RESORT, PO Box 58, St. George's, ☎ 473-444-4224, fax 473-444-1189

GRAND VIEW INN, PO Box 614, St. George's,
☎ 473-444-4984, fax 473-444-1512

GRENADA GRAND BEACH RESORT, PO Box 441, St.
George's, ☎ 473-444-4371, fax 473-444-4800

JENNY'S PLACE, PO Box 1742, St. George's, ☎
473-405-6073, fax 473-439-5186

LALUNA, PO Box 1500, St. George's, ☎ 473-439-0001, fax
473-439-0600

LAZY LAGOON TROPICAL COTTAGES, PO Box 1451, St.
George's,
☎/fax 473-443-5209

LEXUS INN, Grand Anse Road, ☎ 473-444-4780, fax
473-444-4779

THE LODGE, PO Box 3540, St. George's, ☎ 473-440-2330

MARIPOSA BEACH RESORT, PO Box 370, St. George's,
☎ 473-444-3171, fax 473-444-3172

ROYDON'S GUEST HOUSE, PO Box 1404, St. George's,
☎/fax 473-444-4476

SIESTA HOTEL, PO Box 27, St. George's, ☎ 473-444-4646,
fax 473-444-4647

SOUTH WINDS HOLIDAY COTTAGES & APARTMENTS,
PO Box 118, St. George's, ☎ 473-444-4310, fax 473-444-4404

SPICE ISLAND BEACH RESORT, PO Box 6, St. George's,
☎ 473-444-4423, fax 473-444-4807

TROPICANA INN, ☎ 473-440-1585, fax 473-440-9797

WAVE CREST HOLIDAY APARTMENTS, PO Box 278, St.
George's, ☎/fax 473-444-4116

Point Salines, True Blue Bay & Lance Aux Epines

CALABASH HOTEL, PO Box 382, St. George's,
☎ 473-444-4334, fax 473-444-5050

CORAL COVE COTTAGES & APARTMENTS, PO Box 487,
St. George's, ☎ 473-444-4422, fax 473-444-4718

FOX INN, PO Box 205, St. George's
☎ 473-444-4123, fax 473-439-0524

LANCE AUX EPINES COTTAGES, PO Box 1187, St.
George's, ☎ 473-444-4565, fax 473-444-2802

LA SOURCE GRENADA, PO Box 852, St. George's,
☎ 473-444-2556, fax 473-444-2561

MACA BANA VILLAS, ☎/fax 473-439-5355

MONMOT HOTEL, ☎ 473-439-3408

MOUNT HARTMAN BAY ESTATE, ☎/fax 473-444-4504

REX GRENADIAN, PO Box 893, St. George's,
☎ 473-444-3333, fax 473-444-1111

SECRET HARBOUR RESORT, PO Box 11, St. George's,
☎ 473-444-4439, fax 473-444-4819

TRUE BLUE BAY RESORT, PO Box 1414, St. George's,
☎ 473-443-8783, fax 444-5929

TWELVE DEGREES NORTH, PO Box 241, St. George's,
☎/fax 473-444-4580

The Southeast

BEL AIR PLANTATION, ☎ 473-444-6305, fax 473-444-6313

CABIER OCEAN LODGE, Crochu PO, St. Andrew's, ☎/fax
473-444-6013

EPPING PLANTATION HOUSE, PO Box 2669, St. Paul's, ☎
473-440-3333

LA SAGESSE NATURE CENTRE, PO Box 44, St. George's,
☎/fax 473-444-6458

PARADISE BAY VILLA RESORT, La Tante, St. David's, ☎
473-405-8888

PETITE BACAYE COTTAGES, Westerhall PO, St. David's,
☎/fax 473-443-2902

The Leeward Coast

SUNSET VIEW RESTAURANT & BEACH HOUSE, Grand Mal,
St. George's, ☎ 473-440-5758, fax 473-440-7001

Grenada

VICTORIA HOTEL, Victoria, St. Mark's, ☎ 473-444-9367, fax 473-444-8104

The North & Windward Coast

ALMOST PARADISE COTTAGES, Sauteurs, ☎ 473-442-0608

GRENADA RAINBOW INN, PO Box 923, Grenville, St. Andrew's, ☎ 473-442-7714, fax 473-442-5332

MORNE FENDUE PLANTATION HOUSE, St. Patrick's, ☎ 473-442-9294, fax 473-442-7853

SAM'S INN, Dunfermline, St. Andrew's, ☎ 473-442-7313, fax 473-442-7853

■ The Southwest

ALLAMANDA BEACH RESORT

Lobby at Allamanda Beach Resort

PO Box 27, St. George's

☎ 473-444-0095, fax 473-444-0126

www.allamandaresort.com

US$100-$200 MC, Visa

Fifty air-conditioned rooms, with balconies facing the sea. All have bath, shower, TV, telephone, ceiling fan and refrigerator. Amenities include restaurant, bar, pool, tennis, fitness center, and conference facilities. Situated right on the beach, this hotel is geared towards activity, with a large quantity of equipment for windsurfing, Sunfish sailing, a Hobie cat and bicycles.

BLUE HORIZONS GARDEN RESORT

PO Box 41, St. George's
☎ 473-444-4316, fax
473-444-2815
www.grenadabluehorizons.com, blue@
spiceisle.com
US$100-$200 MC, Visa

The 32 air-conditioned cottages, with bath, shower, refrigerator and

stove, are set in a large hillside garden on the Morne Rouge Road. **La Belle Creole** restaurant is on-site. Guests may use the pool and non-motorized watersports at the Spice Island Beach Resort, 300 yards away on the beach.

COYABA BEACH RESORT
PO Box 336, St. George's

☎ 473-444-4129, fax 473-444-4808
www.coyaba.com,
US$201-$300 MC, Visa

Coyaba's 80 air-conditioned rooms have bath, shower, TV and telephone. The rooms, redesigned in 2006, are arranged in terraces facing the gardens and beach. In the center is a pool with a swim-bar for the reckless and an adjoining restaurant for the relaxed. Complimentary watersports, tennis and croquet are available, and a free round at Grenada Golf Club. EcoDive are the on-site dive team.

THE FLAMBOYANT HOTEL & COTTAGES

PO Box 214, St. George's

☎ 473-444-4247, fax 473-444-1234

www.flamboyant.com, flambo@caribsurf.com

US$100-$200 MC, Visa, Amex, Discover, Diners

Facilities include restaurant, **The Owl** late night sports bar, pool, dive shop, snorkeling, kayaks, pedal boats, golf at the Grenada golf club, games room, mini mart and wedding packages are available. The 60 air-conditioned rooms, with bath, TV and telephone, have a great view over Grand Anse, but it's a steep descent of over 150 steps to the beach, restaurant and other amenities. Hestel Car Rental is in the main building.

GEM HOLIDAY BEACH RESORT

PO Box 58, St. George's

☎ 473-444-4224, fax 473-444-1189

www.gembeachresort.com, gem@caribsurf.com

US$100-$200 MC, Visa, Amex, Discover, Diners

Gem has 18 air-conditioned apartments of one and two bedrooms. Single bedroom units have a shower; apartments with two bedrooms have bath and shower. All have kitchenette, sitting room, and balcony overlooking the bay, plus TV, telephone and ceiling fans in sitting rooms. Beach towels and chairs are provided. There is an on-site mini-mart, and the beach bar has the **Sur La Mer** restaurant above.

This is a great location on the beach in Morne Rouge Bay. The apartments are furnished – they're on the chintzy side, but comfortable nevertheless. Between the hotel and restaurant is the **Fantazia 2001** nightclub, which is soundproofed.

GRAND VIEW INN

PO Box 614, St. George's

☎ 473-444-4984, fax 473-444-1512

www.grenadagrandview.com, gvinn@caribsurf.com

Under US$100 MC, Visa

There are 55 rooms, with bath, shower, TV, telephone, some with air-conditioning, some with ceiling fan. Five minutes walk down to the beach, 10 minutes to walk back! An on-site pool is refreshing after such a hike. Grand View is an apt name due to the elevated position of this hotel. The **Pirate's Cove** restaurant delights with its food and atmosphere, attracting non-residents as well as guests. **L&A Car Rental** is in the gatehouse office.

GRENADA GRAND BEACH RESORT

PO Box 441, St. George's

☎ 473-444-4371, fax 473-444-4800

www.grenadagrand.com

paradise@grandbeach.net

US$201-$300 MC, Visa

Each of the 240 air-conditioned rooms, with bath,

Fantasy Pool, Grenada Grand

shower, TV and telephone, has a balcony or patio with garden or beach view. This is specially built for the conference trade and the rooms have a condominium look to them. Two pools, two floodlit tennis courts and a nine-hole pitch-and-putt course are among the amenities for guest use only. If I were attending a conference and someone else were picking up the tab I'd stay here. For a family with children, it has much to offer.

JENNY'S PLACE

PO Box 1742, St. George's

☎ 473-405-6073, fax 473-439-5186

www.jennysplacegrenada.com

US$100-$200 MC, Visa, Amex, Discover

Upon opening, a business tends to have a period of grace for a season or three; in this case the honeymoon should last for years to come.

On the northern end of Grand Anse beach, a new guest house – owned and run by Grenada's former Miss World, Jennifer Hosten, and her husband, Shaun – offers a high standard of personal service.

Four brightly furnished suites and one slightly more expensive apartment, each with air conditioning, ceiling fan, kitchenette, balcony, TV and DVD player. Continental breakfast included; the **Turning Point Diner** is right on the beach only yards away from the main building.

LALUNA

PO Box 1500, St. George's
☎ 473-439-0001, fax 473-439-0600
US toll free ☎ 1-866-4-LALUNA

www.laluna.com
US$301-$500 MC, Visa, Amex

As the manager of a rival hotel said, "Laluna, ahh, ze best!" Open since early 2001, it has quickly established itself as one of *the* places to stay. The 16 cottages and main buildings are built and furnished in Balinese style. Each room has its own plunge pool, four-poster bed, large deck and is air-conditioned. Among other luxuries are a remote-controled ceiling fan, TV/VCR, CD player and mini-bar. An Italian chef, who is a perfectionist, runs the restaurant. We recommend reserving rooms as early as possible since repeat bookings are rapidly filling the calendar; drawing the rich and famous, perhaps bored with Mustique, Laluna has almost exclusive use of a tiny bay, at the other end of which is the **Beach House Restaurant**. To get here from Morne Rouge, take the wonderfully named Old Leper Colony Road.

LEXUS INN

☎ 473-444-4780, fax 473-444-4779
lexus@spiceisle.com
Under US$100 MC, Visa

Situated on the busy Grand Anse Road, at first glance it looks uninviting. On inspection, the 19 rooms are basic but functional apartments with kitchens. Good snorkeling from the rocks below the inn. Randy Wilkinson is the local owner and manager. The only drawback is for those with a car; only three parking spaces are available.

Grenada

THE LODGE

PO Box 3540, St. George's
☎/fax 473-440-2330
www.thelodgegrenada.com, thelodge@spiceisland.com
US$100-$200 MC, Visa

The only exclusively Vegan establishment in the Caribbean, The Lodge requires a five-day minimum stay, including breakfast, three-course evening meal, and airport transfers. The Lodge can accommodate six people, has a 25-meter swimming pool and, from its perch atop Morne Jaloux, offers panoramic views over St. George's and neighboring areas.

View from the terrace, The Lodge

MARIPOSA BEACH RESORT

PO Box 1392, St. George's

☎ 473-444-3171, fax 473-444-3172

www.mariposaresort.com

US$100-$200 MC, Visa, Amex

On Morne Rouge Bay just above the Gem Holiday Beach Resort, 30 hotel rooms and 15 Mahogany Run self-catering apartments. The rooms are standard, along the lines of an airport or chain hotel, with air-conditioning, TV, telephone and mini-bar. The pool is one of the best we have seen on the island, and the beach is only a few minutes' walk. Mr. & Mrs. La Vera are charming hosts. For a mid-price establishment this is hard to beat.

ROYDON'S GUEST HOUSE

PO Box 1404, St. George's

☎/fax 473-444-4476

roydons@caribsurf.com

Under US$100 MC, Visa

Six rooms in the guest house, six apartments on the beach. Mrs. De Freitas is a lovely lady and, instead of upgrading the faded rooms of the original, she and her husband have built up-to-date apartments with kitchens a few hundred yards away on the beach. For those wishing to capture the at-home atmosphere of Roydon's, try the guest house. The rooms are on the small side and very plain, but they provide the authentic West Indian experience of dogs and chickens as the nocturnal soundtrack. Meals can be arranged for houseguests. A bus stop is right on the doorstep.

LAZY LAGOON TROPICAL COTTAGES

PO Box 1451, St. George's
☎/fax 473-444-5209
lazylagoon@spiceisle.com
Under US$100 MC, Visa

Bananaquit

Six rooms with shower and ceiling fan. It's described as having a "young and informal atmosphere for the independent traveler" – so informal indeed that when we went to check it out no member of staff was to be found. Another guest showed us the basic accommodations in these attractively painted lilac and yellow cabins. Theproperty is set back in a small garden off the Lagoon Road. The **Horny Baboon Restaurant & Bar** is also on-site.

SIESTA HOTEL

PO Box 27, St. George's
☎ 473-444-4646, fax 473-444-4647
www.siestahotel.com, siesta@spiceisle.com
US$100-$200 MC, Visa

Located on the Morne Rouge Road, with its own pool, although guests may use facilities at the Allamanda Beach Resort, a five-minute walk away. The hotel's 37 rooms have bath, shower, TV, telephone; some have air-conditioning.

SOUTH WINDS HOLIDAY COTTAGES & APARTMENTS

PO Box 118, St. George's
☎ 473-444-4310, fax 473-444-4404
www.southwindsgrenada.com, southwinds@spiceisle.com
Under US$100 MC, Visa

There are 14 air-conditioned one-bedroom apartments with kitchens, and five two-bedroom cottages. The owner has car rental offices at the airport and the Rex Grenadian. This is affordable for those wanting something long-term without a fuss.

SPICE ISLAND BEACH RESORT

PO Box 6, St. George's

☎ 473-444-4423, fax 473-444-4807

www.spicebeachresort.com, spiceisl@caribsurf.com

US$301-$500 MC, Visa, Amex, Diners, Discover

This is an all-inclusive (breakfast, lunch, afternoon tea, dinner and beverages, including house wine) resort on the beach. There are 64 air conditioned suites featuring whirlpool hot tub, shower, flat screen TV, DVD player, telephone with voice mail, Internet access and ceiling fan. Restaurant, bar, pool, business center, water sports, fitness center, bicycles, golf and tennis are among the amenities.

The hotel layout is pleasing without being monumental or grandiose. Elegant stores sell designer clothes at duty-free prices (bring your air ticket as proof that you'll be leaving), a beauty care center and spa complete the pampering.

Staff members are friendly without the dismissive haughtiness sometimes shown to walk-in visitors at other all-inclusives. After a US$10 million renovation, this is the jewel of Grand Anse, and we suppose the jewel is an emerald, since owner Sir Royston Hopkins is committed to eco-friendly tourism. With policies of least waste and recycling where possible, this green resort heads the way in responsible practices.

TROPICANA INN

☎ 473-440-1586, fax 473-440-9797

www.tropicanainn.com, tropicanainn@spiceisle.com

Under US$100 MC, Visa

Of all the budget places dotted about the Lagoon, this gets our vote. The modern block contains 20 rooms with shower and basic furnishing. It may lack the funky atmosphere of some of its neighbors, but it is clean and practical. The ground floor restaurant is well patronized by local people.

WAVE CREST HOLIDAY APARTMENTS

PO Box 278, St. George's

☎/fax 473-444-4116

wavecrest@caribsurf.com, www.grenadawavecrest.com

Under US$100 MC, Visa

Breakfast room, laundry and internet facility available. There are 22 air-conditioned apartments, equipped with kitchen, shower, TV, and telephone.

■ Point Salines, True Blue Bay, & Lance Aux Epines

CALABASH HOTEL

PO Box 382, St. George's

☎ 473-444-4334

fax 473-444-5050

www.calabashhotel.com, calabash@spiceisle.com

US$301-500 MC, Visa

The 30 air-conditioned suites have bath, shower, ceiling fan and most have a whirlpool tub. Wedding packages are available. This is a luxurious establishment set in eight acres of manicured garden on Prickly Bay, Lance Aux Epines. The suites are divided into units of four in duplex style. The beachside garden is tranquil, as the main activity areas are at the rear of the complex. These include a pool, massage center, tennis court and library. **ScubaTech** are the resident dive operators. Celebrity chef Gary Rhodes adds further class with **rhodes restaurant**, as swanky as any London eatery.

CORAL COVE COTTAGES & APARTMENTS

PO Box 487, St. George's

☎ 473-444-4422, fax 473-444-4718

www.coralcovecottages.com, coralcv@spiceisle.com

US$100-$200 MC, Visa, Amex

Eleven units with kitchen, shower, TV, telephone and ceiling fan, occupy a quiet location at the end of a residential road. It's three miles to the nearest shops and supermarkets. The beach is on the windward side of Lance Aux Epines peninsula; the sea has a seaweed floor. Large sea grape and almond trees provide ample shade. A pool, tennis court and snorkeling gear are available.

FOX INN

PO Box 205, St. George's

☎ 473-444-4123, fax 473-439-0524

foxinn@spiceisle.com

US$100-$200 MC, Visa

Having undergone a refit in preparation for the 2007 World Cup of Cricket, this functional property of 22 rooms is as adequate as any found in motel chains across North America. It's very handy for the airport and neighboring beaches.

Grenada

LANCE AUX EPINES COTTAGES

PO Box 1187, St. George's
☎ 473-444-4565, fax 473-444-2802
www.laecottages.com
US$100-$200 MC, Visa

Seven air-conditioned apartments and four cottages with shower, telephone and ceiling fan. Laundry, Internet, TV lounge, game room, kayaks and Hobie cat are available. Tim Braithwaite is the local owner of these cottages. His prices are fair and a great value if there are four people sharing. The cottages occupy a beach garden on Prickly Bay. This is the Hawaiian shirt, compared to next-door Calabash's jacket and tie.

LA SOURCE GRENADA

PO Box 852, St. George's
☎ 473-444-2556, fax 473-444-2561
lasource@caribsurf.com, www.lasourcegrenada.com
US$201-$300 All-inclusive MC, Visa

With 100 air-conditioned rooms, all meals and bar drinks included, you don't have to leave the confines of the resort until you leave Grenada. You can dive, snorkel, play tennis, golf, go to the gym, have a massage, even take an archery or fencing lesson. How about water-skiing, sailing, windsurfing, or volleyball? Classes are given in yoga, Tai Chi and meditation. Every-

thing you could possibly want to busily relax. This is very popular with charter companies, and runs at 75% capacity in the off-season.

MACA BANA VILLAS

St. George's

☎/fax 473-439-5355

www.macabana.com, macabana@spiceisle.com

Over US$500 MC, Visa

Located on the hillside above the Aquarium Restaurant, five two-bedroom and two one-bedroom villas with air-conditioning, fully equipped kitchens, en suite bathrooms, and external hot tubs. A lot of thought has gone into these accommodations, with rustic balconies and decorative murals; you'll want to befriend guests of the other villas to inspect the artwork gracing their walls. Views over the southeast coast of the island are even better from the infinity-edge swimming pool. Their spa treatments, art and cookery lessons prove that tourism thrives on diversity as much as standardization.

MONMOT HOTEL

Saman Drive, Lance Aux Epines

☎ 473-439-3408

www.monmothotel.com, monmothotel@spiceisle.com

US$100-$200 MC, Visa, Amex

Twenty studios and suites form three sides around a communal pool, the fourth side is Gath's Restaurant. The opposite wing has two tower rooms and the place has the look of a Roman villa. Rooms have bath/showers, kitchenettes, and TV. In-room spa and beauty treatments, massage and reflexology are on offer should you wish to pamper yourself.

MOUNT HARTMAN BAY ESTATE

St. George's

☎/fax 473-444-4504

www.mounthartmanbay.com

Over US$500

MC, Visa

A peculiar dwelling built into the cliff-face on a private peninsula, having a grass covered roof and internal water-falls. The house, in early troglodyte architecture, was intended as the retirement home of a British carpet manufacturer. Sadly, he died shortly after completion. The current owner has created a dream vacation venue. Groups of eight persons minimum are required in winter season. Two 4x4 SUVs, a 43-foot twin-engine cabin cruiser and other motorized toys are part of the all-inclusive package. A helipad indicates this is for the affluent, or 22 people that can share the cost. Seven suites are in the main house, a further four in the beach house close by.

REX GRENADIAN

PO Box 893, St. George's

☎ 473-444-3333, fax 473-444-1111

www.rexcaribbean.com, grenrex@caribsurf.com

US$201-$300 MC, Visa

A palatial resort close to the airport, with 212 rooms, it embraces the full range of watersports, tennis, business services and gift shops. Obviously built with the conference trade and incentives in mind. There seems to be a class of people who aspire to the jet set and like to stay in inordinately large hotels with high prices. You will find them here.

SECRET HARBOUR RESORT

PO Box 11, St. George's

☎ 473-444-4439, fax 473-444-4819

www.secretharbour.com, secretharbour@
caribbeanhighlights.com

US$201-$300 MC, Visa

The 20 air-conditioned suites have extra large bathrooms, two four-poster beds, a comfortable lounge area and decks overlooking Mount Hartmann Bay. Windsurfing, kayaking, tennis and a swimming pool are among the amenities. The main building and restaurant are attractive, and a friendly atmosphere accompanies good food.

TRUE BLUE BAY RESORT

PO Box 1414, St. George's

☎ 473-443-8783, fax 473-444-5929

www.truebluebay.com

US$201-$300 MC, Visa

With an all-inclusive resort, you can be forgiven for not straying outside the complex, but you might feel as though you haven't experienced much of the country. True Blue is one place you could stay without doing injustice to the rest of the island, although this isn't an all-inclusive as such. In addition to the gamut of water and land-based activities, there are 38 modern accommodations of different types to

Grenada

suit all guests, whether they are individuals, self-caterers or families. Emphasis is on Caribbean and Mexican cuisine in the restaurant; considered one of the top three in Grenada, its menu is reasonably priced. The **Dodgy Dock** bar is an easy-going venue on the jetty; True Blue is also where the **Moorings** yacht chartering organization has its base on the island. **Aquanauts** are the resident scuba operators; **Indigo Car Rental** has an office on-site. Russ and Magdalena Fielden and their two daughters run True Blue and are happy to make you feel part of their extended family. Children are especially welcome and the ballet classes are an added bonus.

TWELVE DEGREES NORTH

PO Box 241, St. George's
☎/fax 473-444-4580
www.twelvedegreesnorth.com, 12degrsn@caribsurf.com
US$201-$300 MC, Visa

Joseph Gaylord came to Grenada and built this retreat in 1966. A friend with a sextant discovered that the 12° North line of latitude runs straight through the swimming pool, hence the name. There are six one-bedroom and two two-bedroom apartments, each with shower and ceiling fan. Each has its own housekeeper from breakfast until 3 pm, doing the cooking, cleaning, and laundry. Groceries for the week are at an additional cost (about US$100), but some provisions may be returned; given advance warning the management will try to obtain specially requested items. Evening meals can be prepared by the housekeeper for guests to reheat, and several fine restaurants are within walking distance. The shaded garden contains a pool, decks, lounge chairs and hammocks. Tennis, kayaks, Sunfish sailboats and snorkeling gear are for guest use on what is seemingly a private beach. Fishing trips can be arranged on a private boat. There is a maximum of 20 guests and no children under 16 years are allowed. 12° North has its faithful returnees so it can be difficult to find a room in high season.

Joe and his wife Pat are keen historians and on their travels around the island have amassed a collection of Amerindian stone carvings and remains that would put many museums to shame. Joe found some animal bones deep in the cliff next to the property; after carbon dating, they were found to be a species of capybara over three million years old! The bones are the basis of a paper by the American Natural History Museum putting forward a theory that at some time Grenada was joined to the South American continent, and the new species bears the name Hydrochaeris gaylordii in honor of the discoverer.

■ The Southeast

BEL AIR PLANTATION

St. David's

☎ 473-444-6305, fax 473-444-6316

www.belairplantation.com

US$301-$500 MC, Visa, Amex

This hot upscale property has set a standard by which others will be judged. Susan Fisher and her husband, Yves, have painstakingly designed their creation down to the last detail. The **Water's Edge Restaurant & Bar** draws many patrons from establishments island-wide. Above, the clubroom atmosphere of **Bay View Lounge,** which has board games to supplement the beau-

tiful view. A grocery market, gift shop and **Blue Ginger Spa** add to the eclectic nature of the place. The accommodations are spread around 18 acres amid orchards and gardens, blending into the terrain, and lending a village atmosphere. There are 11 air-conditioned villas and cottages with ceiling fans, phone, cable TV, and CD players. All have plush furnishings, unique artwork and tropical plants. Arriving guests will find their kitchens stocked with tea and coffee, cheese, crackers and fruit. Daily maid service is provided. Snorkel gear and kayaks are at hand, although one of Bel Air's maxim is "Set your own pace," so don't be surprised if you end up lounging by the plantation's pool.

CABIER OCEAN LODGE

Crochu PO, St. Andrew's
☎/fax 473-444-6013
www.cabier.com
Under US$100 MC, Visa

Nine rooms with shower, some have ceiling fan. Originally meant as a retreat for artists and for alternative healing, this wonderful place is now open to all comers. The wooden cabins have minimal clutter, with no pictures on the walls to disturb meditation. The beds are very comfortable, with walk-in mosquito nets. The dirt road from Crochu is very uneven and may deter you from making the trip every day in a vehicle. Still, this keeps out casual visitors and insulates guests from the hurly-burly. Bring some books, a guitar, an easel and canvas, your dancing shoes... whatever stirs your soul. The restaurant serves breakfast at US$7 and dinner at US$16 per person.

EPPING PLANTATION HOUSE

PO Box 2669, St. Paul's

☎ 473-440-3333

www.grenadaguesthouse.com

Under US$100

No credit cards

Dave and Jackie Kennedy have converted an old plantation house into an intimate bed and breakfast set in three acres of lush gardens.

The three rooms – one suite comprises two rooms with a connecting bathroom – have ceiling fan and shower, and are decorated in the height of Victorian charm. An inland location ensures peace and privacy, while the hustle of town and beach life is only a bus-ride away. Guests are invited to share the swimming pool or pick fruit in the garden of this Eden-like setting.

LA SAGESSE NATURE CENTRE

PO Box 44, St. George's

☎/fax 473-444-6458

www.lasagesse.com

lsnature@caribsurf.com

US$100-$200 MC, Visa

Twelve rooms with bath or shower, ceiling fan and screened windows. Beach chairs and some non-motorized watersports equipment available. The location couldn't be better:

Set on the beach in a secluded bay, it attracts day visitors, and many locals flock to the bay on weekends. The recent addition of a faux sugar mill to house the main office certainly adds to the plantation feel of the place.

PARADISE BAY VILLA RESORT

La Tante, St. David's
☎ 473-405-8888
www.paradisebayresort.net
US$201-$300 MC, Visa

Nine villas situated on a promontory 85 feet above two secluded beaches, La Tante and St. Pierre. Each villa has both a room and a suite with bathrooms, TV, CD/DVD players and refrigerator. The higher priced villas have a fully-equipped kitchenette and a Jacuzzi (whirlpool) on the balcony. As with other properties in this area of the island, you're tempted to get away from it all and keep it that way for the duration. Sea and land sports (even archery!) are at hand, and hungry toxophilites can score a bull's eye at the Aloe Vera restaurant.

PETIT BACAYE COTTAGE HOTEL

PO Box 655, Westerhall Post Office, St. David's

☎/fax 473-443-2902

www.petitbacaye.com

hideaways@wellowmead.u-net.com

US$100-$200 MC, Visa

These six cottages are set in an ever-evolving garden on the beach. Peter Pilbrow and his partner, Julia Montgomery, first stayed here in the 1990s and made an offer to the then-owner on their fourth evening. You can tell they love working the place as much as they did when just visiting. Constant improvements and tinkering ensure that standards will be kept while they are at the helm. Among the jewels to be found are the chef, the hike from here to La Sagesse Bay, and a nearby beach that receives hardly any other visitors.

■ The Leeward Coast

SUNSET VIEW RESTAURANT & BEACH HOUSE

Grand Mal, St. George's

☎ 473-440-5758, fax 473-440-7001

www.tropicanainn.com

tropicanainn@spiceisle.com

Under US$100 MC, Visa

Located a few miles north of St. George's on a quiet beach at Grand Mal, this is a budget getaway. Run by the same team as the Tropicana Inn, these clean and simple air-conditioned rooms have shower and balcony.

VICTORIA HOTEL

Victoria, St. Mark's

☎ 473-444-9367, fax 473-444-8104

Under US$100 MC, Visa

Five single and five double rooms, with shower and TV. If you plan to make a leisurely tour of the island, this is a great place to break your journey. Only a few miles north of Gouyave, which is a big city in comparison. Victoria is the perfect base if you want to visit the nutmeg processing station in Gouyave, the Dougaldston estate, or hike up to the Tufton Hall waterfall. The people of Victoria seem friendlier and more laid-back than their neighbors to the south. Mr. & Mrs. Fletcher and their staff are warm and hospitable. Our dinner was of mammoth proportions and cost only EC$20, the breakfast of bacon and eggs only EC$13.50.

■ The North & Windward Coast

ALMOST PARADISE COTTAGES

Sauteurs

☎ 473-442-0608

www.almost-paradise-grenada.com

a.p.grenada@lycos.com

Under US$100 MC, Visa

Four colorful cottages sleep two to four people. Each has a large balcony, kitchenette, toilet, and private outdoor shower. Two other rooms available. Establishment is run by Kate, a Canadian, and her husband Uwe, from Germany.

GRENADA RAINBOW INN

PO Box 923, Grenville, St. Andrew's

☎ 473-442-7714, fax 473-442-5332

rainbowinn@spiceisle.com

Under US$100 MC, Visa

Ten rooms with shower and balcony, about a mile inland from Grenville and close to a gas station. It has been managed since the 1970s by Neitha Williams, known to all as "Aunty Nits," who is renowned for her delicious cooking. The Rainbow Inn has won awards in the tourism industry over the past 10 years.

MORNE FENDUE PLANTATION HOUSE

St. Patrick's

☎ 473-442-9294, fax 473-442-9888

caribbean@spiceisle.com

Under US$100 MC, Visa

Eight new rooms have been added to this delightful old plantation residence. The main house dates from the early 1900s and was for many years the home of Nurse Betty Mascoll. The late Princess Margaret stayed here in the 1950s. It is often included as a lunch stop by tour companies and taxi drivers.

Morne Fendue Plantation House
(Grenada Board of Tourism)

Breakfast and dinner is served to overnight guests. Owner Dr. Jean Thompson is a delightful hostess and the gardens reflect her charm.

SAM'S INN

Dunfermline, St. Andrew's

☎ 809-442-7313, fax 809-442-7853

Under US$100

Sixteen air conditioned rooms with restaurant and bar on the premises. The inn is popular with school groups.

We have tried to inspect and list as many places to stay as Grenada has to offer. There are some deliberate omissions, while others may be inaccessible due to renovation after hurricane damage. If you find a place you feel worthy of inclusion, please let us know.

After Dark

For an island not particularly known for its nightlife, there's every excuse here to sit back and do nothing when the sun goes down. However, nocturnal entertainment can be found at the southern end of Grenada.

Fantazia Night Club on Morne Rouge Bay has a local clientele and reggae bands regularly. The **Aquarium Restaurant's** huge speakers aren't just for decoration; it's a spot that can really rock.

At **Flamboyant's Owl Sports Bar**, weekly crab races and steelbands are as entertaining as the wide world of screen sports. **True Blue Bay Resort** also has live music on a couple of evenings every week. Most of the larger hotels have some sort of music night; reggae night might be Thursday this season, but could just as well be Tuesday the next.

Bananas Restaurant and Nightclub has taken off as the latest hot spot on the island. It's certainly filled with enthusiastic partygoers at weekends.

Still not satisfied? Find the nearest rum shop and join the boys at the bar for some serious white rum and laughter.

Grenada's Grenadines

History

You may wonder why some Grenadines belong to St. Vincent and others belong to Grenada. The answer lies in the 1700s and Britain's attempt to keep hold of her empire.

When the British gained control in 1763, all of the Grenadines south of St. Vincent were put under the charge of Grenada. Ten years later, raiding parties by American privateers presented a real threat. In some instances,

the Americans would land by night and supply arms to the local Caribs. William Leybourne, Governor-in-Chief of what were then called the Southern Caribbee Islands, protested to London that St. Vincent should have a separate governor.

Appointed to the post was gentleman planter, Valentine Morris. He arrived in 1774, as the Boston Tea Party was occurring in Massachusetts and Leybourne lay on his deathbed. Within three years, Governor Morris wrote to the Admiralty in London making a request that the small islands of Bequia, Balliceaux, Mustique and Canouan be annexed to St. Vincent. This was granted just in time, as the French recaptured Grenada in 1779.

 Four years on and Britain had control of Grenada again. A bureaucratic nightmare was wrinkling the brows of the French and British planters by this time. Finally, in 1791, the Admiralty made a division between the two territories. Based upon latitude, they drew a line on the map giving St. Vincent the lion's share of the Grenadines. Only **Carriacou** and **Petite Martinique** ended up belonging to Grenada, but the boundary ran across the northernmost tips of both islands. That is why, even today, the area on Carriacou known as Gun Point and the headland on Petite Martinique known as the Breeza belong to St. Vincent.

Carriacou

■ Orientation

View of Bay, Carriacou (Grenada Board of Tourism)

Carriacou is 34 nautical miles north of Grenada. The island is seven miles long by three miles wide and covers about 13 square miles, making it the largest of all the Grenadines. Crossing from St. George's takes 90 minutes. Hillsborough is the only town on either Carriacou or Petite Martinique. The island population numbers around 7,000, and you'll find several restaurants and shops, two banks, a bakery, a post office and a heap of rum shops. Main Street runs parallel to the beach and gets about as much traffic. Need a water taxi? There will always be a few

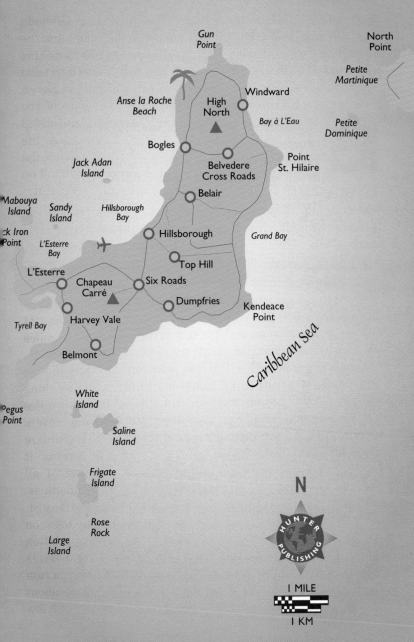

Carriacou

Gun Point

North Point

Petite Martinique

Windward

Anse la Roche Beach

High North

Bay à L'Eau

Petite Dominique

Bogles

Belvedere Cross Roads

Point St. Hilaire

Jack Adan Island

Belair

Mabouya Island

Sandy Island

Hillsborough Bay

ck Iron Point

L'Esterre Bay

Hillsborough

Grand Bay

Top Hill

L'Esterre

Chapeau Carré

Six Roads

Dumpfries

Kendeace Point

Tyrell Bay

Harvey Vale

Belmont

Caribbean Sea

Pegus Point

White Island

Saline Island

Frigate Island

N

Rose Rock

Large Island

HUNTER PUBLISHING

1 MILE

1 KM

men waiting along the jetty to carry you away in their brightly painted speedboats.

Carriacou is much hotter and drier than Grenada, and lacks the lush vegetation. The highest points on the island are connected by a wooded ridge. High North reaches 955 feet above sea level and Chapeau Carre only one foot less. Despite its size, you can explore in a number of ways: on foot, by mountain bike, by bus, taxi or rental car or by boat.

 The earliest records date from 1656 in the documents of a Dominican missionary, Jean Baptisite du Tetre. Du Tetre lived with the Caribs on Dominica for 25 years and, fortunately for history, he traveled the Windwards. At that time Carriacou was referred to by the Carib name, "Kayryouacou," believed to mean "island surrounded by reefs." It was shortened to its present name in the early 1700s.

Du Tetre noted that French turtle farmers were habitual visitors. Before too long, the first permanent European settlers arrived from Guadeloupe, after their plantations had been destroyed by ants. They brought with them Carriacou's first slaves, numbering around 1,200, and cultivated cotton. Much of the early information on all these islands came from the journals of missionaries. The first priest on Carriacou, Father Maisonneuve, wrote in 1771 that his 12 acres and 10 slaves produced 3,000 pounds of cotton. Around that time there were 50 proprietors living on Carriacou and eight on Petite Martinique. A contemporary census reported 107 whites on the island and 3,046 slaves.

 In 1781, the first Catholic Church was built, but was in ruins 12 years later. Here again the priest is the source of information. Father Guis owned 19 slaves and one white servant. He had five acres in Hillsborough and another 16 acres at Bay-à-l'Eeau on the windward side. He recorded that in the year the church was lost this little island produced 967,800 pounds of cotton, and its tiny neighbor, Petite Martinique, brought in an astronomical 30,224 pounds.

Alongside the Carib and African, three European cultures have helped shape Carriacou. L'Esterre is as much French as Hillsborough is English. However, with names like Craigston, Bogles and Dumfries, the Scottish influence is evident. Two hundred years ago, Carriacou had the largest concentration of Scottish residents, planters and shipwrights of any island in the whole of the Caribbean.

■ Festivals

February

Carnival and **Shakespeare Mas**. Carnival on Carriacou starts in mid-February at midnight with drumming. While every island's Carnival has its own personality, Carriacou's distinctive feature is its Shakespeare Mas. Partici-

Dancers, Carriacou
(Grenada Board of Tourism)

pants dress as pierrots and recite Shakespearean verses. If they forget their lines, they are beaten in a slapstick manner. The event can be quite competitive and on occasions the local police have had to step in.

April

Kite flying competition. For one weekend near Easter the sky is filled with the bright colors of kites. Anyone can join in with stunt kites or an artistic design of their own.

Maroon Music Festival & Big Drum Nation Dance. Celebrated at the end of April. Three drums are tied together; two bass drums with a treble in-between and played by open palms. Drumming was a method of communication between slaves on different estates, and outlawed by the planters. Now held at Belair Estate as a heritage celebration.

August

Carriacou Regatta. Beginning of August. Begun in the 1960s as a way of reviving local boat building skills; nowadays, the races draw entrants from all over the Grenadines and plenty of partying is guaranteed. For more information on how to take part, ☎ 473-443-7930.

December

Parang Festival. Held the weekend before Christmas, this is a 1977 revival of the traditional house-tohouse serenading by string bands. Friday night opens with comedians and the song competition (with a

Quadrille Dancing

first prize of EC$2,400). Songs are political, historical and sometimes hysterical. The weekend is filled with contests for brass bands and string bands. **Quadrille dancing** and **Big Drum dancing** mean sore feet for some. The festivities come to a climax with the appearance of Santa Claus himself.

■ Getting Here

By Air

It is possible to fly from Grenada into Lauriston Airport, Carriacou, via **SVG Air**, **TIA** and **Mustique Airways**. The daily 20-minute flight costs approximately US$70 per person round-trip on SVG Air. TIA and Air Mustique are charter airlines, so you need to make arrangements with them directly. Flights can be booked from Bequia, Canouan and Union islands into Carriacou and Grenada; services generally originate in St. Vincent. You can contact Lauriston Airport in Carriacou at ☎ 473-443-7362 or 473-443-6677. Inter-island tickets can be purchased at John's Print Shop, Main Street in Hillsborough, or ☎ 473-443-8207.

Airlines Serving Carriacou	
Mustique Airways	☎ 784-458-4380, fax 784-456-4586, reservations in the USA, ☎ 800-526-4789, fax 717-595-8869, www.mustique.com
SVG Air	☎ 784-457-5124, 784-457-5777, fax 784-457-5077, www.svgair.com
TIA	☎ 784-485-8306, 246-418-1654 (in Barbados), fax 246-428-0916

By Sea

The most common method of reaching Carriacou is by ferry.

The *Osprey Express* takes 1½ hours from St. George's.

The *Jasper*, a wooden schooner, leaves Ashton, Union Island, on Monday and Thursday at 6:00 am, arriving at Carriacou one hour later. The fare is

EC$20 and you need to pass through Customs and Immigration before boarding.

If you want to travel up the chain of Grenadines and do it cheaply, the ***Barracuda*** is an old cargo transport that covers the route three times every week. If the seas aren't too rough and you're feeling adventurous, this is a true island experience, complete with chickens, goats and refrigerators. Take a water taxi from Carriacou to Union to meet the boat, but check under Union Island information (see pages 242-243) for the schedules.

■ Police, Immigration & Medical Services

 Police and Immigration are at the end of the jetty in Hillsborough, ☎ 473-443-7482. For emergencies dial 911.

Hillsborough Health Centre, ☎ 473-443-7280. **Princess Royal Hospital**, Top Hill, ☎ 473-443-7400. For an **ambulance**, dial 774.

Emergencies at sea are reported to the Coastguard at ☎ 399.

■ Yacht Services

 Tyrrel Bay Yacht Haulout supplies fuel, oil, water, chandlery and repairs, ☎/fax 473-443-8175, tbhy@usa.net, or by radio on VHF channel16.

Windward Marine is next door to Tyrrel Bay haulout and has a location in Windward. Contact Billy Bones, Tyrrel Bay, ☎ 473-443-8500, fax 473-443-6992; Windward, ☎ 473-443-8756.

■ Tour Operators

Big island or small island, on your first visit you can lose your bearings or miss out on important things to see and do. Take a couple of hours for a guided tour by land or on water. It gives you an overview of places and things you might want to go into at greater depth.

For land tours, contact the **Carriacou Owners and Drivers Association**, ☎ 473-443-7386, VHF channel 16. The set rate for a 2½-hour tour is EC$180.

For sea excursions, Brian Fletcher has a 40-foot Morgan sloop, *Cinderella*, on which he gives day or overnight tours of the Grenadines, ☎ 473-443-7277, fax 473-443-7165.

Reggie Haemer and Captain Bubb have a 41-foot Morgan ketch, *Chaika*, ☎ 473-443-8468, or 473-443-7752.

Carl McLawrence and his sloop, *Good Expectation III*, are ready to sail when you are; ☎ 473-443-7505.

For water taxis to Petite Martinique or Union, Island call **Snaggs**, ☎ 473-443-8923, VHF channel 16; or **Scooby**, ☎ 473-443-6622.

> *Carry a long-sleeved shirt and pants when sailing. The air is noticeably cooler as the sun sinks and, if you're sunburned from the day, you'll feel a chill.*

■ Car Rental

We tried two rentals on Carriacou, both in Hillsborough.

Martin & Wayne Jeep Rental, ☎ 473-443-7204. The Bullen brothers provide insurance with their rental agreements. They also own Carriacou's only gas station. We took a car back with a little steering problem; within 15 minutes it was fixed and we were back on the road.

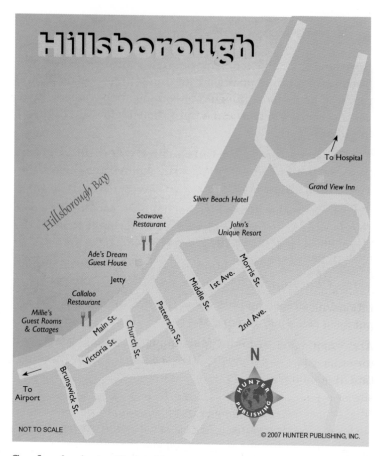

Sunkey's Auto Rentals, ☎ 473-443-8382, sunkeywp@yahoo.com, gave us no problems with the hire, use and return of the car. Insurance was not an option in the rental agreement, however. Sometimes you just have to trust.

Barba's Auto Rentals is in Tyrrel Bay and convenient for yachties. ☎/fax 473-443-7454.

■ Bike Rental

Try **Wild Track Cycles** in Hermitage, Tyrrel Bay, ☎ 473-443-6472.

■ Exploring

The roads criss-crossing the island can be credited to early French settlers. Supposedly, they hauled cannon from one side to the other, depending upon which direction British ships were approaching from. Today, these old roads make for good hiking and are well shaded by a canopy of old-growth vegetation.

Start at the **Tourism Office** in Hillsborough to obtain a map. You'll need one, whatever mode of transport you choose. Across the street is the **Carriacou Historical Society Museum**. This is privately owned and houses artifacts from Amerindian culture, through the sugar and cotton period, to modern paintings and writings by local artists. Hillsborough does have the remains of a botanical garden, but Hurricane Janet stole most of it. Adding insult to injury, mealy bug infestation took a terrible toll in 1999; only now is it beginning to be put back into shape.

At the southern end of town is the **Anglican Church**. The rectory was originally part of the great house of Beausejour Estate. It is sometimes called "The Fort," as it once had been the site of a fortification. A half-buried cannon can be found in what is now the cemetery. Again, Hurricane Janet is responsible for extensive damage to the building.

The village of L'Esterre is the former home and studio of Carriacou's treasured folk artist, **Canute Calliste**. If you would like to see a collection of his paintings, stop in at the Carriacou Museum, where his daughter works.

CANUTE CALLISTE

We had heard of Carriacou's folk artist, Canute Calliste, and seen his paintings scattered throughout the Grenadines. On reaching this island, it became part of our mission to understand what made him tick. Sure, we could have just bought one of his works and then gone to the beach, but in the spirit of adventure we sought him out and touched base with a legend.

Canute, or "CC" as he was known locally, was nearly ninety years old and robustly guarded by his daughter, Clemencia Alexander. Her loving protectiveness of her father made us instant friends. Under her watchful eyes, tourists and journalists were permitted or denied access to her father for interviews and possible exploitation of his paintings.

At the age of nine in Tyrrel Bay, so the story goes, he was visited by a mermaid, who sent him scurrying home to his mother. He never went to school again and so never learned to read or write. Painting became his means of expression, and he considered it a gift from God.

With the colors from dime-store acrylic paints, he conjured up images of Carriacou culture. The mermaid quickly emerged as his signature. Her hair changes, as do her movements and expression, but she is there, as if leading Canute through the world of the enchanted. He captured the essence of peoples uprooted from both Scotland and Africa, then melded on this spit of land by sugar, cotton, rum, and seafaring.

Canute said he could turn his hand to almost anything. He had built boats, his home, had been a fisherman, and was a selftaught fiddle player and painter. He fathered 22 children and has countless grandchildren. What he excelled in was building a story of his country's past through paintings.

While we visited we asked who lettered and titled the paintings. He replied that his wife had done so, but she had passed away the previous year. Clemencia told us he hadn't painted for several months, yet had started again that very week. Perhaps he had shed his veil of mourning, or the mermaid had woken his tired eyes and once more guided his hands to the brush. Over three days, he completed 17 paintings and continued to work during our visit.

He painted on scratchboard, primed with white. His work is primitive and childlike. It depicts boat blessing, the blessing of the fishing fleet, weddings, mermaids, carnival, regatta, invasion, and the Jab-lesse (the devil). It brought him international recognition as an artist and he even went to Buckingham Palace to play his fiddle for the Queen.

His paintings sell in the region of US$300. Clemencia collected as many as possible on film as a catalog of his work. Now he is gone, two of his grandchildren have heeded the call of visual expression. They show a similarity of style to Canute, but their world is one of cars, television, speedboats and technology. Only from Canute Calliste can we learn what the merfolk or people of the sea and the people of Carriacou have held sacred for generations.

There is talk of reproducing some of his work as prints. For now the only reproductions are postcards on sale at the Carriacou Museum and giftshops in St. George's.

Harvey Vale and **Tyrrel Bay** are basically one and the same; the Vale is the land and the Bay is the water. This is a preferred mooring area for yachties. Divers hunker down here as well. It is a calm and safe harbor to wait out the battering of hurricane season. There are several bars and eateries along the strip; at the far end is the boatyard for marine repair. Next door, the **Carriacou Yacht Club** has a restaurant and one of the few laundry facilities on the island. Forty feet from the shore on Harvey Vale is an **Amerindian well**. The mineral water is reportedly good for the health. It is purported to be an intensive internal cleanser. It's wise to avoid taking the cure before climbing into a small aircraft or boarding any sea-going vessel. Beware the curse of the Carib!

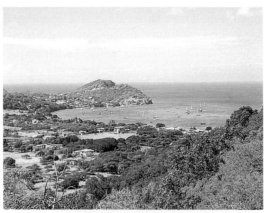
Tyrrell Bay

Continue on to **Belmont** and up to **Six Roads**. You can then hike the road up to **Chapeau Carre** for views at 954 feet above sea level. Or take the road down past the island's land-fill dump (not as bad as it sounds) to the old estate of **Dumfries** and the **beach of Sabazan**.

The Bells, from Dumfries, Scotland, were among the first owners of the estate and its mill. Records from 1792 show a ship's doctor, John Bell, arriving and buying the estate. There is an unidentified Bell listed as buried on the property. A brick chimney sticks up above a canopy of trees as if trying to break free of the undergrowth. On closer inspection, the old sugar mill is full of equipment in disarray. After sugaring, the mill was used for distilling lime oil.

On the east coast lies the village of **Windward**. Here live the descendants of Scottish shipwrights. The tradition of boat building began to die out when fast speedboats came onto the scene. Fortunately, this honorable trade was revived in the 1960s when retired yacht designer, Linton Rigg, took up residence on the island.

The Princess Royal Hospital sits majestically on the central ridge of Carriacou known as **Top Hill**. This is a great vantage point for viewing the Grenadines and escaping the heat. Close by are the windmills and ruins of **Belair Estate**, now a National Park.

Beaches

 All the beaches on Carriacou are public. Remember that the windward side of the island is going to be rougher than the leeward; its a case of Atlantic Ocean versus Caribbean Sea. A surfer would choose the windward, a snorkeler the leeward.

The beach at **Hillsborough** is long and white, with enough going on to provide gentle distraction if you aren't an earnest sunbather. To the south, **L'Esterre** beach is more secluded and shady, with one restaurant and beach bar. To the north is the very secluded and beautiful **Anse La Roche Bay**. Take a water taxi from town or a bus to Bogles and then hike down past the Kido Ecological Station. **Windward** also has a good beach with a spectacular view of Petite Martinique and Petite Dominique.

If you are looking for the Robinson Crusoe experience, hire a water taxi to take you to **Sandy Island**, just west of Hillsborough Bay. This is the perfect tropical islet that we all fantasize about, with a scattering of coconut trees and a coral garden surrounding its aquamarine waters. Be aware of the fragility of both islet and reef. Many boaters have dragged anchors through the coral and storms play havoc with the trees. Be sure you have an ample supply of bottled water, snacks and sunscreen; and what you pack in, pack out.

Any of the water taxis along the jetty will be happy to arrange a drop-off and pick-up service. Agree on the price before you go.

White Island is a pristine islet with a coral reef. If somebody beat you to Sandy Island, then try here. It lies off the south-west corner of Carriacou and is best reached by water taxi out of Tyrrel Bay.

View of White Island

KICK 'EM JENNY

Kick 'Em Jenny is a submarine volcano northwest of Grenada near a small group of cays known as The Sisters. Older maps refer to this area as Diamond Island or *Ile Diamente*. Another French description in use was *Cay Que Gen*, meaning "the island that shakes."

You can't see it, but it's there, rising 1,000 feet off the ocean floor. In 1962 it was 762 feet below sea level and the following year it was only 630 feet below the surface.

In July 1939 the first eruption of Kick 'Em Jenny was reported from Sauteurs. It took place over a 24-hour period and sent rocks, water and smoke into the air to a height of 150 feet. The eruption caused earthquakes, lightning and tsunamis or seismic sea waves along Grenada and the Grenadines. A tsunami washed as far eastwards as Barbados, covering its western road. A second eruption, six hours later, sent vapor clouds billowing up 1,800 feet above sea level.

Since 1939, 10 eruptions have been recorded by seismographs. In June 1974, eruptions were seen above the surface and in March 1990, the sea boiled turbulently around the summit of the volcano. The volcano is blamed for turning fish belly-up in Levera Pond during 1996. This is most probably what experts call "variations in fumarolic activity."

Kick 'Em Jenny is monitored from Sauteurs and, like other active volcanic areas in the Caribbean, alerts are issued when there is cause for concern.

■ Scuba Diving

The dive sites off Carriacou are used by dive operators on Grenada as well. There is usually a small surcharge for the transportation, but then Carriacou's dive operators charge a little more than their competitors on the big island. It doesn't make much difference financially which island you make as your dive base.

 Sandy Island has an extensive reef to a depth of 70 feet, with many fish, sea turtles and lobsters. **Jack Iron Point** is good for beginners, with a reef populated by turtles and rays. A small wreck of a tugboat lies 30 feet down off **Maybouya Island**, near Hillsborough Bay, with eels and rays. **Pago Das Garden** by Frigate Island provides a good depth for beginners at between 40 and 80 feet.

Experienced divers will enjoy **Sister Rocks** to a depth of 100 feet. The similarly named, but more spectacular **Two Sisters of Ronde Island** goes down to 180 feet and has an abundance of coral and marine life.

Average Prices for Diving	
One-tank dive	US$40-$50
Two-tank dive	US$75-$95
One-day Discover Scuba	US$75-$90
Four dives + certification	US$220-$270

Prices differ for longer courses, specialized courses and night diving.

Dive Shops

ARAWAK DIVERS
Tyrrel Bay
☎ 473-443-6906
www.arawak.de

CARRIACOU SILVER DIVING LTD.
Main Street, Hillsborough
☎ 473-443-7882
www.scubamax.com

■ Where to Eat

It's a small island, but there are plenty of choices for a good meal. Most hotels offer dining of some kind, whether it is limited to their overnight guests or open to the public.

Restaurant Directory

BOGLES ROUNDHOUSE, Bogles, ☎ 473-443-7841
CALLALOO BY THE SEA RESTAURANT & BAR, Hillsborough, ☎ 473-443-8004
GREEN ROOF INN, Hillsborough, ☎ 473-443-6399
JOHN'S UNIQUE RESORT, Hillsborough, ☎ 473-443-8345
SEAWAVE RESTAURANT, Hillsborough
SILVER BEACH HOTEL, Hillsborough, ☎ 473-443-7337

BOGLES ROUNDHOUSE
Bogles
☎ 473-443-7841
US$26-$35 MC, Visa

Superb food in new-age surroundings. Dinner reservations are required in advance, in the morning at the latest, as ingredients are bought fresh that day. The manager prepares a feast, so come hungry. An excellent place to celebrate that special occasion – a birthday, an anniversary, a proposal.

CALLALOO BY THE SEA RESTAURANT & BAR

AUTHOR
PICK

Hillsborough
☎ 473-443-8004
US$15-$25 MC, Visa
Monday to Saturday, 10 am-10 pm.

The best deal on the island. The lunch was so good we had to go back for dinner, and then cocktails the next day. The seafood selection of lobster, lambi or grilled fish is a delight. Try the Dumfries cocktail for a taste tingle. A banana smoothie at EC$8 should cool the most fevered brow. Reservations are required for dinner in high season.

GREEN ROOF INN
Hillsborough
☎ 473-443-6399

US$15-$25

The Swedish chef prepares local dishes with a heavy accent on seafood. In high season it gets busy in this intimate setting, so reservations are required. Dinner is not available in off-season.

JOHN'S UNIQUE RESORT
Hillsborough
☎ 473-443-8345
US$15-$25
Daily, 7 am-midnight

A bit of a mixed bag, this one. The rice and peas were edible, but the fish we had was not. The waitstaff had a "don't care" attitude, but then the owner was off the island. We'd be happy to hear any reports to the contrary.

SEAWAVE RESTAURANT
Hillsborough
Opposite Ade's Dream Guest House
Under US$15
Daily, 7 am-9 pm

Small restaurant with local food at low prices. Good place for a light snack and cooling drinks.

Hillsborough Beach

SILVER BEACH HOTEL

Hillsborough

☎ 473-443-7337

US$15-$25 MC, Visa

Very pleasant. We were made to feel as if we were the only people on the island. The day menu is light but filling. Rotis and fish cakes make a tasty lunch. The Shipwreck Bar serves potent piña coladas. Situated on the beach. You could sit here all day.

Silver Beach Hotel

■ Where to Stay

Carriacou is big enough to have a wide choice of accommodation. Divers may prefer to stay on the beach, while others may prefer to nestle on the hillsides. One advantage of such a small island is, wherever you stay, you are only minutes from anywhere and everywhere else.

Paradise Inn, Carriacou

Accommodations Directory

ADE'S DREAM GUEST HOUSE, Hillsborough
☎ 473-443-7317, fax 473-443-8435

ALEXIS LUXURY APARTMENT HOTEL, Tyrrel Bay
☎/fax 473-443-7179

BAYALEAU POINT COTTAGES, Windward
☎/fax 473-443-7984

BOGLES ROUNDHOUSE COTTAGES, Bogles
☎/fax 473-443-7841

Grenada's Grenadines

Traditional Chattel Cottage Porch

CARRIACOU YACHT CLUB, Tyrrel Bay, ☎ 473-443-6123, fax 473-443-6292

GRAND VIEW INN, Hillsborough, ☎ 473-443-8659, fax 473-443-6348

GREEN ROOF INN, Hillsborough, ☎/fax 473-443-6399

JOHN'S UNIQUE RESORT, Hillsborough ☎/fax 473-443-8345

KIDO ECOLOGICAL RESEARCH STATION SANCTUARY Bogles, ☎/fax 473-443-7936

MILLIE'S GUEST ROOMS & COTTAGES, Hillsborough ☎ 473-443-7035, fax 473-443-8107

PATTY'S VILLA, Hillsborough, ☎ 473-443-8412

THE SAND GUEST HOUSE, Hillsborough, ☎ 473-443-7100

SCRAPER BAY VIEW HOLIDAY COTTAGES, Tyrrel Bay ☎/fax 473-443-7403

SILVER BEACH HOTEL, Hillsborough, ☎ 473-443-7337, fax 473-443-7165

TOM'S BACKPACKER RETREAT, Tyrrel Bay tom@grenadines.net

ADE'S DREAM GUEST HOUSE

Hillsborough

☎ 473-443-7317, fax 473-443-8435

adesdream@spiceisle.com

Under US$100 MC, Visa

They have 16 air-conditioned rooms with kitchens and seven rooms with fan that share bathroom and kitchen facilities. Located in the heart of Hillsborough above a supermarket.

ALEXIS LUXURY APARTMENT HOTEL

Tyrrel Bay

☎/fax 473-443-7179

Under US$100 MC, Visa

Apartments with basic furnishings ideal for those diving or on other activity-based vacations.

BAYALEAU POINT COTTAGES

Windward

☎/fax 473-443-7984

www.carriacoucottages.com, goldhill@caribsurf.com

Under US$100 MC, Visa

Four rooms with shower & ceiling fan. Dave and Ulla run this intimate venue. They have a restaurant on-site and provide laundry service. Windsurfing, kayaking, and trips aboard their 28-foot power boat are available.

BOGLES ROUNDHOUSE COTTAGES

Bogles

☎/fax 473-443-7841

www.boglesroundhouse.com

Under US$100 MC, Visa

This is a truly amazing place. If you can't stay, then go for dinner (reservations are required); if you don't go for dinner, then drop in just to check it out. Built from local stone, old trees, driftwood and other discarded items, the roundhouse is the main building and restaurant, and resembles an egg. There are three self-contained cottages with compact kitchen, shower and separate water closet. The beds have walk-in mosquito nets. At the end of the garden, a few steps lead down to the beach. The Roundhouse is the brainchild of Kim and Sue Russell, whose life together deserves its own book. At present they are living on a working barge somewhere on the canals of England.

CARRIACOU YACHT CLUB

Tyrrel Bay

☎ 473-443-6123, fax 473-443-6292

carriyacht@spiceisle.com

Under US$100 no credit cards

Four rooms with basic furnishings intended for first-night and last-night yachties. The restaurant and bar provide a cool, relaxed atmosphere during the day and a thriving social scene in the evening.

GREEN ROOF INN

Hillsborough

☎/fax 473-443-6399

www.greenroofinn.com

Under US$100 Breakfast included. MC, Visa

Five attractive rooms with showers and ceiling fans. Overlooking gardens and the sea, this lovely inn was built in the ruins of an old house. It is on the road out of Hillsborough towards the village of Bogles. The rooms are bright, airy and comfortable. It is worth making a reservation for dinner at the restaurant if you aren't staying at the inn. Dinner is served in high season only.

GRAND VIEW INN

Hillsborough

☎ 473-443-8659, fax 473-443-6348

www.carriacougrandview.com

Under US$100 MC, Visa

Six rooms and seven apartments, with all modern furnishings. Restaurant, bar and pool are on the premises. In an elevated position overlooking Hillsborough and the center of the island, it is far enough from town to afford peace and quiet, yet only a five-minute walk to the beach or 10 minutes to the center of town.

JOHN'S UNIQUE RESORT

Hillsborough

☎/fax 473-443-8345

junique@caribsurf.com

Under US$100 MC, Visa

Modern apartment block opposite the Silver Beach. Some units have kitchens. The dinner was less than unique.

KIDO ECOLOGICAL RESEARCH STATION SANCTUARY

Bogles

☎/fax 473-443-7936

kido-ywf@spiceisle.com

Under US$100 no credit cards

Three bungalows for couples, families or groups. The restaurant offers vegetarian meals, but also serves fish, cheese and eggs. Breakfast and a take-out lunch cost about US$10 each; dinner is just under US$20 per person. Kido lies at the northern end of Carriacou, a mile or so beyond Bogles, along a very uneven dirt road. Funded by the European Union and ecological groups, it exists to train local people to be nature and hiking guides and act as wardens in the **High North Nature Park**. Ecotours offered include turtle watching, hiking, bird watching, snorkeling, and whale and dolphin watching. The architecture of the buildings borrows from that of the Bogles Roundhouse.

MILLIE'S GUEST ROOMS & COTTAGES

Hillsborough

☎ 473-443-7035, fax 473-443-8107

millies@spiceisle.com

Under US$100 no credit cards

Rooms available in town.

SILVER BEACH HOTEL

Hillsborough

☎ 473-443-7337, fax 473-443-7165

silverbeach@caribsurf.com, www.silverbeachhotel.com

Under US$100 MC, Visa

There are 16 rooms divided into eight cottages, all with shower, TV, telephone, ceiling fan. They look comfortable. One night is given free for every seven nights stay. Free transport to and from jetty if requested in advance. Located on the beach at the northern end of Hillsborough. The restaurant serves good local cuisine.

PATTY'S VILLA

Hillsborough

☎ 473-443-8412

A historically preserved traditional West Indian building on the beachfront. Two self-contained apartments for two people within walking distance of restaurants, rum shops and the museum. An ideal place to see the green flash.

THE SAND GUEST HOUSE

Hillsborough

☎ 473-443-7100

Under US$100 no credit cards

Rooms in the center of town.

SCRAPER BAY VIEW HOLIDAY COTTAGES

Tyrrel Bay

☎/fax 473-443-7403

scrapers@spiceisle.com

Under US$100 MC, Visa

Six air-conditioned apartments with kitchens. The rooms are in the main building above the restaurant and gift shop. The beach is across the road. And there you are, ready for adventure.

TOM'S BACKPACKER RETREAT

Tyrrel Bay

tom@grenadines.net

Under US$100

Five rooms in an A-frame house at the top of the hill above the Carriacou Yacht Club. Owned by a Danish family.

Villa Rentals

BELAIR GARDENS COTTAGE

Belair

☎ 207-338-5922

belaircottage@caribsurf.com; bjsawyer@adelphia.net

Pastel chattel cottage two miles outside Hillsborough. One bedroom, with another double bed in a loft space, it can sleep four at a pinch. The kitchen has all the basics for cooking and a laundry service is available. Set in a private three acres next to a forest. US$490 weekly in high season with a one-week minimum booking; great value at US$350 per week in off-season.

DOWN ISLAND

Hillsborough

☎ 473-443-8182, fax 473-443-8290

islander@caribsurf.com

An assortment of villas, cottages, and apartments in Carriacou from US$400 per week.

SAND X BEACH HOUSE

☎ 473-443-8382

sunkeywp@yahoo.com

House and Jeep available at US$650 per week or US$115 daily.

■ After Dark

Carnival Parade

The night scene on Carriacou is what you make it. These islands are generally pretty quiet, except on special occasions like Christmas, New Year's Eve, Carnival, Shakespeare Mas, Regatta and Parang. During high season, with more tourists around, rum shops and bars get more business at night.

Don't hesitate to frequent the local rum shops and bars, as the friends you make locally will make your experience all the more enjoyable. It's in these places that you'll hear gossip, whether whales are in the area or if something special is brewing. Most of the locals get up with the sun, so don't expect an all-nighter.

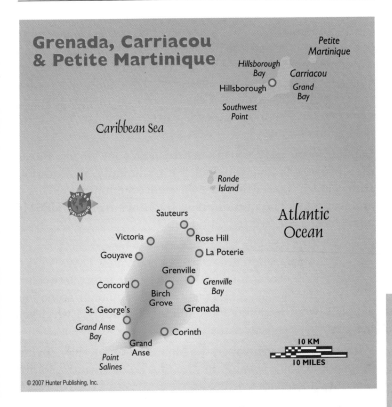

Grenada, Carriacou & Petite Martinique

Petite Martinique

■ Orientation

Petite Martinique lies five miles east of Carriacou and is home to 800 people. The sea provides employment for most of the island men. Fishing, water taxis, ferries, container ships, boat-building and smuggling are all part of the tapestry of life on the island. Importing and exporting business is accomplished bypassing customs because of the distance to St. Vincent's Petit St. Vincent. It's only a five-minute boat ride. Anything from champagne to refrigerators can be had on the island at an affordable price.

Petite Martinique, locally known as PM, is truly a one-horse town. There is one school, one medical facility, one bank (open Tuesday and Thursday only), one post office and one church. One gas pump serves the boats and the handful of vehicles that travel the two miles of roads. Look for the one taxi/bus driver on the island. That's Coco. Anyone should be able to get hold of him for you.

Landing at the jetty, you are in the island's one village, **Paradise**. Turn left and you find the community of **Madame Pierre**; turn right to find the two small communities of **Citen** and **Kendace**. The ethnic background on Petite Martinique is a mix of African, Scottish and French.

This is not an island of second homes, resorts, swimming pools, tennis courts or boutiques. There is little here except fine, hospitable people living between a 700-foot mountain peak and the aquamarine waters dappled by surrounding cays and small islands. Everybody here knows everybody's momma.

PM has its own carnival on the Monday and Tuesday during the week of Lent. During the two-day Easter regatta, Petite Martinique's sailors are sure to give any visiting competitors a run for their money.

■ Getting Here

Other than by private yacht, Petite Martinique can be reached only by ferry from Carriacou or water taxi from neighboring islands.

The *Osprey Express* ferries from Grenada to Petite Martinique, stopping at Carriacou en route. Departures from Carriacou to Petite Martinique are at 10:30 am and 7 pm, Monday to Friday; 10:30 am on Saturday; and 9:45 am and 7 pm on Sunday. Departures from Petite Martinique to Carriacou are at 5:30 am and 3 pm, Monday to Saturday; and at 3 pm on Sunday. The journey takes 30 minutes and costs EC$20 one-way, EC$40 round trip.

From Union Island or any of the other Grenadines, you can negotiate a price with a water taxi driver. You don't have to book him for the return journey as there are plenty of Petite Martinique drivers that can take you back. A good place to ask is the Palm Beach Restaurant. If one of the Clement brothers can't take you, then they'll certainly make arrangements. Allie Roche also has a speedboat, *Footstep*. He charges EC$60 per person one-way from Petite Martinique to Union Island or Windward, Carriacou. Traveling between Petite Martinique and Hillsborough, Carriacou is EC$120 per person.

For a tour of Petite Martinique by car, call **Coco Mitchell**, the only taxi driver on the island, ☎ 473-443-9021. It lasts close to an hour and costs EC$30 for two. For such a small place, there is a lot to see and learn.

Having trouble with your sailboat? **Windward Marine** has a branch here; contact the Clement brothers, ☎ 473-443-9022. For fuel, oil, provisions, water and ice for your boat, contact **B&C Fuels Enterprise**, ☎ 473-443-9110.

In case you need the **Health Clinic**, ☎ 473-443-9198. The doctor travels from Carriacou on Wednesdays only and is available from 11 am to 3 pm.

A WORD TO
THE WISE

Wearing dark colored clothing attracts mosquitoes at daybreak and dusk. Keeping fruit in your room also lures these tiny pests. Another good way to get bitten is to stand near bright lights with exposed limbs.

■ Exploring

It doesn't take long to see the whole island. To feel the spirit of the island and the warmth of its inhabitants may take several trips.

The land is hilly and dry with wild cotton growing in places. Yes, even Petite Martinique was colonized by planters. Marie Galante cotton was grown commercially from 1867 through the 1970s and exported to Great Britain. The windward side is uninhabited and not accessible by road. In the south, the tiny communities of **Citen** and **Kendace** are home to legends of buried treasure and human sacrifice – just ask Coco, he'll fill you in on the details.

The village of **Paradise** is the heart of the boat building and fishing industries. Historically, Petite Martiniquians were boat builders. The "smuggling" that they are known for is due to the lack of a customs official on the island. We prefer to describe it as a healthy import/export market run by free trade entrepreneurs. This is the way commodities are moved around the islands. Fish, liquor, cigarettes and electronic goods are all shipped by boat. Don't presume by the word "smuggling" that narcotics are involved; they are illegal here as with the other islands of Grenada and St. Vincent.

Paradise has a pretty white sand beach, but there are other tiny deserted cays where you can spend your time. The translucent water makes for excellent snorkeling around these spits of sand. With little around these Grenadines, the water, beaches and reefs are about the cleanest the Caribbean has to offer.

To the north of Paradise is the community of **Madame Pierre**. This is where "de red ones" live. In the 18th and 19th centuries, poor Scottish and Irish indentured servants were brought in to Barbados, St. Vincent and Grenada and were known as "redlegs." They tended to keep to themselves and pocket communities of their descendants exist to this day. Madame Pierre is a prime example. The houses at this end of the island have gables with decorative fretwork or gingerbread.

On the hillside overlooking Paradise is a museum. Perhaps not the smallest museum in the world, nor the strangest, but this curiosity should make you smile. There is a reproduction wattle and daub building as big as a tool shed, housing old pots and pans, smoothing irons and orca jawbones. The entrance fee is EC$1. The curator, who happens to run the Classic View

Guest House, told us the plaster of the walls was made with cow dung, *"mix with piss and dirt, de sun dry it up."*

■ Snorkeling

Petite Martinique is a superb shore base for snorkeling adventures. water taxis will transport you to any of the several cays, such as **Mopion** and **Petite Dominique**. The latter is owned by the Clement family of the Palm Beach Restaurant. It's best to obtain their permission and use one of their water taxis to carry you there. They can arrange a picnic lunch for you upon request. Be sure to take bottled water and plenty of sunscreen.

You can try out snorkeling in St. Vincent's Grenadines from this location. **Petit St. Vincent** is only five minutes away by boat, **Union Island** is a 30-minute ride, and the **Tobago Cays** closer to an hour. You don't have to go through customs or immigration and the Tobago Cays are exquisite.

Palm, Petite St. Vincent, Petite Martinique, Carriacou, Union Island & Mayreaux

Negotiate the price before leaving Petite Martinique. Make sure you establish whether the rate is EC$ or US$; if it is per person or for the boat, regardless of the number of passengers; and that it includes the return fare. When going as far as the Tobago Cays, it's best to have the boat wait for you. The Cays are uninhabited and if you don't have a ride back, then you will be playing Robinson Crusoe for at least a night. Always, always pay the captain after the return leg of the journey.

Remember, the reefs are fragile. Do not touch any coral, as oil from our fingertips is known to damage this frail lifeform. Do not remove anything nor leave anything behind except footprints. It is illegal for visitors to use spear guns or take lobsters. Please observe these regulations. And have fun.

■ Where to Eat

PALM BEACH RESTAURANT & BAR
☎ 473-443-9103
US$15-$25 MC, Visa

Petite Martinique Village (Grenadines.net)

Monday to Saturday, 8 am-10 pm, Sunday, 2-10 pm

Free water taxi service is provided for dinner guests staying on Petit St. Vincent. This is a beachfront property with thatched dining areas close to the shore. The food and service are high-standard for breakfast, lunch and dinner, and their hospitality is genuine. Bacon and eggs costs EC$20, a sumptuous burger at lunch is EC$8, in the evening the lobster dinner is EC$70. Vegetarian dishes are available on request. Dinner reservations are advised in high season.

MELODIE'S RESTAURANT & BAR
☎ 473-443-9052
Under US$15 MC, Visa

Situated on the beach next to Palm Beach Restaurant. We stayed at Melodie's Guest House and spent a fun evening in their bar on karaoke night. For Petite Martinique, the house was packed. By the time you read this, the restaurant should be up and running. Patrice says his menu will be light fare of salads, sandwiches, rotis, chicken, fish and lambie dishes.

■ Where to Stay

 Petite Martinique takes care of its guests and if you arrive without a reservation, that's not considered a problem. There are only a handful of families and you feel as though you're arriving at one big family reunion. You instantly slide into a comfort zone.

As a guest, please note that rainwater is collected in barrels and cisterns. There are no freshwater rivers or streams and, thus, fresh water is in constant demand. Please do your part to help conserve water.

MELODIE'S GUEST HOUSE

☎ 473-443-9052, fax 473-443-9093

melodies@caribsurf.com

Under US$100 MC, Visa

Ten rooms with shower, TV and fan, share a fully equipped kitchen and dining area. Half the rooms face the beach and have balconies overlooking the sea. On the ground floor, there is a restaurant and bar. The owner, Reuben Patrice, is a charming host and oversaw the Saturday karaoke evening. This was the perfect excuse not to have an early night. I must apologize here to all who witnessed the appalling renditions of *Under The Boardwalk* and *Blueberry Hill*.

SEASIDE VIEW HOLIDAY COTTAGES

☎ 473-443-9007, fax 473-443-9210

Under US$100 MC,Visa

Three cottages next door to Melodie's Guest House and owned by Reuben Patrice's uncle, Francis Logan. These self-contained cottages are situated directly behind Mr.Logan's well-stocked supermarket on the beach. A sign offers scuba diving, but don't take for granted it is PADI.

Grenada's Grenadines

CLASSIC VIEW GUEST HOUSE

☎ 473-443-9234

Under US$100 no credit cards

Two rooms share a shower and have very basic furnishings. Perched high on the hill overlooking the harbor, Carriacou, Petit St. Vincent, and Union Island. The grounds contain one of the smallest museums you're ever likely to visit. The hosts will prepare breakfast for EC$9, Oil Down (see page 379) for lunch at EC$12 and dinner entrées from EC$15-25. Prices are per person.

■ After Dark

Typical of these southern Caribbean islands, Petite Martinique has a quiet night life, unless it is Carnival, Regatta or a holiday time.

Yet we did have a wonderful time at **Melodie's Bar** in the evening. Melodie's also provides nightlife for the employees of the Petit St. Vincent Resort. If you've never experienced karaoke before, this is a brilliant introduction. Hear some familiar tunes sung with a West Indian accent, mon.

By 11 pm, all is quiet, save for the ebbing and flowing of the sea on the shore. This is a great opportunity to read some book you haven't had time to read at home. Don't expect too much from the book exchanges in the hotels and restaurants in these islands if you're picky about your writers. We found a good night's sleep most welcome after a long day in the sun.

Diving Emergencies

A WORD TO
THE WISE

St. Vincent & the Grenadines and Grenada dive shops have excellent safety records, yet we feel an obligation to provide the following information in case an emergency should arise.

Typical decompression sickness symptoms include itching, skin rashes, pain in the joints, breathing difficulties, dizziness and, in extreme cases, loss of consciousness.

Immediately contact a recompression chamber in Barbados, Trinidad or Martinique, keeping in mind that Martinique is French-speaking.

■ Recompression Chambers

Barbados

- **Barbados Defense Force (BDF)**, Garrison Street, St. Michael's, ☎ 246-436-6185

Trinidad

- **Mount Hope Hospital**, ☎ 809-625-2104, 809-625-1691

Martinique

- **Le Maynard Hospital**, Service D'Urgence Hyperbare, ☎ 596-55-22-00

Air Ambulance

- Mustique Airways, ☎ 784-458-4380
- SVG Air, ☎ 784-457-5124, 473-444-0328
- TIA, ☎ 246-418-1650

Divers Alert Network

- ☎ 919-684-8111

Addendum

Index

Index